JOURNALS FROM A WARRIOR'S MOTHER

THE FALL TO THE CLIMB

Collector's Edition

Chrissy L. Whitten

Illustrated by Tammy S. Edwards

Copyright © 2022 by Chrissy L. Whitten
www.chrissylwhitten.com

All rights reserved. No part of this publication may be reproduced, distributed or transmitted in any form or by any means, without prior written permission.

Publisher's Note: This is a narrative nonfiction memoir. The events and conversations contained in this book have been documented to the best of the author's ability.

All scripture quotations, unless otherwise indicated, are taken from the Holy Bible, New International Version®, NIV®. Copyright © 1973, 1978, 1984, 2011 by Biblica, Inc.^{TM} Used by permission of Zondervan. All rights reserved worldwide. www.zondervan.com. The "NIV" and "New International Version" are trademarks registered in the United States Patent and Trademark office by Biblica, Inc.^{TM}

Scripture marked (NKJV) is taken from the New King James Version®. Copyright © 1982 by Thomas Nelson. Used by permission. All rights reserved.

Cover design by Tammy S. Edwards & Chrissy L. Whitten
Illustrations copyright © 2022 by Tammy S. Edwards,
   tammyedwards63@yahoo.com
Photographs on pages 33, 52, 55, 56, 68, 76, 82, 188, 241, 242, 245,
   276, 340, & 346 by Kelli Marone, NILMDTS Affil. Photographer
Photograph on page 64 by Cindy Haley
Image on page 85 by Cassandra Clark
Photograph on page 360 by Silver Dollar City Photography
Author portrait on page 381 by Ginger McKinney Reinoehl
Graphics on pages 40 and 114 by Darla Baker-Hurst
Remaining photographs by Chrissy L. Whitten
Edited by Staci D. Mauney, prestigeprose.com
Formatted by Danelle G. Young, danelleyoung.com
Book Layout © 2016 BookDesignTemplates.com

The Fall to the Climb/ Chrissy L. Whitten. -- 1st ed.
ISBN 978-1-7365322-3-2 (paperback)
ISBN 978-1-7365322-4-9 (e-book)
ISBN 978-1-7365322-5-6 (Collector's Edition)
Library of Congress Control Numbers: 2022922036 and
   2022921958 (Collector's Edition)

DEDICATION

God,
   You keep providing and moving me to do what is needed for this book project. I drag my feet at times. Adversities and distractions make it easy to avoid the finish line. Thanks for never giving up on me and meeting me where I am. I love you with all my heart and soul!

Michael, Lilian Grace, Piper Allegra, and Daphne Mae,
   I know it's not always fun when I'm trying to juggle all the things. Thanks for supporting me through the ups and downs. I love you to the moon and back and for all eternity!

Warrior Tribe,
   My life would not be the same without you. Thanks for pouring into me and stepping up when needed. I love you more!

Scared but holding on tight to God

INTRODUCTION

After losing Lilian Grace on August 5, 2010, God prompted me to continue journaling and sharing on CaringBridge. *The Fight*, my first book in this series, took you from Lilian's birth to her departure and a few months into my grief beyond. This book (number two) picks up there as I try to work through my grief during our first year without her.

I was attempting to figure out where life was taking me; what I should be doing now that Lilian was gone; how I was going to keep it together when I felt crushed, broken, and disoriented; and who I was going to be after such a life-altering trauma. Revisiting these journal entries reassured me God has and always will be woven into all. No matter where I am in life, He provides.

May God stir your spirit and inspire you to keep fighting forward in your journey. As in book one, I share songs, Scriptures, and inspirational thoughts in these entries. I hope these tools will help you through your own trials. Old and new tools help us climb and descend as life's terrain changes elevation.

My big takeaway from this book is that life's journey has climbs and falls that are meant to bring healing, growth, and change. Without change, it's difficult to progress as a person. Though I'd love to avoid many experiences, they are part of me—scars, brokenness, failures, and successes. I'm starting to see the beauty in all of them and surviving each as a badge of honor.

They have shaped me for the better. The times they debilitate me are moments when I can't accept change. I keep trying to go back to who I was or where I've been—neither are meant to exist again in the same way.

Welcome (back) to book number two. I almost stopped

working on the *Journals from a Warrior's Mother* series more than a dozen times. I didn't think anyone would care if I didn't carry on with this project. But God—He won't let me stop. I can't stand in His way or abandon what He started in me over a decade ago. He has plans, and I'm blessed to keep being a part!

My work with Calm Waters Center for Children and Families and The STEAM (Science, Technology, Engineering, Art, and Mathematics) Engine has helped fund my second book. It's not a cheap venture to self-publish, but God provided. May you find God in everything daily. Thank you for being here. You are not alone. God's got you! Be a warrior who leans on God's strength while moving forward one step at a time!

Love,
Chrissy

CONTENTS

DEDICATION	3
INTRODUCTION	5
104 › Persevere	11
105 › Two-Month Angelversary	13
106 › Layers of Healing	17
107 › STOP!	19
108 › Water Works	23
109 › Beauty Will Rise	27
110 › The Answer	31
111 › Two Roads	35
112 › Dress Up	39
113 › Masked Up	41
114 › Broken	45
115 › Three-Month Angelversary	49
116 › Believing, Battling, & Learning	53
117 › Fish Tank Faith	57
118 › 103 Beads	61
119 › Thanksgiving	65
120 › Completely Held	73
121 › Four-Month Angelversary	77
122 › The Dancer	83
123 › Healing at the Altar	87
124 › Another's Battle	91
125 › Unfinished	93
126 › On the Radio	97
127 › Christmas Eve Lost & Found	103
128 › Christmas Day: Peace on Earth	111
129 › Borrowed Angels	117
130 › Five-Month Angelversary	119
131 › Outside the Society Box	123
132 › Set the World on Fire	127
133 › Mountains	129

134 ›	The Climb	133
135 ›	Inside Out	135
136 ›	Wonder	141
137 ›	A Way to Celebrate	147
138 ›	Snowstorm Enlightenment	151
139 ›	Six-Month Angelversary	157
140 ›	Processing & Tears Flowing	163
141 ›	Father's Love Letter	167
142 ›	Fresh Eyes, No Blinders	171
143 ›	I Will Carry You	173
144 ›	Seven-Month Angelversary	179
145 ›	Challenge Yourself	183
146 ›	Race On	185
147 ›	Two Trains	189
148 ›	Speed	193
149 ›	Eleven-Month Birthday Anniversary	195
150 ›	Eight-Month Angelversary	199
151 ›	The Next Miracle	203
152 ›	Warrior Princess Trail Run	207
153 ›	Glory in the Cross	211
154 ›	Keep Fighting	215
155 ›	Details	217
156 ›	First Birthday Anniversary	223
157 ›	Nine-Month Angelversary	227
158 ›	Mother's Day	235
159 ›	It Is Well	239
160 ›	Never Wave My Flag	243
161 ›	Destiny in Purpose	247
162 ›	Project Details	249
163 ›	Tenth-Month Angelversary	257
164 ›	Returning Love	261
165 ›	Blessings	265
166 ›	Works in Progress	269
167 ›	Healing Stick	271
168 ›	Sarcasm & Irritation	273
169 ›	Adding Margin	275

170 › Sickness Amid Grief	277
171 › Bad Days	281
172 › Quietly Processing	283
173 › Father's Day	289
174 › Fighting Rules & Priorities	293
175 › Processing Wins	297
176 › Be the Change	303
177 › Eleven-Month Angelversary	309
178 › Treasurable	317
179 › Top Priorities & Front Seats	321
180 › Bumps & Blessings	325
181 › Stripped Away	329
182 › Roots & Leads	333
183 › Listen, Pray, Dream	337
184 › Chipped Shoulder	341
185 › Before the Morning	347
186 › One-Year Angelversary	353
A NOTE FROM THE AUTHOR	359
BOOK COVER LEGEND	361
MEMORY VERSES	373
PLAYLIST	377
ACKNOWLEDGEMENTS	379
ABOUT THE AUTHOR	381
MORE FROM CHRISSY L. WHITTEN	383
REVIEW PLEA	384

SEPTEMBER 30, 2010

104 › Persevere

Memory Verse 1

⚔ *"His divine power has given us everything we need for a godly life through our knowledge of him who called us by his own glory and goodness. Through these he has given us his very great and precious promises, so that through them you may participate in the divine nature, having escaped the corruption in the world caused by evil desires. For this very reason, make every effort to add to your faith goodness; and to goodness, knowledge; and to knowledge, self-control; and to self-control, perseverance; and to perseverance, godliness; and to godliness, mutual affection; and to mutual affection, love. For if you possess these qualities in increasing measure, they will keep you from being ineffective and unproductive in your knowledge of our Lord Jesus Christ" (2 Peter 1:3–8).*

Nancy March posted this earlier: *"Just received word that Trishtan is being moved from a regular room at Texas Children's Hospital (TCH) to the Pediatric Intensive Care Unit (PICU) for observation. Last time, about two weeks ago, she didn't have to be in the PICU. Trishtan has a urinary tract infection (UTI), fluid on her heart and lungs (starting to drain), and breathing problems. She's definitely a fighter. Please keep her and her mother, Denise, in your prayers. Continuing to ask God to be Big!"*

The above Scripture reminds us that God provides everything we need. Knowing Trishtan is in the PICU brings back the memory of walking my own Lilian Grace to the PICU at St. Francis. I get a little choked up because I knew "it" was it— she'd never be going home with us.

I pray with all my heart that God will hear our prayers and heal sweet baby Trishtan. How many things do we go through without realizing that He just wants us to lean on Him and trust that He will keep providing? This too shall pass . . . no matter the outcome.

🕯 *Heavenly Father, thank you for being incredibly patient and teaching us to persevere through what life throws at us!*

OCTOBER 5, 2010

105 › Two-Month Angelversary

I typed this earlier today while flying from Arizona! Please enjoy!

I'm flying on the two-month angelversary of my daughter earning her wings. I didn't plan it this way. Our wings are completely different, yet they symbolize something special. My daughter flew toward a new life where she feels no pain, sorrow, or suffering—to a place where she has a new body without any complications, defects, or struggles. She gets to be with many angels who have earned their wings before her. They are so lucky to spend time with her. Lilian Grace lived out her purpose so gracefully and strong. Her story will live on through all of us as we gather what we've learned and move forward with a purpose.

As for my wings, they are theoretical and man-made. I am flying into a new chapter! I'm starting my own business helping individuals accomplish their goals in the physical and well-being realms of life. I am lucky to be opening a personal training and group exercise studio in downtown Sand Springs, Oklahoma. This has been a dream of mine for a very long time. I don't think I'd be doing this if my daughter hadn't shown me how to fly and trust God completely.

I think we all get so scared of living life that we get in the way of letting God do His thing. We have desires and dreams for a reason. He wants us to have the desires of our hearts. He has a will and purpose for each of us!

Flying home is more to me than just getting on a plane

from Phoenix to Tulsa. It's about growing my wings and letting God be my wind to keep me going where He needs me to be. What's keeping you from growing your wings so you can take flight into the life you were meant to live?

I just remembered something that happened two days ago when my girls (Marsha Johnson and Cristin Handlin) and I visited Disneyland. We were trying to get to Pixie Hollow, and I ended up at the gift shop at the exit. I couldn't seem to get away from that gift shop. I guess I thought I had time!

Anyway, we finally ended up at Pixie Hollow. Come to find out, we were too late to take pictures with Tinker Bell and her friends. Well, I was disappointed because I really wanted to get a picture with Tinker Bell.

I looked through the tall grass of Pixie Hollow to see if I could get a good look at the fairies. Cristin found a hole for me to get a good pic of Tinker Bell, and I did! She was a gracious one, because she caught me taking a pic, and she smiled big and waved right at me.

It was like Lilian was there to say, "Hey, Momma, I can't be right with you, but I'm near!" We did get to walk through Pixie Hollow and take some wonderful pics. It was a beautiful moment knowing that my daughter might not get to be with me, but I could enjoy life knowing she isn't far away.

I shed a few tears, but my joy shined through. I'm continuing to work through the healing layers one by one. I want to keep flying and living! At the end of Pixie Hollow was the perfect sign for you and me. It is too perfect not to be from my baby girl, who was the best Tinker Bell ever. It says, "Fly with you later!" Now that's something to look forward to with hope and faith!

THE FALL TO THE CLIMB

🕯️ *God, you keep being Big! I can't wait till the day I can fly with you, Lilian, and my other loved ones! Till we can fly together later, I will keep flying and making the best of this life!*

Memory Verse 2

🗡️ *"Take delight in the LORD, and he will give you the desires of your heart. Commit your way to the LORD; trust in him and he will do this: He will make your righteous reward shine like the dawn, your vindication like the noonday sun. Be still before the LORD and wait patiently for him" (Psalm 37:4–7).*

A message from my Tinker Bell

Chrissy L. Whitten

OCTOBER 6, 2010

106 › Layers of Healing

I feel like a monsoon is coming out of my eyes. God sure knows how to relieve my heart, even if I'm not a willing participant. I can see Him healing my next layer of grief even when I think I'm not ready. He's wonderful like that.

I spent the night with one of my best friends and her baby boy last night. We had an amazing time, yet it opened me up for the next layer to be healed. I held her baby boy last night and even this morning, which brought many feelings and emotions. As I was driving to the bank this morning, all of a sudden, memories came flooding in one by one—memories of holding my sweet Lilian Grace for the first time. She was itty bitty. I can still feel the warmth and love we exchanged that day and the moments that followed until my last time holding her.

Breathe! Breathe! Breathe! This layer hurts tremendously. I've fought tears all day. I even shared our story with someone today. I was composed, yet tears came afterwards. Also, I spoke to my pastor and dear friend about things I'm not willing to face right now.

Come to find out, I'm having to face them no matter what. There are things Michael and I experienced that weren't fun. People surprised us, and now we have to deal with it all. I talked to Michael today, and we both cried. We aren't sure what we are going to do, but we know we are going to have to face some things and make some decisions.

Please keep us in your prayers. We never know when we are going to be hit with major emotions. We both are hurting just like many of you. We have so much stored up. I think the best way to describe it is like this: it's like training for a marathon and not getting to run the race. You put all this effort into prepping for it, but now you have to be a spectator instead of a participant.

I started going back through a lot of emails and Facebook messages I've been putting off, because I know I have to relive some moments. I'm not responding to all of them, yet I want you all to know how grateful we are for your support.

As I read yesterday's entry, I should have known that I'd finished one layer of healing. Each time I come to terms with a layer, God starts right in on the next one. He knows me better than anyone. I must keep trekking through. The tears are lighter at this point.

The walk down the hallways of St. Francis with my baby girl wrapped fully in a baby blanket was a rare moment. It was the first time I had been able to walk anywhere with my baby girl without all the cords, wires, and machines. Oh, the gift of walking with her alive without the extras would have been pure bliss.

Instead, I had to be content walking her with no heartbeat. When we got to the funeral home's van, I could have stood there forever embracing her. Knowing it would be the last time I'd hold her precious little body—with no power to change the situation—I decided not to take long. I had to be okay with it. So as I let her go, I let go of the worst of the pain of losing her.

Her life is a phenomenal story that keeps helping people and lessening my pain. I am so proud of her life. Please keep telling me stories of what she has done for you and will do. For this mother, it makes her not being here more bearable. She continues to be a missionary even in her passing.

Thanks for letting me ramble as always. I love you all!

OCTOBER 11, 2010

107 › STOP!

I keep going and going and going until I find myself about to lose it in the Walmart parking lot. What got me to that point? Well, I've continued to overcommit and cram my schedule so that I won't feel the full grief process. It's just plain hard, no matter how willing I am to give it over to God.

This morning's sermon, "Teach Us to Pray," was tough—our pastor talked about how God made it known to pray to Him as Father in the New Testament. Pastor Matt spoke about being a father himself and realizing just how the Father sees us and wants to watch us grow. Thank You, God, that I didn't wear mascara because the tears kept coming.

A key point he made today—and I've said it before—there is nothing we can do that would make God love us any less, just as there was nothing Lilian Grace could have done or said that would have made me love her any less. I wanted her to stay so badly, but I knew she wasn't meant to live here like us. She was meant to exist, fight, and encourage all of us. She never disappointed me once. I will love her with all my heart and everything that I am and will be.

Thankfully, God, our heavenly Father, doesn't let anything we do or say separate us from His love. He loves us unconditionally. He becomes a proud Papa when we get out of the way and do His will. Understanding He knows our purpose and keeps being proud of us blows my mind, heart, and soul. He rocks like no other!

Back to the Walmart parking lot where I found myself on the wrong side of it. Oh yes, I was one of those crazy people who walks up and down the parking lot having no clue as to where she parked her car. I started thinking about multiple things like working on my many projects; opening my new business on Wednesday; working at the church and dealing with my grief. It struck me hard—I almost lost it right in the center lane of the parking lot.

Tears welled up in my eyes as my heart pounded a million beats. What did I finally say? STOP! You will not lose it now—not in this parking lot where cameras are filming you. Devil, you will not break me. God, I need You now more than ever. I cannot do this without You! STOP the noise! I am too blessed! It's going to be all right—this too shall pass.

I did find my car. I didn't lose it, but I came close. PRAISE GOD! I need to remember constantly to be still and let God. When I'm on the verge of losing it, I'm usually trying to skim a level of the grieving process.

If you find yourself trying to skim or skip a level in the process, keep in mind that you might miss out. Our heavenly Father is a wonderful parent who wants to prepare us for all the bumps along the way. He isn't going to give us everything we want. He will give us what we need when we need it. Jump in and learn from Him.

I'm far from being okay. Today was a nice reminder for me. As the days pass, I feel different. I feel one emotion after the next—some days hit Michael and me harder. Today was a rough day.

Each moment I experience without Lilian, the harder it can be for me. Dang it, tears just keep coming. I'm tired. I'm happy. I'm exhausted. I miss her. I love her. I feel like a crazy woman more times than not. More importantly, no matter what I'm going through, God's love makes it all worth it—even the painful days.

I don't know what you are going through at this moment, but remember the verses God gave us when He answered the question *why* for me—and perhaps even for you:

Memory Verse 3

"So that Christ may dwell in your hearts through faith. And I pray that you, being rooted and established in love, may have power, together with all the Lord's holy people, to grasp how wide and long and high and deep is the love of Christ, and to know this love that surpasses knowledge—that you may be filled to the measure of all the fullness of God" (Ephesians 3:17–19).

I praise His holy name for giving me a clear answer and for not ever leaving me alone—especially through the tough times. If you are wondering how Michael and I are doing, know that for right now we are parents who are trying to walk and live while our daughter is with her heavenly Father. There's no time limit on missing her, grieving, or being ready for each level. It will happen when it happens, and it will take as long as it takes.

I'm just human, wondering when I'll feel more normal, stop having moments of numbness, or lose it at any moment. I see life through different eyes than pre-Lilian. I see more of the world and the people with their paths than I could have before—some good, some bad, and others I'm not sure about at all.

I pray to God about you and your struggles in life—sickness, health, surgeries, treatments, new adventures, poor, rich, diseased. The list is endless. I see each of us heavily burdened with life and schedules. I'm forever learning that I've got to STOP more! Life is hard, so why add more all the time?

May we all stop and let our Father teach and prepare us for our mission! Yes, we all have one. Each mission looks different, but each results in showing God's love and expanding His kingdom.

🕯️ *Dear Father, oh yes—my Daddy from above—You rock in all aspects of life. You give us exactly what we need. I pray that anyone reading this right now would be lifted up—that You would give them exactly what they need as Your will is done in their lives. You know every nanosecond of their past, present, and future. Please pick them up with their struggles into Your ever-so-loving arms and comfort them with all the comfort and love they need. Help them to see just how wide and long and high and deep is Your love. You are keeping eternity open for all of us right now because You saw that we were worth the sacrifice so we could be with You for eternity. My heart glows with thanksgiving and awe for You. Guide each of us through the messes and joys of life. In Your glorious name. AMEN!*

OCTOBER 12, 2010

108 › Water Works

No matter how fast you run, you can't escape a breakdown moment. I found myself still struggling yesterday—in and out with tears mixed with indescribable emotions. Last night was the first time since Christmas that I can recall having the capability of driving to Cushing. With this info processing, I wondered why, until the past year came crashing down in my brain—three surgeries while experiencing the most precious baby I've ever known.

On the way to Cushing, I was counseled by a couple of friends. I didn't know how I would react when I got there. I was going to watch my niece, Cali Ann, play soccer. It's not her nor Caleb's fault. I can't seem to get myself to do anything right now. I have to take baby steps in certain areas so I don't completely lose it. One thing at a time!

Watching her play was wonderful. I had survived until I looked at a message on my phone. I've been praying for a young woman, twenty-eight years old, who had just gotten married last year. She wanted kids so badly, then got pregnant with twins. The twins were born early on September 26 and earned their wings the same day. The mother, a young woman named Leslie Joy Evans, ended up in a coma with other complications from the birth and passed away also. Today will be their service—Leslie along with her twins, Marisa and Mac.

I pulled myself together during the soccer game to make it to my mom and dad's. I knew this was going to be the hardest part because I was pregnant the last time I was there. Lilian Grace was not with me then nor now. I gathered myself enough to get in the car to take my niece, nephew, and sister-in-law home to see all their cool new stuff. Luckily, I was on my way home before the tears rolled down in sheets.

The tears fell slowly at first until I thought about Leslie's husband. I've lost a child, but I have not lost both a child and my spouse. Oh my, the tears are coming back as I type. I have no idea what he's going through. I can only imagine, which doesn't even come close to the pain he's feeling. My pain for Lilian Grace is nothing compared to his. Yet last night I found myself thinking more about Leslie. She got to go home to be with her babies. She departed from this world—from the suffering, pain, and holes in her heart where her children were placed.

I collected myself after processing Leslie's situation, going to my parents' house, and acknowledging these past months. A song I used to play over and over again hit me the hardest. I was singing it at the top of my lungs when I found myself struggling to breathe. The back of my throat felt like something was lodged there. My lap was wet from the relentless tears. I had to pull over short of the medium-sized hill heading into the light at Mannford.

I was out of control. I couldn't say anything to make it better. The hospital trauma hit me hard. Missing her took a hit at me. Not being able to make her better here on earth was another blow. It all came crashing down with a vengeance. I sat there in my car on the side of the road—screaming at the top of my lungs while trying to breathe in between it all. This was the hardest I've ever cried.

I knew it had been coming, yet I wouldn't let myself go. I was afraid I wouldn't be able to come out of it. Thankfully, God, my heavenly Father, knows my needs and used a song as an antidote to liberate the emotions needing released.

At some point, I saw red and blue lights coming at me from behind. Oh yes, a police officer stopped, not knowing what he was about to find. I rolled my window down, struggling to find words at first. I couldn't stop crying. I finally told him I'd lost my daughter. Since I ended up breaking down, I thought it best to pull over to avoid causing a wreck. He agreed it was a smart choice.

He ended up asking me a couple of common questions I get asked: Is there anything I can do for you, and how can I help you? All I could answer was that no one could help me but God. I wish you could help me, because this pain hurts more than any hurt I've ever felt. God is so gracious to give me His strength and comfort—just like He provided last night and every moment. He knew my heart and soul needed a deeper level of release than I'd been allowing Him to do.

As the police officer left, I found myself a mess yet smiling—because I knew I needed this. I understood this level was going to be hard. I think what bothers me most is when someone tells me "WE" are going to get through this. Well, "WE" are going through different levels. There is no way that we can be on the same level. I comprehend more after being educated with Leslie's story. I couldn't say "WE" to them. I can only say I am going to get through what I am feeling and experiencing—just as you do on your journey.

Think about this—losing your child is not like losing someone else's child. Losing your mom, dad, or loved one is different from losing someone else's mom, dad, or loved one. I'm learning this for myself. Our relationships reach different depths unique to them. We can still grieve alongside someone, but we aren't them at the end of the day.

After everything, I know why going to Cushing was so

hard for me. Exactly a year ago today, October 12, I found out I was pregnant with Lilian Grace and had hopes and dreams for my precious baby. I imagined how it would look for my family to share in it all. Little did I know my reality would be far from my hopes and dreams.

Rising above the previous days, I come full circle. A year ago, I was excited to be pregnant, thinking nothing could touch me. Today, I find myself not pregnant nor with my child I was pregnant with at the time. Still God blesses me through everything. I can smile through the tears and pain because I have new hopes and dreams that God, through Lilian Grace's life, has given me to live out. Praying we all get through our own pain and sorrow while trusting God to get us through. I will stop on that note! I love you all. Running will take you away from things, but you eventually have to stop to rest—and everything will catch up!

OCTOBER 16, 2010

109 › Beauty Will Rise

Steven Curtis Chapman did an amazing job on the song, "Beauty Will Rise." I owe him a huge thank you for making such an honest and raw album and including this song. Though he wrote it about his life, it's relatable to everyone. I see and hear story after story of people struggling. We shall never truly get over what we've gone through, but we will learn to deal with it—with the various holes in our hearts. For Michael and me, Lilian Grace left a huge one in each of our hearts.

Sitting in my studio today, I stared at the black-painted Phoenix my sister created on the bright orange wall. At various points in life, we've all been burned by fires. Whether we choose to rise from our ashes to fight another day is up to each one of us. The reason my slogan for The Phoenix Experience (my business) is *Burn, Renew, and Soar* is that I feel like I've repeated this process over and over in my life.

Praise God for loving me abundantly. I can see beauty rising amid the ashes and His glory in each experience. Though some fires have been hotter than others, each one makes me stronger. Surviving Lilian Grace will always be a deeper scar on my heart than any other scar. She was completely worth the depth of it.

I'm glad the bad days aren't every day! He gives me strength like none other on many days. Today was a tough day for me, yet I was in mission mode. Nothing could touch me nor destroy me. I went to see a dear friend, whom I worked with at Oklahoma State University Extension, in the trauma intensive care unit. She was in a horrible car accident this week. She is a tough woman—a fighter—who has gone through many fires in her life.

Please pray for her as she fights for her life. The doctors put her into a coma to paralyze and assist her body to succeed in the upcoming numerous surgeries. Thinking about her life, I saw how every little stupid thing I get upset about just goes out the door. I've been frustrated and mad at various people. Why? I can't give an answer.

No matter what people do to us, we will always love them deep down. On days when tragedy happens, we forget why in the world we were angry in the first place. God really amped up my work load this week. The fire burned, but I'm emerging from the ashes a stronger person—a wiser woman!

Looking back at each time the ashes surrounded me, what do I see? I see a better version of myself. I am far from perfect, but I see God burning away my shortcomings. Every one of us should look at the ashes around us and ask ourselves these questions: Do I see a better version of myself? Do I see beauty rising? Am I who God needs me to be? Do I see the glorious Father's hand?

He is wiping away all my tears. This layer was tougher than most. The fire was stronger. The tears were more abundant, yet I'm appreciating His glorious hand helping me see what I need to recognize and correct. He's given me revised eyes to view life from different angles as I fly above it all.

I hope whatever fire you are in that you see yourself as stronger afterward. God will help you rise and see life from a different angle. You may feel like you're still in the fire, but you're flying unaware of the altitude you've achieved.

Regarding the trials and tribulations I call fires, I pray we go through each of them and rise from the ashes! May God continue to work on us all and help us be the best versions of ourselves! I love you all! Remember to rise from the ashes—wallowing defeats the purpose of the fire!

Burn ~ Renew ~ Soar

OCTOBER 19, 2010

110 › The Answer

Sleep—must find time to sleep! The problem with sleep is the part before it actually happens. The part where I have to deal with myself—my thoughts, losses, weaknesses, and everything. It's that time where you can't get yourself to stop thinking. You just lay still trying not to think about what really needs to be thought of or processed.

I see one positive thing after another during daylight, but the night brings a whole new thought process. It robs me of the positive and gives me sadness, loneliness, negativity, and more. All I can do is pray that God protects me as He silences these thoughts. I pray He can replace them when the dark sets in with happiness, joy, companionship, positiveness, and more.

We each continue to have things that rob us in life. God just wants to be here for us. He wants to get us to a better place—a better us. The song "Answer" by Sarah McLachlan inspires different meanings for me each replay.

The first section is a sense of God speaking to us. He's the answer when we are at the end of our rope. He wants to be here for us no matter how much time passes until we finally lean on Him. He's our balance! When I hear the part about taking my whole life, I see myself talking.

I need Him in my life! I know nights and life are unkind to me, yet I know there's always something better in any situation. No matter what we go through, it will all be worth it in the end. Trash, pain, sorrow, junk, and disappointment are all what they've been defined to be. When it comes down to it, it's the trash, pain, sorrow, and disappointment that needs to be removed from our head space and heart so we can be free.

I am scared to get raw. I'm afraid what staying in bed will do for me. Will I get out of bed when I let myself be raw? I believe God has made me strong! He's molded me into the person who can get her butt out of that bed even when she wants to stay in it.

I will eventually let myself stay in that bed to promote a deeper level of healing. I will finally let myself get raw! I know I've got my peeps who will drag me out of bed if I become paralyzed. This makes my heart and soul happy! Do you have peeps who will drag your butt out of bed? If not, it's time you start finding some who will. It's easy to be there for someone to hand them a Kleenex, but it's hard to be there for someone to drag them out of bed.

I read today that grieving can take more than twenty-four months. I have no idea how long it will take me, but I'm okay with allowing myself all the time I need—no time limits nor pressures to be composed or perfect. Can you give yourself a break? God is here for us and wants to carry the load!

I wore one of my shirts today—the women's Solace Church one with Ephesians 3:20 on the back. God works in crazy ways by taking time to be here for me in the smallest details. When I was at the bank, Don (an employee there) told me about Ephesians 3:14 after seeing the verse on my shirt. I told him my story behind Ephesians 3:17–19, about my time with Lilian Grace and after.

I decided to look up Ephesians 3:14 after wondering how I would make it through this part of my grief journey. God's perfect timing with this verse reassured me. I read on to verse sixteen, and my heart was comforted.

THE FALL TO THE CLIMB

Memory Verse 4

🗡 *"For this reason I kneel before the Father, from whom every family in heaven and on earth derives its name. I pray that out of his glorious riches he may strengthen you with power through his Spirit in your inner being" (Ephesians 3:14–16).*

Now how cool is that? I'm not worried about going to bed tonight because I understand that He's got my back! He's giving me strength. When I start to do it all on my own strength, I fail miserably. I am completely worn out! Yet again I find myself handing it all back over to Him. I am only weak when I try to do it on my own. He is the answer!

If you find yourself worn out, tired, frustrated, or overwhelmed, always give it all to Him! He will be there no matter what! He will be your strength to get you through EVERYTHING! He's the answer you've been looking for during your struggles. He never fails us! Lots of love sent your way.

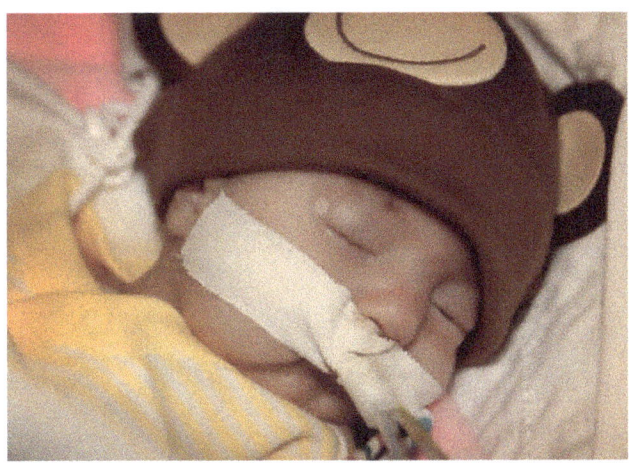

Lilian rests as she prepares to meet Jesus.

OCTOBER 25, 2010

111 › Two Roads

Six months ago, our beautiful daughter came into the world with a great purpose—a mission! She was here to help us see life in a different way. She taught us to fight no matter the circumstances we face each day until we take our last breath.

Today, October 25, 2010, I find myself on a unique path involving parallel roads. On one road, I grieve immensely. I see no end to the loss I've experienced. I never know when something little will tear me down. I see the bad in people and the world. Yet I see the present and hope for tomorrow to be better.

On the other road, I walk strong and tall—with forward motion. I see the future and want to experience it all. I trust God completely and know His plan is magnificent. I see the good in people and know they are learning and growing.

Both these roads exist side by side. I wish I could only walk the strong and tall way, but the Lilian Grace experience opened my eyes completely. There's no shutting any of it off. I see everything for what it is, whether scary or amazing!

A half year since my baby girl arrived earth-side, and time seems to fly when just trying to survive. Night tends to come quickly. I tend to stack my days to distract myself. Funny thing is, I still have to deal with everything and everyone.

I'm okay with this now. Over the next year, I know that each passing day will be tough. I will relive moments when

I carried my daughter in my womb and go back to places she accompanied me after birth. I must create new memories that pair well with our memories made this past year.

Last week, I found myself scared after attending a surprise party. I was unsure how I'd handle being around eighteen people plus their kids. I did better than I had previously estimated, minus some moments of withdrawal. A few times, I saw mouths moving and couldn't hear what anyone was saying. Silently, I had my own anxiety/panic attack. Anyone looking at me had no clue about my state of mind, which was nice.

I preferred to have a mini meltdown inside my mind, instead of an outside showing. As the night progressed, it became easier. A new birthday party memory was formed to pair with the last birthday parties with Lilian. Time and work will reduce the pain.

Next, I attended my first Oklahoma State University (OSU) football game in over a year. I was pregnant at the last one. I found it funny when the same couple who sat by us last year were seated in the same spots. God helped rewrite another memory for the strength and reassurance of attending more games.

I was good until a little girl went by us in an OSU ruffled dress. I immediately remembered Lilian's ruffles on the back of her OSU onesie. My mind visualized Lilian wearing her OSU gear at the hospital after she passed away for her Now I Lay Me Down to Sleep (NILMDTS) photo shoot—fragile, lifeless, yet so beautiful even in death. I got really quiet, and my eyes watered. It took everything I had left not to lose it in the stands. It didn't help that OSU lost the one game I attended.

Anyway, I ended up sleeping all day on Sunday. The outing depleted the rest of my strength. On repeat, I don't have to have it all together. I've got to lighten up on myself. I walk two paths (wanting to be with Lilian and trying to remain present and purposeful here) knowing it will get easier at some point. I don't need advice. I need to live.

One thing to help others around me—please don't ask if I'm pregnant or trying for another baby. My daughter just passed away a couple of months ago—going on almost three. Another baby will not make it better—period. I put this here to educate friends or family members of parents who have lost a child.

Plus, it's even good advice when speaking to a divorcee. You don't ask them if they are getting remarried or trying to get someone to marry them. You don't say it will be better when they have their next spouse. Sorry, I just find this humorous. It reminds me of when people thought I might not ever get married. It came to a point where I'd get asked, "When am I going to attend your wedding?" I'd respond back with, "When am I going to attend your funeral?" I just didn't get why it was so important I get married. Same thing for having kids. We—society—get so caught up on the next level that we forget about the level where we are currently. Can't we just be satisfied with our present?

Soapbox sidebar complete—back to Lilian Grace. Out of all the lessons I learned from her, enjoying the present is one of the most important. I don't have to do what everyone else expects. What matters most is that Michael and I have our little family. Though our extended family is important, Michael is my number one. He continues to help me through the hardest trials.

Seeing Lilian Grace depart from this earth has paralyzed me at times. I find myself still here—walking and breathing. PRAISE GOD! Losing someone so special is what it is for me, and it's different for you—we're handling it in our own ways. I hope everyone recognizes that no one's pain is worse than someone else's. Shame on the person who tries to make their grieving worse than someone else's. It's selfish and unjust.

When I share with you all what is on my mind, I'm just letting you in to my grief. God has taught me so much from various people's reactions. I hope in your grief—for whatever you are grieving—you look to God for help. I'm like a broken record, but it's true. He is the way, the truth, the light!

On this special day for our daughter, I continue to pray for the medical field and children who are sick—for cures, comfort, and happiness for all. To my trisomy 18 families, hang in there. We are beyond blessed to have our wonderful network helping support us. May God give you peace, sleep, and hope! Love you all!

OCTOBER 30, 2010

112 › Dress Up

I'm crying like a crazy woman—grieving for my daughter who doesn't get to experience her first Halloween. Michael did the opposite of me this weekend. He's hunting while I've booked three major events. My motto of keeping myself busy to make it easier to deal with had to work. Unfortunately, the night still comes where all calms down, bringing a deadly silence.

Tonight, I went to the first of three events—Hallow-ZOOeen with my dear friend Sherry. We had a blast. I sugared myself up with too much candy and PF Chang's Sprite, resulting in a hurting tummy, but not as much as my heart hurts.

I witnessed kid after kid dressed up and looking so cute. I reminisced about the days Lilian Grace dressed as Tinker Bell and the Little Mermaid. Oh, how those images make me snicker. I was good with being around people, but I'm finding myself crying right now being alone. To find comfort, I glanced through Lilian's pictures. I loved dress-up time and photo shoots with my princess.

I love the invention of pictures! I'm thankful to God for gifting us with them for such times when our minds struggle to look back. Missing her seems to be at a record high. Every holiday can be tough by watching others live the reality I'm missing out on. You visualize one way in your head how it's supposed to go, then wake up to a whole different reality. It sucks! We take our available opportunities to gather for granted—only appreciating it more when it's lost.

Our little mermaid with her favorite accessory—the red wig

I was blessed to share stories about Lilian Grace several times and praise God for people willing to listen. I did get 103 gorgeous days with her and a thousand-plus pictures to cherish. I stand in awe of God considering those 103 days weren't supposed to happen.

As you celebrate Halloween 2010, take it all in, from dress-up to playtime adventures. I have two more events this weekend to watch families celebrate. It will be another experience to conquer, proving I can make it. Seeing families play and dress up together makes my heart happy. Though Lilian can't be here, I'm making myself have fun again. Our 103 days together weren't easy, but we made it fun by making the moments count! Are you living?

I hope you have a Happy Halloween with good, safe times. Lilian Grace was set to dress up in a Build-A-Bear's Sleeping Beauty costume this Halloween. She would have made a beautiful Sleeping Beauty. Her body was sleeping as she drifted to heaven. From this mother who yearns for her baby girl to be here for dress-up, I love you all!

NOVEMBER 1, 2010

113 › Masked Up

God's love shines down on me all the time. Thanks for the continued prayers and thoughts. The weekend was much easier after the initial night of lil trick or treaters! We are blessed with people who lift us up and don't tear us down—true blessings. Michael and I managed to persevere through the tough weekend.

Behind my mask, I quietly teared up only twice during our church's Trunk or Treat 2010. A little girl dressed as the Little Mermaid triggered me, but I smiled through the tears. On that note, I literally smiled for the camera behind my mask—too funny!

Surprisingly, the experts were right when suggesting we make new memories to replace the ones I dreamed and hoped for with Lilian. Each step will draw more tears and sadness, but eventually that will lessen—fingers crossed. I don't have all the answers, but I do know getting out helps.

Another helpful experience was a dear friend of mine sharing her and her son's first Halloween. Paxton got to be the Woodstock to my Lucy. It was perfect! Thank you, Brianne and Paxton, for sharing your special first.

I'm worn out and happy! I've posted lots of pictures. The best thing Michael and I did tonight was be gone from our house when trick or treating started in our neighborhood. I had a fear about it. I just couldn't watch people with their kids walking down the streets going door to door—a tradition I've desired yet haven't had the chance to experience.

I returned to HallowZOOeen with a worthy adventure, adding my husband and the Downings. We had a ball taking pictures and meeting up with new friends, the Jurneys! The night ended with a showing of *Date Night* with lots of laughter. I loved it.

Laughter is beautiful and much needed. We sometimes forget the importance of giving ourselves a good laugh. Laughing makes everything better! When you find yourself overwhelmed or down, LAUGH—it's one of God's greatest gifts to our souls!

I hope you all had a wonderful holiday. I praise God for His grace, mercy, and love! PRAISE GOD! A friend posted this Scripture on her update, and I thought I'd share:

Memory Verse 5

"A cheerful heart is good medicine, but a crushed spirit dries up the bones" (Proverbs 17:22).

When you have a broken spirit, don't just live with it and stay where you are—let God heal your spirit to make it new! Love you!

To my sweet Tinker Bell,

This Halloween wasn't the same without you here, but your daddy and I learned how to survive. We wish we could have dressed you up. You always made everything look fabulous. I got to see other little girls dress up exactly as you had; they just didn't pull it off as grand as you did.

You looked perfect as Lady Gaga, Minnie Mouse, Tinker Bell, and Lil Mermaid. You even showed us "Girl Power" on the Fourth of July. Thank you for always being such a good sport in dressing up. I know you wanted to roll your eyes a few times, but you just gave me that sassy smile instead.

I love you with everything I have. When I saw other little girls dressed as angels, I thought of you. You don't have to dress like one of them because you are a true angel. I close my eyes and picture you looking perfect in every way. I keep seeing you in random pictures that have been taken here on earth.

I saw you when Cristin (Handlin) and I were at Disneyland; with Cali (Cooper) and me at her soccer game; and today with Detra (Hollie) and me at Trunk or Treat. You are a very bright light leaving me in awe of God through you. Thank you for coming to visit here and there as you bring more smiles.

I miss you more than anything in my life. I hope you know how loved you were. You touched so many. I beamed with happiness as many talked off and on about you.

I must go, but know that you were missed on this trick-and-treating holiday! Keep shining bright!

Love,
Your Mommy

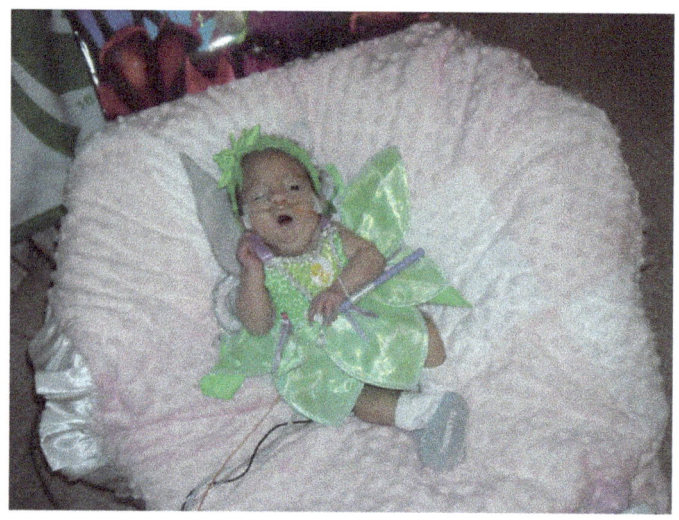

Lilian Grace exhausted from being magical!

NOVEMBER 2, 2010

114 › Broken

Last night was a moment of deep release for Michael and me. He finally uploaded videos from our home camera. What was on it? A family member's wedding and Lilian Grace—two pivotal milestones creating big changes in our lives forever.

Watching just a handful of videos was tough, but I'm glad we did. Bottom line from all the footage—the hopes and dreams of our future were crushed. What we thought would be, will not ever be. What's currently different from the videos? My family member is rebuilding and trying to move forward with life after the marriage ended. Lilian Grace is highlighted, but she's no longer with us, and we keep adjusting to life without her.

What have I learned from these videos? To embrace the moments we have now, hope for the future, and expect God to get me through the reality we call life. It's challenging to watch a family be crushed from divorce or a loss. Ultimately, you have multiple people trying to stay above the water or keep their feet walking forward as they battle disappointment and loss.

My head has been in full drive after more tears and my husband completely melting down and losing all control of his emotions. Thoughts about what my family used to be like and how close we all were taunted me. My family's spirit had been crushed long before Lilian Grace. We've been stuck, just like many of you, in chaos and uncontrollable life changes.

The last couple of years have been tiresome. I've watched not only my family but several others go through traumatic times, almost destroying their family structure. I wish I could travel back to when life wasn't as hard or heavy and the only decision to make was whether to take a bath or a shower!

I can't erase the past, though I'd be the first to line up if the option presented itself. Instead, I must embrace the past. Though my family, friends, places, experiences, and myself are not what we were, I can accept that and meet them all right here.

Life is hard enough without adding to the chaos. Life continues no matter what mood or shape we are in. Truly letting go is one of the hardest challenges in life. Trust me, I've held on too long before releasing many strongholds. Holding on is only misery to us and doesn't impact the ones causing unwanted change and outcomes in our lives. They keep on living and making choices to benefit themselves, disregarding how it impacts others.

I almost jumped out of my body with excitement when I saw Lilian Grace with her daddy. We got it on video! Praise God! Though it's hard to watch them dance together, I'm ecstatic for the chance to replay this. I just wish more moments were recorded. I am thankful many are forever burned in my memory bank!

Please keep us in your extra prayers this week. Friday will be the three-month angelversary of our baby girl earning her wings. Michael's blood pressure has been bad already with multiple nose bleeds—not little ones. I hate that I can't help him feel better. He did finally scroll through the NILMDTS photos—documenting our special moments with Lilian Grace as she earned her wings and after.

Last week's *Grey's Anatomy* episode hit us hard. It's

crazy the timing when a lesson from a TV show is applicable to life. The characters suffered such a traumatic experience at the end of last season. Starting off with the new season, we find them trying to keep living while walking through their grief. One said in a preview that she's just broken.

Many of us can relate to this—BROKEN. It's the best way to describe Michael and me. We are broken. The fabulous news is that God is putting us back together one piece at a time. He wants this for all of us—to be healed from trauma and brokenness.

We won't be the Michael and Chrissy we used to be. You won't be who you used to be. Things will not be how they used to be. I'm learning to be okay with this truth because God is transforming me into something better than what I was. He's making good from bad. I can close my eyes and imagine Him using His loving and gracious hands to piece me back together.

When I look back, may I continue to smile about the good times while learning from the bad ones. May I let my expectations melt away so God's purpose can be fulfilled in my thoughts and soul. There's no going back—we can't change it. Our present is a new reality. May we wake up and adjust accordingly. Welcome to the present, and thank God, the past stays there.

God is Big! He will not let the messes of life overtake us. Keep stepping aside to let Him heal you throughout your mind, heart, and soul! Love always!

NOVEMBER 5, 2010

115 › Three-Month Angelversary

In a little over one hour, it will have been three months since Lilian Grace last coded. I remember her last fighting moment when three in the morning struck on August 5, 2010. The song "No Air" lingered—it was the alarm I used to remind me to pump more breast milk. Ironic since, at the time the song played, they were performing CPR on her.

I'm not sure why it feels so fresh. I wish the other memories would drown it out, yet they don't, and the tears and pain are unstoppable. The only time I get a true break is when I'm at the studio—drifting away for a short moment—training and helping transform people through workouts I've designed.

I relive being curled up on the cushioned guest couch in Lily's hospital room and telling myself, I trust You, God! I trust You, God! I trust You, God! I knew God was answering our prayers. He was going to heal Lilian Grace, and He did—certainly not the way we wanted it to happen, yet He healed her for eternity.

I've stated before about how God granted my prayer—my daughter doesn't have to know suffering, heavy burdens, and more. I still yearn for her precious little body to be in my arms—alive.

As I look at my empty arms and feel great pain, there remains no little baby girl—our squeaker. My arms feel her presence like she's still here, but she is not—the emptiness intensifies my emotions. When she earned her wings fifteen hours and nineteen minutes later that same day, I held her in my arms. The ache in my heart and soul is unbearable. I wish I didn't have to feel this at all and that people didn't have to watch us deal. I know this too shall pass, but missing her is debilitating.

Thank you for always keeping us in your minds and hearts, reminding us that we are not alone. I appreciate those who keep reading my words, allowing me an outlet to release my emotions. Every time I type an entry, I feel better. God sends me lovely little God moments to share and make me smile as He moves me with His grandness.

I will be posting the NILMDTS pictures later today. Please do not feel like you have to look at them. These are very emotional—raw and real. Kelli from NILMDTS was generous to give her time and gifts to capture such a rare moment in our lives.

I wasn't going to post them, but a huge desire to do so would not dim. Three months ago, we shared a moment with doctors, nurses, other hospital staff, and the photographer that left such a hole. When you see the photos, you will see the love Michael and I share with each other and our daughter. We couldn't hide our emotions in the reality of the final moments with her before letting go so her sweet spirit could fly.

I will let you know when I upload the pictures to a new or old album on Facebook. I may put them in an album from long ago. Certain pictures display how hard the tears flowed. Hoping this can give you partial or full closure since you've been supportive and need to process your grief.

At first, the photos crushed me more than anticipated yet brought joy after the fact. I realized not many people get the beautiful opportunity to be present with their child if they pass away—capturing it all on camera! Flashing back through my life has been rough—almost unbelievable how crazy it's been. I couldn't make it up if I tried.

My sister-in-law sent me an inspirational story that made me cry. Her email included a poem titled "Quilt of Holes"[1] that exemplifies my life. I pray my quilt (life) lets God's image and light shine brighter than me. He makes the journey worth continuing as He reaches the lost! Every person is worth being included in eternity.

> *To my angel,*
>
> *I dedicate a song, "Goodnight My Angel" by Billy Joel, to you as it serenades and haunts my soul. Can you believe it's been three months since we said our goodbyes until next time? It still feels like yesterday.*
>
> *I hold you close to my heart—cherishing all our rocking and swaying as beautiful songs of praise, hope, love, and joy were sung or played with you in my arms. I'm not too far away. Eternity sounds heavenly with you there waiting for our reunion. I won't rush it, for I know you will always be a part of me. You are in perfect hands with our Maker.*
>
> *Happy third-month angelversary, Lilian Grace! I love you to the moon and back and for all eternity! May God give you a huge hug and kiss from all of us!*
>
> *Forever,*
> *Your Mom*

---

[1] Linda Winchell, "The Quilt of Holes," (2009), https://www.poemhunter.com/poem/holes-in-my-quilt/.

Thanks for hanging in there to this point. I hope you look up the story and that it and the song by Billy Joel stir your spirit. Please continue to lift up families who have lost their children or spouse. They're fighting silent battles every day, trying to survive or to just breathe. I keep you all lifted up because life is not easy. God continues to be Big for us all! Praise His holy name forever and for all eternity! Love you all!

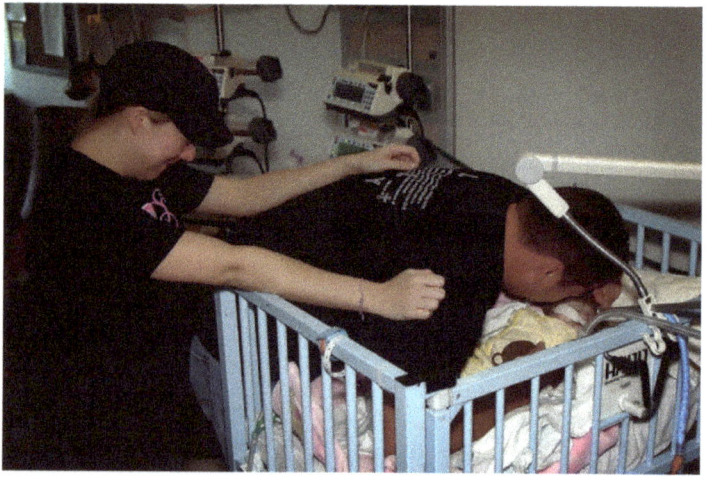

Before letting go so her sweet spirit could fly

NOVEMBER 6, 2010

116 › Believing, Battling, & Learning

The NILMDTS photos can be found in the album "Life" on my Facebook page. Keep in mind how extra special and real they are as they display all our emotions while we experienced our worst fear—losing her to death.

I felt a strong desire to share these with you. Please have tissues near when viewing all of them. Hoping this brings closure for you about Lilian Grace's mission here on earth.

For a good portion of my life, I've been an open book. I never knew just how open God would have my life be. I deeply appreciate that He gave me such a miraculous gift. Lilian Grace was the smallest and greatest missionary I've ever had the privilege to meet here on earth.

My husband has been such a rock for our family. I know he fights just as I do in our daily life. Some things people worry about or emphasize just don't matter as much to us anymore. Knowing that Lilian Grace is the most amazing thing to happen helps us through the junk and chaos.

I pray God moves you to appreciate more of your life as you live it out. Break away from your chains and live the life God intended for you. Even through the tears, I'm stepping a step forward every day.

I keep praising God for giving me good from the bad. Trisomy 18 or any chromosomal disorder is evil and unfair. We, who have had to live with it every day, love our babies unconditionally, just as our heavenly Father does. We fight each day either wondering if today will be their final day or missing them because they were called home early.

Don't get me wrong—God gives us enough strength to keep seeing the beauty in our children's lives. We are worn out, yet God refuels us to find a shred of fun or happiness. May all of you experiencing something similar know God carries each of us. Even when we jump out of His arms, He waits for us to either jump back in or allow Him to pick us up from the crumbled messes.

Thank you for battling with us!
Thank you for believing God is Big!
Thank you for learning valuable lessons alongside us!
I say thank you a million times over to all of you.

May God comfort you after seeing our blessed family in pictures. Lilian was able to finish out her mission—God's will for her life—when we learned to let go. Love always! I'll leave you with several verses to reflect on. Hope in God's glorious ways and ultimate goal.

Memory Verses 6–8

🗡 *"He said to me: 'It is done. I am the Alpha and the Omega, the Beginning and the End. To the thirsty I will give water without cost from the spring of the water of life. Those who are victorious will inherit all this, and I will be their God and they will be my children'" (Revelation 21:6–7).*

🗡 *"After that, we who are still alive and are left will be caught up together with them in the clouds to meet the Lord in the air. And so we will be with the Lord forever" (1 Thessalonians 4:17).*

🗡 *"I eagerly expect and hope that I will in no way be ashamed, but will have sufficient courage so that now as always Christ will be exalted in my body, whether by life or by death.*

For to me, to live is Christ and to die is gain. If I am to go on living in the body, this will mean fruitful labor for me. Yet what shall I choose? I do not know! I am torn between the two: I desire to depart and be with Christ, which is better by far" (Philippians 1:20–23).

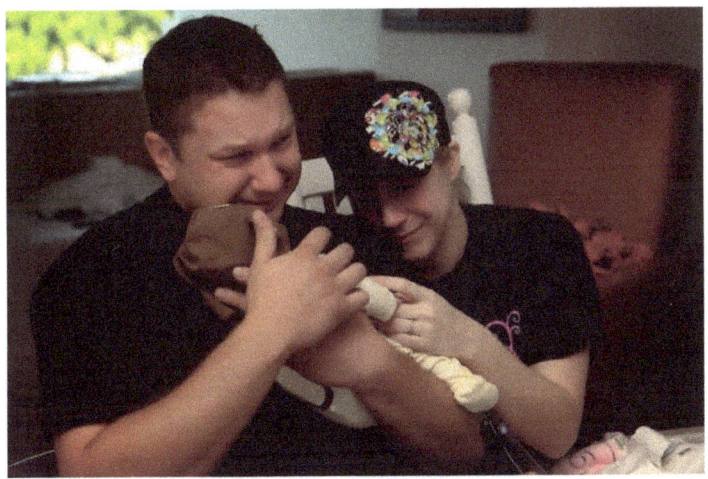

Our worst fear—losing her to death

God is Big.

NOVEMBER 16, 2010

117 › Fish Tank Faith

Swimming, swimming, swimming, swimming—must keep swimming! Michael's sister, Leslie, and our brother-in-law, Kyle, gave us their fifty-five-gallon freshwater tank and four fish. Watching fish has been known to calm the soul, but I never really thought it would work.

The basics of the whole deal is to take time to sit down and stop talking. You give God a chance to work on you while you are still. I've been staring at the tank off and on for almost two weeks. Not all has been fun because I've had to start facing aspects of my journey that I've avoided or denied for thirty-two years.

I'm a compassionate person who thrives on being a worker and helper. I've found that there are many people in this world who use others—I'm not counting myself out. We all, at some point, are guilty of using others or have been used. I digress—back to the fish tank journey.

We added other tropical fish to the mix, which made the tank environment more interesting. We have two big fish who rule the tank, protecting their territory and the food. The followers attempt to bombard the bigger fish yet fail.

A couple of fish like to hide away from it all—going without food to avoid any confrontations. You've got the type A fish who is everywhere and in everything. Another fish is out and about just enough to say, "Hey, I'm here." Then there's the one who wants all the attention as soon as someone is near. We can't forget the one who is open yet scared, with even the slightest movement causing a quick jerk and escape. Wow, I could say names of people in place of each fish if the tank represented my world. We're all swimming through life, trying to survive.

Through all my projects and jobs lately, I'm having to accept I'm not who I used to be. Yes, there are some similarities that do exist—yet I'm not the same, and neither are any of you after Lilian and the circumstances you've gone through.

I think half my problem—maybe this is true for you as well—is spending too much time trying to put the pieces back together once they've been broken. Have you ever tried to glue broken pieces back together? It's never the same again, even if you do a superb job of gluing it.

What else isn't the same? Mostly my eyesight—my baby girl ripped my blinders down, making me truly see people and places for who and what they really are. I have been trying to swim backward, avoiding realities—wanting to go back to when it was less painful. God had a different plan for you and me.

It's easy to avoid and not deal with life's realities. As I kept staring at the fish tank and focused on one "fish" at a time, I started working on healing old wounds. I thought of people I know who have hurt me. I wish we could all get it right 24/7, but we are only humans. Even through our failures, we can keep trying and swimming until we get things right.

I'm sadly discovering that a number of people do not respect me in my personal and professional life. It seems that if they can't use me, then what am I good for? I'm only straying a second here because I really don't want to deal with them. To be positive, I thank God for the people in my life who aren't users. I am blessed with amazing people who swim alongside me and others—helping along their way.

Do I know there are people out there who don't know any better? Yes, I think I do. I want to give them the benefit of the doubt. I blame my perception instead of accepting the truth.

What should I do? What should you do? We should stop trying to make people, jobs, places, past moments, and other things meet unreasonable expectations. We need to accept who or what they are and keep swimming. We can't expect the past to be the future. We've got to release people's shortcomings, habits, and failures when it's time.

The facts can't be changed—Lilian Grace is gone. I can't bring her back. I can refocus on the good stuff and praise God that I got to meet her and be her mommy—even though heaven separates us.

Why don't we leave the shipwrecks of life—death, divorce, hurts, or disappointments—to swim in fresher water representing the present? I can't change what people have done or how they have handled things in my life. What I can do is let go—free myself—like escaping a fisher's net.

I'm not sure why this needed to be written today, but I trust God. I've been saying it more these days—I trust You, God! I trust You, God! I trust You, God! In order to continue swimming, I must make the choice to face issues one at a time while releasing the strain they put on me.

I look around my house; it's not the same. I must get my act together and organize it even though I'm crying and processing. I've got to stop doing what I often do—open my mouth before I think about my schedule.

I pray we all start releasing the nets—the past and the weights that pull us down daily. We'll find out that we get more sleep, lose weight, and live when we do. Love you all and thanks for all the feedback from Lilian Grace's photos. God was right that I should share them with you.

My baby girl continues to be a rockstar as His plan rocks on. I appreciate those who say they don't know what to say or their honesty of not understanding. The fact is that I need love, attention, prayers, and hugs, which you freely give. I need real and loving people who aren't trying to get ahead or aren't trying to say they are worse than us. Thank you from the bottom of my heart! I love you for lifting us up, instead of telling us what we aren't doing for you. You know who you are, and I pray daily for you.

There is a difference between being selfish and taking care of yourself without neglecting others. God continues to teach us through Lilian Grace's life. I appreciate mothers who take care of their babies yet make time for other relationships. I see lots of mommies getting it right. Thanking the Lord for your examples!

The therapeutic fish tank

NOVEMBER 17, 2010

118 › 103 Beads

Lately, I've been blessed to witness amazing friends working through God's will. He keeps inspiring individuals through Lilian Grace's story, which brings me great pride and joy for my daughter and fabulous heavenly Father! In the following months, I will ask you to share about how God's will unfolded for you through Lilian Grace's life. I'm excited to work with you to help others while giving God credit and honoring my daughter's legacy. God is timely in providing what I need to succeed in His ever-loving plans.

At tonight's home team's prayer request time, unexpected emotions filled the space. In our group, we are blessed with special people whose hearts follow the Lord. My heart always sings and happy tears flow when I speak about Lilian Grace, who keeps touching people's lives even after death. Wow! I'm blown away and praising God to the depths of all eternity! I'm one lucky mommy!

Continuing with blessings—my dear friend Cindy (Haley) has inspired me with her commitment, love, and talents. She doesn't realize she's special, yet God demonstrates His extravagant plans often throughout her life. She's been a blessing to our Warrior Princess Foundation by making beautiful necklaces to help raise money to assist trisomy 18 and trisomy 13 families with costs related to medical services, equipment, unexpected funerals, milk supplies, and more.

I asked Cindy to write up a short story to explain the significance of the 103 beads on the necklaces to Lilian's life and the cause—please read the story. It may make you cry so grab some tissues just in case. One hundred percent of the forty dollars goes directly to the foundation. Cindy has donated her time and supplies. Praise God for her heart! Love you all!

> *A little over a year and a half ago, I attended my ten-year high school reunion and caught up with Michael Whitten, to whom I hadn't spoken in all of those years. If you had told me then that all of this time later, he and his gorgeous wife, Chrissy, would be on my heart every single day since, I would've thought it strange.*
>
> *The first time I saw Chrissy, she was all alone on the dance floor, busting every move in the book, completely fearless, inviting others to join her! I knew at that moment that she was an incredible person and that I wanted to get to know her. During the following year, I had that opportunity when precious baby Lily came to be.*
>
> *As everyone else who knew of her did, I fell head over heels in love with Lilian Grace and had the honor of praying for her throughout every day of her life. In that time, I also grew to love and cherish her parents, whose testimony of strength and courage in the face of unspeakable loss and pain inspires me to be a better wife, mother, and Christian.*
>
> *Throughout the 103 days of Lily's earthly life, I struggled with my inability to "do" anything of any consequence to help the Whittens. On the day that Lilian earned her heavenly wings, I spent the day in quiet prayer time, and God revealed to me an idea for a memorial necklace, which could be used to raise money for Lily's fund.*
>
> *You see, I make jewelry as a hobby, so my initial response to this idea was that it may come off as a tacky suggestion; therefore, I kept it to myself for over a month.*

God kept wrestling with me, though, so I looked into what making the vision I'd seen in my mind on that fateful day would entail.

Lily lived 103 glorious days. In my mind, I saw one crystal for each day of her life, each representing the birthstone for all 103 days, and a charm at the center. That's six clear crystals for April, thirty-one emerald crystals for May, thirty pearls for June, thirty-one ruby crystals for July, and five peridot crystals for August.

Well, the crystals I typically use are only 4 millimeters wide, so I doubted that 103 would be enough to create a necklace that was at least 16 inches long, which is the standard necklace length. Guess how long 4mm multiplied by 103 works out to be—16 inches!

I knew at that moment that God had his hands in this, so I contacted Chrissy. She was excited about the idea and chose an angel wing for the charm to represent the wings her darling daughter had earned.

I feel so blessed to be able to donate several editions of these necklaces over time to Chrissy and Michael so that they may reach out and support the families of other T18 babies. These two are truly storing up treasure in heaven!

In the words she typed in this story, you get a sense of her heart. She makes me proud to call her a dear friend. She is making ten necklaces for the first round. Please send me an email if you would like to buy a necklace—first come, first served. The first ten purchasers in round one will get the necklace within two to three weeks. A gorgeous photo of the necklace is included in this entry.

Thanks again for reading and supporting us the way you do. Be ready for more amazing opportunities to bless others. Coming soon:

🍪 *Timmy's Tasty Treats to Topple Trisomy 18* cookbook: All the way from New York, another dear friend of mine, Stefanie Hilarczyk, has brought together trisomy 18 kids and their families' recipes. Family recipes from both my and Michael's side are featured to represent Lilian.

🛍️ Scentsy party: The foundation gets 25 percent of sales.

🏃 Warrior Princess Trail Run on April 25—celebrating Lilian's birthday: We're teaming up with RunnersWorld to put on this event with volunteer opportunities!

👪 Women of Faith Conference "Over the Top" on November 11–12, 2011, in Oklahoma City at the Ford Center: Recruiting 103 women to attend in honor of Lilian Grace! Let me know if you'd like to participate.

If there is something burning in your heart and mind that you feel moved to do, please send me an email, and we can work together on it. I'm open to many ideas to raise money to help our fellow trisomy 18 and trisomy 13 kids and their families. Praise God for all the current and future opportunities!

Fundraiser necklace

NOVEMBER 24, 2010

119 › Thanksgiving

Thanksgiving—count your blessings—take a gigantic deep breath! God has blessed us beyond measure, yet a few blessings feel bittersweet. I try to stay positive! I try to stay connected! Try—I try—I try, but I find myself exhausted as usual at the end of the day. Blessings keep popping up right and left, yet they still drain my energy.

Not only would tomorrow have been Lilian Grace's seven-month birthday and our first Thanksgiving, but her older sister would also have been four on my mom's birthday—November 27—had she been born. I've had a hard time appreciating the fullness of Thanksgiving for some time since that horrible miscarriage in 2006. Even my great-aunt Geneita passed away on this special day years ago, making the holiday bittersweet in more than one way.

I remember years ago when Thanksgiving was filled with delicious stuffed turkey, salty mashed sweet potatoes with fluffy marshmallows, buttered homemade rolls, and grape Kool-Aid. We would play football with cousins, make leaf piles and jump in without a care in the world, and follow the leader through the creek and woods. Laughter, prayers, songs—you name it—if it was joyous, it was part of our tradition, and my blessings overflow because of all those memorable moments together.

Now—well, now Michael and I will be trading in the past and exploring new adventures this Thanksgiving holiday. Branson better be ready! For our Thanksgiving meal, we will eat with our hands at the Dixie Stampede. The next two days, we will play, laugh, sing, and listen to all things Silver Dollar City—marking Michael's first visit ever. I still can't believe he's never been.

Is this my ideal Thanksgiving? No, it is far from it. If I looked at what my life could have been like, I'd have three children—a four-year-old, one-year-old, and seven-month-old, filling our house with laughter and joyous moments. We would, of course, watch the Macy's Thanksgiving Day Parade. I would have learned to make a very traditional turkey meal with all the works for our little family to enjoy. We'd pile all the fresh and dried leaves together in the backyard and take turns jumping in—what sweet joy.

We'd eventually see our extended families after we finished with our own little family traditions. Some hide and seek along with football playing would occur. Michael would be grateful and proud of my energy and desire to create such a precious holiday with a homemade meal (since cooking has been a struggle of mine as of late—try the last few years).

Instead of the perfect Thanksgiving, my arms are empty, but my heart is full. I've been lucky enough to meet one of my children—to see and experience her smiles, laugh, cries, and movement. No one is making a special dinner today. I'm here trying to piece together my blessings and lessons. I'm trying to step aside so God can adjust my eyes, feet, heart, and soul. This is different ground than I expected. This is definitely not where I saw us spending the holiday.

I can't imagine when this will feel different or more normal. I don't even know when progress will start. I do know that I am grateful for my heavenly Father's patience with me. He just cares that I'm trying. I'm trusting Him even through the fogginess, pivots, struggles, pitfalls, and hang-ups—through it all. One percent of God is big enough for me and all of us.

Counting my blessings—people to be thankful for. I have a set of people in my life who are unique and divinely created to walk with me and build me up. They assisted me in getting up this mountain. I couldn't do life without them.

I have a set of people who get it right in their own unique way—who challenge me and inspire me to be stronger than I thought possible. I wouldn't grow in this way without them in my life.

I have a set of people who show me how not to do things. I've learned through their trials, which spares me from participating and failing. I'm thankful for the lessons they've taught me.

There are people I've never personally met, yet I learn from those who knew them and were impacted by their journey. I have to add them to the list of people I could not do life without—their footprints have forged a path for my walk.

For those who communicate with me often, keep in mind that I process things out loud. If you think I'm crazy, you might be correct. I'm your average turkey—gobbling around the forest floor while trying to find my way.

There are people who can get on my nerves, as I'm sure I do to them. I unquestionably have a hard time hiding my emotions—and I gain wisdom from each encounter. I'm not happy when I get in my crappy moods and start griping. Unfortunately, this is still part of my process at this time. I appreciate your listening ear and loyalty, even if it's the one-hundredth time I've repeated myself. I promise it does help!

When looking back at my thirty-two years, I see things I wish I didn't see. Yet what would my life be without any of it? Would I be who I am today? I have issues just like the next person. I guess I'm just learning how to accept new truths in order to move forward—not so easy to do, but it is possible. I'm still here, so I presume God has more in store for me.

I want you all to know how blessed I truly am. God has given me a beautiful roof over my head; a daughter who rocked this world and now resides in heaven; decent health (even in the not-so-fun stuff) with eyesight, hearing, thinking, and breathing; a heart that loves unconditionally (hopefully always); physical abilities in walking, running, and moving; compassion and a passionate soul; abundant family and friends; new adventures; jobs; owning my own business—and the list goes on. I thank God—to the fullest of all eternity—for giving me so much.

I may not always accept a blessing, but I appreciate each one in time. I pray and hope you and your family and friends enjoy this beautiful holiday. To the shoppers who will be crazy enough to wake at the butt crack of dawn, please be careful and enjoy the day—injury free. To all the eaters, may you pace yourselves and not go too crazy. You are what you eat, and that's reflected in the amounts of food and trips through the line! Now a letter to my angel . . .

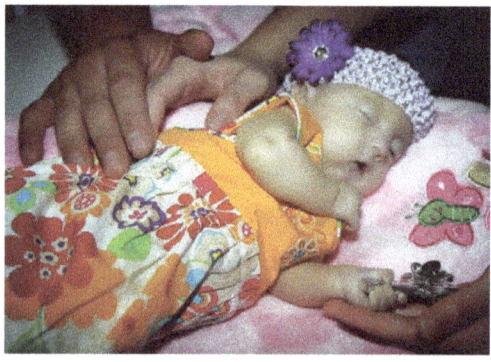

Thankful for this sweet miracle and blessing!

Oh, to my Lil Squeaker,

I wish you could be here to enjoy this jam-packed holiday season. I must say that it's been very lonely without you here. I miss your squeaks, poopy diapers, and medicine frenzy. Most of all, I miss your gorgeous, smiling face, even when I knew you didn't feel good and hurt so bad.

Mommy and Daddy couldn't help you, but your heavenly Father did. I owe Him gratitude for making such a perfect lil angel. Yes, Mommy is talking about you, Warrior Princess. I love you more than words can describe.

Thanksgiving is a holiday where we give thanks. It's a time where we count the blessings God has given us. The greatest one God has given me is you, baby girl. You are everything I could ever hope for or imagine. Because you fought and gave everything, you taught us how to live and follow through with God's plans—a true blessing.

Lilian Grace, I want to thank you for being such a blessed example—living up to your Warrior Princess nickname. I praise God for letting us be your parents—an honor that comes with many emotions.

I wish you could be here for an extra special Thanksgiving meal. Your daddy and I will be doing something your daddy wanted to do a long time ago, minus you—though I know you'll be here in spirit. By the way, I caught a glimpse of your bright light shining through the curtains at the studio this morning. I tried to take a picture. Thanks for saying hello! Anyway—thank you again for living God's will out loud for all of us to experience. I love you to the moon and back and for all eternity!

Love,
Your Mommy

Before I forget, I've got another dear friend putting together her second cookbook to help trisomy 18 families. Lilian Grace is featured in this wonderful cookbook along with recipes from her great-great-grandma Edith Cooper and great Nan West. I can't wait to get my copy! They are only twenty-five dollars. Through the sales of *Timmy's Tasty Treats to Topple Trisomy 18*, Stefanie (Hilarczyk) will be giving the Warrior Princess Foundation up to two-thousand dollars after books are sold. I can't wait to start blessing our trisomy 18 and trisomy 13 babies and their families.

Here is the story I had Stefanie write to share more detailed information. I am blessed to know her and other special people who are trying to make a difference in my life. God is Big and blessing us all one after another—enjoy and love to you all!

> *Our son, Timothy Hilarczyk Jr., was diagnosed with mosaic trisomy 18. It is a very rare genetic disorder. Trisomy 18 occurs in about one in every three thousand births. Most of these babies are stillborn, which happens more with boys than girls. There are three different types of the disorder—full trisomy 18 (with most children dying soon after birth), partial trisomy 18, and mosaic trisomy 18. Unlike Down Syndrome, which is also caused by a chromosomal defect, most trisomy 18 developmental issues are medical and life-threatening.*
>
> *When my husband and I learned about this syndrome in 2009, our hearts were broken. We had tried for three and a half years to give our daughter, Lorelai, a playmate. After seeing some fertility doctors and scheduling my IUI, I found out I was pregnant. Boy, was I surprised! We knew Timmy was a miracle. Every day, we thank God for our children.*

Timmy is monitored by a team of doctors and receives early intervention because of his developmental delay. We have done a lot of praying. Timmy had one corrective eye surgery but fortunately did not need craniofacial or kidney surgery, which is common for children with this disorder. At the end of the day, it all makes sense when I see our kids hug each other or when Lorelai tells me how much she loves Timmy! Hearing him begin to talk lately has been so much fun! Timmy is a brown-haired, blue-eyed heartbreaker. He is the most lovable little guy I know. He loves to snuggle with his sister. And he loves to make people laugh. His smile could make the sun rise. He is such a little fighter—as soon as anyone tells him he can't do something, Timmy always finds a way to prove them wrong! He is a tiny guy, but what's inside can fill an ocean. He is PERFECTION to me!

This all got me thinking one day. We have been very lucky so far; Timmy has shown great improvement in his overall health. With his therapy at home, his development is moving right along! Sure, we have hit some bumps in the road, but they have been small. However, while we celebrate Timmy's success, there are still other mommies and daddies waiting for their children's next feeding or breathing treatment, helping their children open their hands because they have clenched hands, waiting for their children's next heart surgery because of defects they were born with, putting them in wheelchairs because they cannot walk, or even waiting for them to die.

Many of these families need respite care so they can take a break. They need support after a child has passed away. The foundations require money to help these families. They rely on financial support to fund research and educate our communities.

We have been blessed with so many helping hands over

the last year. We have such an amazing, supportive family. All the prayers, thoughtfulness, letters, cards, and phone calls from friends and family have been overwhelming. So I came up with the idea of creating a cookbook to honor all of these little people! The proceeds from the sale of this book will go to help families in need of financial support and for research so that maybe one day trisomy 18 will be a treatable disorder. I believe that trisomy 18 can and should be treated like any other disorder—hearing the words "incompatible with life" is NOT acceptable. So I ask today that we all stand together and FIGHT for these children because WE are their VOICES.

I would like to thank everyone for helping me with the vision for my second book. These journeys also lead me to new people. Some were very new to their loss, but everyone shared their loved ones with such grace. These mommies and daddies continue to amaze me with their warmth and courage. I again have learned so much from these women. I even got to meet some of these families, which was amazing, and make memories that I will cherish as one of the proudest moments of my life. I admire all of you for your strength, courage, and joy you have for your children and the pure joy you have for being their parents. If the world could hear these stories, what a sweeter place it would be. Thank you again. All my love to each of you! I am so glad you are my friends and my "trisomy family." ~ Stefanie

NOVEMBER 28, 2010

120 › Completely Held

"Held"—Natalie Grant's angelic, pure voice stirs memories of the recent Women of Faith Conference I attended with supportive women in my life and brings tears to my spirit as if it were written just for my life.

This Thanksgiving weekend has been woven with many unspoken revelations. It's been a time of revolution for myself and those around me since we can all quickly get caught up in the daily comings and goings of life—forgetting how much God holds us and gets us through. I want to stop and praise my ever-loving heavenly Father for not only promising to hold me but for continually holding me no matter what this life brings.

In Branson, I met a lovely lady named Shirley, who had sadly just spent her second Thanksgiving without her husband, Gary. She told me the second Thanksgiving since his passing has been the hardest. A few others have told me the reason—because we expect ourselves to be better and further along in our healing journey.

I believe my running into Shirley at Dress Barn was not an accident but a divine appointment. I gave her my card and added my CaringBridge web address. I wanted so desperately for her to see my precious baby girl, but I could not get pictures to come up—I guess it wasn't meant to be at the time. Hopefully, she's had a chance to check out my CaringBridge site and started reading my entries. For whatever God has planned, I pray it be done!

I saw the sadness in her eyes—the longing to be reunited with her husband. I do believe she will be reunited with him in eternity, just as Michael and I will be with our kids. I'm finding that I need to shift my focus to being held more than trying to fight through the struggles on my own. God's arms are huge and comforting—full of everything I could possibly ever need or want to make it all better.

My crying episodes seem to come at bedtime when my environment goes dark and life slows down. I've been trying hard to figure it all out—emotions and reality swirling. I want to fix myself, find an angle or outlook—something—anything—to magically make it all go away in a snap. I smile through tears, knowing I can't make it all just go away.

I don't need it to go away. I need to process more while being held securely and honestly. With everything I've gone through in life, God makes it turn out for the good. It's so easy for me to fall back, dwell, and convert to my independence—my way—my terms.

Oh, Lord, please continue to push me and others—professional interrupters—out of Your way and our own! I love how You keep holding us through life's daily struggles and the disappointments we face.

To be held means You have not given up on me. I've survived everything in life thus far because You have held me while teaching, believing, and trusting me. You've been my all-powerful, loving God—giving me people who teach, show, and love—oh, so much love—to fuel my way.

I can't change anything. I can't bring my baby girl back. I can't make people be who they are not. I can't make it all better for me—for you—for anyone. I can only keep trusting God that tomorrow is a new day; yesterday is over; and today is almost done.

I've listened to Natalie's song, "Held," continuously while typing this entry—about twenty or more times. The line that talks about the meaning of being held and surviving after something sacred is ripped from your life—that line stirs up memories. Life, family, and values were sacred and secure until all were shaken and torn from my life. God pulled me through and has given me more. His promise of holding me has rung true daily.

My heavenly Father has shown me how much deeper, wiser, and stronger my life, eyesight, and love have grown because of my experiences, adventures, trials, and disappointments. I have a ways to go to adjust, understand, and accept how to let God hold me in everything. I'm not ready to let go of my strongholds—my grip is tight.

We are all guilty! Let's try to curl up in our heavenly Father's arms and let him hold us while we heal, process, and accept tomorrow. He wants to hold us! I'm jumping in His arms to be held completely and fully while He heals my brokenness—making me whole once again.

God, thank You for Your unconditional love and promise of eternal life. I appreciate You for holding me no matter the time, place, circumstance, or state You find me in—especially when I tend to always wear myself out instead of choosing your arms first for renewal of energy, strength, and ability when facing whatever comes. May we not hesitate to jump into Your arms to be held and loved for all eternity.

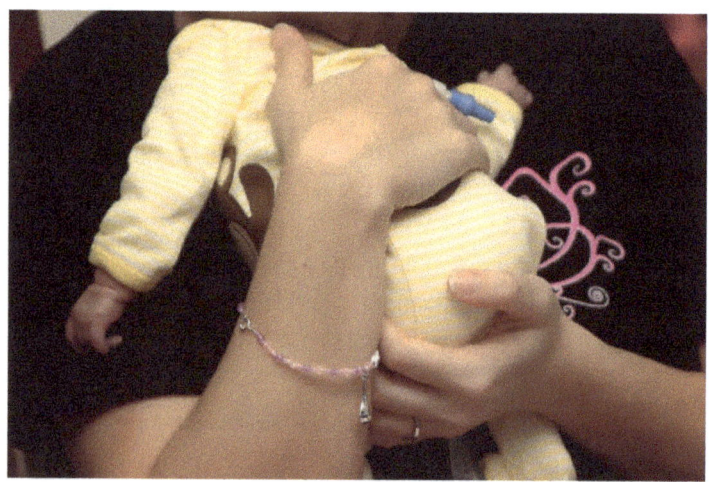

Even though she was gone, I held her tightly while God held me.

DECEMBER 6, 2010

121 › Four-Month Angelversary

As of yesterday, Lilian has officially been in heaven longer than she was here on earth with us. I had a mixed-up day. My goal of hanging out with a family member turned into a huge fight. My intentions were not to attack that person. My anger got in the way when my hearing was impaired by past hurts and unresolved anger. The things I really needed to say were lost in unwanted anger and yelling.

I apologize for not getting the right words out. Instead of helping, I made it worse for you. When I spoke to sixty-plus people at a funeral about hope, I brought up my hurtful actions. I'm realizing I am not in a place to fix things this early in my grief journey. There's much healing to be done.

How many of us try to fix things while hurt and angry and find ourselves making it worse? I've decided I can't help my family, Michael's family, friends, or past coworkers through their problems. A reckoning of truth and acceptance is needed to move forward. I'm in the angry state of grief—unsure of the length—but I may have to lock myself in the house.

I'm not angry that Lilian Grace lived and left us so drastically. I'm frustrated and mad that I'm not the person I used to be—I can't go back. I'm beyond mad; she ripped the blinders from my eyes when she took her last breath. For four months, I've been searching for those blinders to put back up—denial felt easier. Guess what? No such luck.

We all have problems. I'm not sure why we try to make ours seem worse than others—it's not a competition. We all suffer with our own pain—our own load. I've had many state that their problems aren't as bad as ours. Yes—yes, they are. When we face our problems, we have to realize that they are our problems and not someone else's to fix. Some of our problems can only be fixed by us. No one else can fix them for us, no matter how hard they try.

My husband is not one to share his thoughts, emotions, or struggles. And I tend to try and help him by translating for him like it's my job. Well, I need to back off. I need to stop expecting to be able to logically talk it out while holding on to past anger. It's not my place—he has to process it when he's ready. Besides, he thinks he'll be wasting his time by talking it out.

A lady at the funeral I spoke at came up to me afterward to share her fisherman's story. She loves to cast and reel fish in. She said God had told her to put her problems on the hook; tie knots on the line to make sure they stay there; cast them out; grab some scissors; and cut the line, assuring she can't take them back—they're gone forever. Let's do that—it sounds nice!

Michael and I attended a special holiday service at Floral Haven to hear about getting through the holidays for those who lost a loved one in 2010. To my surprise, we've been doing the right things for us. It may not seem right for everyone else, but it's right for us since we both are still standing despite a time where family and traditions flood the months of November and December. Though our little family of three can't be together, we must adjust.

After hearing from others who are grieving Lilian in their own way, I must address a few things. YOU have not "lost" Michael or me. You have to understand we can't possibly be the same people we were before Lilian was born. We are working our way through it all. We are broken—like many around us. Time and God will heal our wounds! Please stop with the "I've lost you all." Please try to understand and don't make us feel bad for being changed by our circumstances.

We have lost our daughter—she is never coming back. One day, we will get to spend eternity with her, but she is no longer here on earth.

I've decided when we do the opposite of what everyone else wants us to do, they think we are wrong and neglecting them. Let me be bold in stating that Michael and I are here for people all the time—family and friends. The problem is when certain people assume or even expect us to clean up their messes, and we can't! Unless someone is willing to face reality and accept their role, no one can help them. Actually, it's up to the individual to be willing to do the work and change.

Let me make this statement clear—this is for ALL of us to read. If you are getting life decisions right, keep moving in that direction. If you are needing a change in your life, start changing it yourself. We—including myself—keep trying to do the same things and expect different results. It's time to take a different path by being different! No one can make you happy—you have to take responsibility.

I hurt my husband yesterday by not controlling myself. Self-control has always been a battle of mine when it comes to controlling my emotions and consuming too many sweets. I heard a message from someone I hurt stating they were planning to leave our church. Who can be proud of this? I acknowledge that I misspoke and left other words unsaid, which caused damage. Even in the craziness of my loss, it's unfair to allow someone else to have that much influence on your own relationship with God. If we all did this, the church wouldn't exist.

I'm tired of watching people make choices that end in

misery—walking through life thinking everything will be given to them because they are owed. Some people expect others to bail them out of any situation—never realizing they have to wake up. I've counseled people who know what they should be doing but purposely choose differently without a care. I can't forget the ones who skip around life from one thing to the next, searching for something to fill the holes in their hearts, then finding themselves with more hurt, pain, and suffering.

Bottom line—I'm tired of hurting people by trying to help. Who am I to think I have the power to help? I don't have any power. I don't have the self-control to stay calm enough when I mishear words while trying to help. I'm finding some people like being miserable because they are afraid of having nothing to complain about. There is a Way of life that doesn't center around pain, suffering, and misery. When storms knock us down, it centers around hope in the One who calms storms!

Remember, unless someone is willing to step up to do the work, none of us can help them. They will continue to repeat situations until a reality check shakes them. I got my own reality check yesterday.

Sadly, I can't take back what was said nor the damage from the unfortunate fights. I can shut up and let God help. He places the right people in our lives to help. I know now that I can't stop people from saying things that cause the anger to swell up in me. I can learn to control my mouth and give it over to God—remembering that people are responding to their own hurts, anger, and shortcomings. I could be more understanding since I do the same thing.

Not sure if this helps anyone, but I know I need to work on not letting others bring out my crazy side—I'm not sure why, but they do. It's not their fault. I let it happen.

May we all mend broken relationships this holiday season! I'm working on letting wrongs and misspoken words go. The biggest issue I face this holiday season is how to adjust to the new eyes God gave me after knowing Lilian Grace. I'm learning from the insights and accepting that I can't go backward. Love you all.

> *Happy four-month angelversary, Lilian Grace!*
>
> *Sorry you had to witness Mommy fighting like an idiot while picking up the broken pieces in my heart. None of this is a quick fix, but I'm willing to work through the good, bad, and ugly to be better!*
>
> *Love,*
> *Mom*

I encourage you to listen to "You Hold Me Now" by Hillsong. There's eternal meaning to this life, and one day believers will be forever free from what hurts us. I don't want to be broken but seeing this picture of Lilian Grace toward her earthly ending reminds me that suffering and pain are temporary. God holds my baby girl just as He holds me now in my shortcomings and weaknesses. There's hope that burns brighter than my brokenness, anger, and frustrations. I look forward to a day without darkness—to live in peace!

82 Chrissy L. Whitten

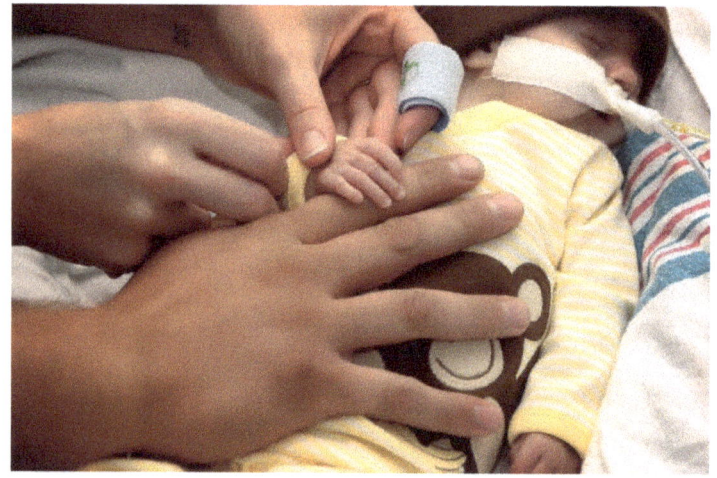

Holding hands

DECEMBER 10, 2010

122 › The Dancer

Memory Verse 9

⚔ *"He will wipe every tear from their eyes. There will be no more death or mourning or crying or pain, for the old order of things has passed away" (Revelation 21:4).*

At this moment, I find myself bawling tear after tear after tear. I have prayed more this week than in a long time with people who are at the beginning of their grieving journey. My heart aches for them and the indescribable challenge ahead. There are mornings after sleeping or drifting away in a daydream when you have no idea how you will feel, be, or do when you wake up.

You may find yourself vastly different than most who surround you. You know you aren't really who you're expected to be. You have moments when you think you will ride this wave like a pro surfer—maybe today you'll have it more together for those around you when, in fact, you barely talked yourself into getting out of bed.

Some will understand, and others will look at you like a deer in the headlights. We all have our own way of walking through life. Just keep getting out of bed and walking with God's help and guidance through the foggy season!

God blessed me with eyes that seem to be magnified greater than 20/20, increasing my people-watching skills. What do I see? I observe people struggling to figure out their true identities. I catch others trying to run from their fears. I spot more than a handful trying to fill the void in their heart with distractions that don't satisfy. We're all human—sometimes selfish and other times just existing.

Knowing there are new members joining the grieving journey is overwhelmingly painful because I empathize with their brokenness. I can only give one comfort that surpasses all—God, the Great Comforter!

One of my very dear friends, Cassandra Clark, took a picture of The Dancer—one of my favorite Willow Tree angels. I started collecting these beautiful wooden angels in 1999. The Dancer—the one in my collection I've had the longest—has always caught my eye.

I've included a picture in this journal entry. The dancer has transformed and taken on many characteristics during my life. In this season, she reminds me to sit quietly and soak up God's hand in everything. As she stares off into the distance, I like to imagine how she's being reenergized by her heavenly Father from her "be still" moment—looking like she's listening intently for what He has to say.

A dancer works hard—she's dedicated to the core and does not give up. She learns to move with the new beat of an instrument or song—no matter if it's happy or sorrowful—as she learns and coordinates a beautiful dance. Oh, and if the dreaded word *injury* were to happen, she fights, finding ways to rehabilitate and return to the stage.

I love how she is captured in the photo. It brings layers of vibrance, strength, stability, and peace to the figurine. She's satisfied with what's been heard along with her new understanding. She sits and debriefs, coordinates, structures, and choreographs so that one day she can live a warrior's life. She can perform on a world stage or in solitude for only herself.

How many of us are afraid to talk about the "truths" in our lives? How many of us run away? How many of us pretend it's okay when it's not? How many of us lie so much we believe our own lies? More importantly, how many of us truly ask our heavenly Father for guidance? Sit on the block, just as my dancer sits in the picture below, and seek Him first. He will answer in His timing if you remain in His will!

Willow Tree figurine, The Dancer

For those at the beginning of your grieving journey, I pray for God's overwhelming peace over your mind, body, and soul for tonight, tomorrow, and all eternity. I know mothers who have lost their trisomy 18 babies; a wife who lost her husband; children who lost their father; and friends who've lost a brother or sister. My heart breaks for you all as the flood gates open and weeping pours out.

For those continuing to grieve a loss—whether it's been one day, months, years, or decades—my heart breaks. Revelation 21:4 reminds me He will one day wipe all this pain away. Oh, for that day—what a day it will be.

For the rest of you who have decisions weighing you down—there are a multitude of you—always look to God and trust Him for guidance. Remember, God is not a God of confusion! You are loved and being lifted up in prayer.

Please lift up in your prayers those who are suffering. I pray God uses this entry—whoever reads it—to pour His love and everything you need over you!

DECEMBER 12, 2010

123 › Healing at the Altar

Another wound in my heart was healed at church today. I saw a dear friend of mine, Jennifer, head down to the altar. She lost her brother this past week and her father not too long ago. I immediately followed her without knowing God was drawing me there to heal my wound.

I was praying with her and could hear the words coming out of my mouth—they were amazing—definitely not mine but my heavenly Father's. I tried to keep pushing through, knowing my flood gates were about to burst open. I grabbed on tight to her, realizing this moment wasn't just for her but also for me.

Pastor Matt (Blair) joined us and started praying. All I could do was fight back the tears, astonished this was happening. I was there for her, but not by myself, not by any means. God knows me well—I would not have gone down the aisle for myself. He knew exactly how to get me there on my knees in sympathy for another.

I put up an emotional fight like no other. By the time I was uncontrollable, God was saying, "Let go, sweetheart, just let go—it's time." Time for what? Oh, time to deal with this layer of healing. For if we don't let go of each part when the time comes, we get stuck. I never want to be stuck.

My warning signs for healing moments are these precursers—moody and frustrated; desire to bail; run in the complete opposite direction; preoccupied. Fact—these make healing ten times harder when it all comes crashing down after living in denial.

Did I lose it on my knees? No, it was when we got up and hugged tightly as I whispered into her ear. I could hear the words coming out of my mouth once again but knew these were meant for both of us. I couldn't let go of her. I was afraid I couldn't stand on my own two feet. The tears came flooding in, and my breath seemed to leave me. I couldn't stand. I couldn't breathe. I just had to feel and deal on the spot—no more hiding or fighting back.

In the rawness of the moment, I accepted that I really couldn't bring Lilian Grace back no matter what I did. Physically, she really was gone. Michael and I are on different ends of the grieving spectrum. I want to keep her memory alive by doing numerous little things around the house and in our lives. Yet when Michael sees these things, he is reminded that she's not here. I don't know how to live without talking about her or memorializing her. I think Michael is asking me not to talk about Lilian like she's still here. Have I been doing that? She was alive—I have hundreds of pictures to prove it. She will always be my daughter, even though her heart stopped and she passed on. I now recognize that my feelings, wants, and needs may be making it harder for myself and others around me. She's no longer here; I know that.

Back to holding on to Jennifer—I couldn't let go as my control issues were addressed. I don't have control of anything, no matter how much I'd like to think I do. For when we realize we don't have control, we must fully trust God by stepping forward, not knowing what will come of it when He takes over and heals us more.

From the point of sitting down and crying out of control while not being able to breathe, all I can remember is the fact that I got walked out of the sanctuary. I thought, *Oh my, I'm actually doing this in public—not at the computer—not in my prayer closet. I'm actually in front of a lot of people.* As I sat down and noticed the amazing women around me who were taking care of me, I realized I'd been caught up in trying to be so strong for everyone else that I forgot about myself.

No wonder my sleep has been a few hours at a time; my house looks like a hurricane blazed through it; and the laundry is stacked in all five baskets. I haven't been cooking. I've been struggling to do the things I committed to doing—though in my mind I thought I was rocking along fairly well. Really? To admit I'd been a complete mess, fighting for some strand to hold on to, completely shook me.

Today was a reality check containing displays of what releasing can do. I cooked lunch; cleaned the whole house (including a couple of rooms for deep, much-needed cleaning); washed five loads of laundry; and finished all the Christmas decorations. In a few minutes, I will go see if there are any more decorations to buy at Walmart. Now—now—now, I feel more like Chrissy—the Chrissy I remember, who cared enough to take care of her family; made the home look beautiful; cooked a good-tasting meal; completed all the laundry; and took care of herself, as well as those around her.

I've always been here! You've seen me deal with many things, yet the problem was that I was failing miserably at home and self-care. Yes, I've had some learning moments, but this—this was busting through a brick wall I had put up before Lilian Grace ever got here.

For those of you who find yourselves completely drowning or all over the place, stop and let go. Trust me! If you can't, just trust God. He yearns and desires to take care of your every need. I praise Almighty God for giving my friend Jennifer the strength to walk down to that altar, because she gave me the opportunity to let go and be held like I've been trying to tell other people to do. Telling first, then experiencing—oh, the experience is so much better than I imagined. God held me today as I took a huge sigh of relief and release. God graciously healed a doozy of a wound today, and I thank Him infinitely.

What's holding you back from healing? Let the fear melt and just let Him work. I love you all and thank you for the much-needed continued prayers. I am breathing. I know there are many, many more layers to go through, and each requires the same thing—letting go! Good luck getting out of your and God's way!

DECEMBER 16, 2010

124 › Another's Battle

Calling all prayer warriors—we need you to lift up baby Trishtan and her mommy, Denise. Below is an update from my dear friend Michelle, written by Trishtan's mommy. Love you all.

> Trishtan has been in the TCH PICU for about three weeks, being intubated the whole time. She was supposed to have heart surgery to fix the ventricular septal defect (VSD), but the day she was scheduled to have the surgery, her white blood count was too high because of a UTI.
> So lots of antibiotics and waiting. So this week the surgery was hopefully going to happen, but then she was spiking fevers, and they couldn't find the source. They thought maybe it was the tube down her throat and decided to take the tube out. Which they did last night, and she did really well, but this morning she was laboring with her breathing, and her heart rate was increasing into the 160–170s.
> They noticed her throat was swollen, so they gave her some steroids to reduce the swelling, but that didn't work the way it was supposed to. So they decided on reintubation, reluctantly. But they didn't want to risk her throat completely closing up on her. They had to have anesthesia come down and reintubate her, and one of the operating room (OR) surgeons said it looked like she had a collapsed airway. UGH! So she is reintubated again—going to have ear, nose, throat (ENT) doctor come and take a look at her.

Denise is really upset; she is mostly disappointed that she didn't get to hold her at all. She was looking forward to a day of holding her little girl that she hadn't gotten to hold since she was intubated. Please, please, please, pray for sweet Trishtan and for Denise (who is a single mom).

Pray the swelling goes down and that she is fever free for forty-eight hours so she can have the necessary heart surgery she needs. Sadly, the trisomy journey is unpredictable. There are no guarantees or promises—it can be a guessing game. Breathing is all we have right now. It can change within seconds. Take life and time to heart and let that reverberate as we join Denise and Trishtan's battle.

DECEMBER 18, 2010

125 › Unfinished

Jodie (M2, a.k.a. my second mom from my college days) sent me a wonderful song to listen to since it's been a rough week for Michael and me. Just when we think we have it together, we don't. We went to Michael's company Christmas party the other night on Thursday, December 16. The last time I was officially with some of his coworkers and their wives was when Lilian Grace was in the hospital.

I kept having this urgency to hurry the night up so I could get back to the hospital to my baby girl. I had to continuously remind myself of the following:

1. We were in Oklahoma City, Oklahoma—not Tulsa, Oklahoma.

2. Lilian Grace is not struggling for her life—she earned her wings and flew high!

3. The day I left the children's hospital after walking Lilian Grace to the van, the need to be there was gone—no more magnet to that place.

4. Enough time has passed that I thought I should remember all the above!

No matter how many times I reminded myself that night, I could not shake it. I held it together long enough to get to the hotel. (I almost typed *hospital*.) Michael wasn't so happy with me. He couldn't understand what my deal was until it hit him at three in the morning.

So much happened this past year; we wish it would all go away—be erased. Interesting thing about life—no matter how much you ignore it or wish it away, it's still there. We have to face the broken pieces one at a time. It's sad when people get in their own way. We want broken relationships to be healed right now, but the other person may need more time to come around than we do.

What I'm trying to say is, we can't reconcile for them, just like people can't make us forgive and forget something. I wanted so desperately to be okay at that Christmas party, but I couldn't shake that night; we had to be apart from Lilian Grace, not knowing if that night would be her last. All I wanted was to be with her, even if it was for just another second!

The brain, heart, and soul are funny things. Just because we say we're fine or there's not a current problem doesn't dismiss the pain and memories people struggle with. We must continuously process when each moment/memory arises, and that's okay. I keep learning this lesson over and over and over and over again—hoping it will stick permanently within my memory.

I don't need a million reasons why I don't want to do something; why I can do some things and not others; or why I may never again do some of the things I used to do. If I don't want to do something, that should be reason enough. My brain, heart, and soul have their own agenda sometimes. Who would have thought a Christmas party with people I was around during Lilian's living days could cause me to struggle so much? I knew it would be tough, but I didn't know how much. I like to think that the Holy Spirit does a great job of warning me. Triggers can happen with a sound, a smell, or an environment.

Now back to the song M2 sent. The words are perfect for me right now as tears stream down my face. They explain where I am today—actually, on most days. The song "You Haven't Seen the Last of Me" sung by Cher is very powerful.

If I could sing this, I'd sing it to several people—most importantly, to Satan. The most powerful weapon I have in my life is my heavenly Father. He's making me into the woman I need to be. He is the reason why this is far from over—I'm far from over. He will call me home when I'm done. Until then, I will carry out His will for my life.

I feel like after all the surgeries, near-death experiences, chaotic circumstances, and more that God is not done with me yet. He has more for me to do. It's why I have survived. I may not get it right all the time, but I'm trusting Him to guide me to the "right" more times than not.

I'm still praying I stay out of God's way. I'm still a work in progress, yet I feel like I'm moving toward something on this crazy ride. For those who have decided not to be a part of my life, I hope our broken relationships heal over time. May you take the healing path for your life. Things may not be the same, but let's not float in limbo while continuing to hurt each other.

For those I know who are dealing with their own struggles—the things that have them on their knees—I pray for you daily. God will give you strength through whatever breaks you, makes you struggle, and continues to push you down. When you are on your knees—LOOK UP—TRUST GOD—know that you are strongest on your knees! PRAY and TRUST are the two biggest weapons God gives us.

Today may drag on as problems seemingly grow, but this too shall pass in God's good timing. I'm trusting God! He's the strength inside me. Don't count yourself out just yet. I'm not counting myself out!

DECEMBER 21, 2010

126 › On the Radio

One of my favorite 4-Hers, Eric Alspaugh, who is turning into a wonderful young man, sent me a song that reminded him of Michael and me. He's impressively mature for his age. Thank you, Eric, for sharing this song. It made me cry as I listened to it the first ten or so times.

I just listened to it again and find myself smiling now. Regina Spektor, a favorite artist of mine, sings "On the Radio" beautifully. Her lyrics are about being young and full of love while trying, laughing, crying, and breathing until you can't. Our lessons learned and gifts should be used to help or invest in others. Life is not just about us. I want to use this journey with Lilian Grace to further God's kingdom. There will always be broken people and trials. I want to take the parts needed to build, grow, and change those around me.

My holiday season this year isn't what I would call normal or traditional. It's been like no other I can remember. To be truthful—neither have some of our prior holidays when we tried to keep up with memories of happier times. We try so hard to make ourselves fit into the ideal way we think things should be, yet we neglect to take a break to deal with the issues at hand.

Michael and I don't have all the answers. We make mistakes just like the next guy or gal. What's helping us rise above the world this year? We've accepted it's not the same—it's not what we want—but it will never be the same. We are taking a stand to take a break—to stop and acknowledge we have to take time to heal instead of making ourselves trudge through gatherings to be socially acceptable, as if nothing ever happened.

We've chosen to get away this year so we can spend some much-needed time together, allowing God to continue healing us while making space for things to work themselves out. Why fight so hard to look like we all have it together? Who does that really help? No one! Life, circumstances, and situations are different than years past.

I spoke to a wonderful Christian lady whom I get to call my grandmother-in-law, Margaret Miller. We had an awesome conversation, and I knew God was helping us both through the words that were spoken and the topics we covered. Even knowing God has given me a heart to see people for who they are or could be doesn't mean I'm the one to fix it all. Sometimes, we are meant to be the planter and another the waterer. Sometimes, we have to move on, praying another person will come along to help them.

I feel like this song affirms that we are doing the best we can. We feel worse while adjusting—it's complicated and sometimes messy, but it would be much worse if we didn't try. Through various attempts and challenges, we sometimes get stung by people who are afraid of change. The world is full of hurting people who are drowning in disappointments day after day because they fight back the healing to avoid change. They're fearful of the unknown beyond change.

I don't want to be paralyzed by fear in any aspect of my life. Being stuck in a situation is not acceptable to me. I will continue to lean on God and trust in His promises. He rocks at taking care of me. I praise Him with a million to infinity shout outs in the mountains, universe, and heaven.

God taught us through Lilian's life to take the love that

grew between the three of us and share it with others; to keep showing everyone that it's okay to grieve; and to accept that you aren't who you once were—you'll be better once your journey is complete. The love that we received from Lilian was powerful and full of God's wonder. I want everyone to know how amazingly miraculous it feels to be a parent. I pray He will bless you with a special child you can care for, even if they aren't your own.

I've mentioned being frustrated when someone says their pain is greater than mine. Let me continue to share what I'm learning from that. If you're broken and hurting, shouldn't you be learning from it and changing? What is the big picture? Your pain is your pain. My pain is my pain. There's no reason to compare our pain to another's.

I know that when my daughter's life ended here on earth, my heart broke. It has continued to break on so many levels, yet I'm learning that each breaking point is part of a beautiful process. All those broken pieces were meant to break. God has used her life and departure to break me of things I haven't wanted to deal with or let go of.

All the brokenness, tears, screams, nightmares, dreams, and shifting relationships are making me better. The cracks and shattered glass in me needed to occur for growth and forward movement. What bothers me more than anything is when people remain knocked down, not becoming who God intended them to be. Some don't even know it, but their actions reveal issues of feeling unworthy. Every one of us is worthy! Every single one of us is worth it because we are God's children!

I'm not going to get it right all the time, but at least I'm trying to learn to laugh till I cry and cry until I laugh while I grow into who I need to be. I've learned a lot about myself in the last two weeks—even the last few years—but during these last two weeks, I let the bitterness, pain, and anger seep into areas they didn't need to be.

I had to take my own advice and face the bitterness, pain, and anger head on so I could see where it lingered. I snapped at some people because I couldn't see clearly. My poor blood pressure skyrocketed, and I looked like a complete fool for not being able to cope with even little things. I got sick and decided it's time to accept some things in my life and know it will be better for myself and others in the end.

Little things can be tricky—they eventually fill a bucket and overflow. Whether you want to or not, you still have to deal with the little to large things in life. It all catches up to you eventually. We can be professionals at pushing it all down deep inside. We think if we don't talk about any of it that it will go away. My bitterness, pain, and anger verified I was running from something and pushing it all down! God continues to use my daughter's departure to teach me valuable lessons.

What is God trying to break in you to help you become the person He created you to be? What experiences have ripped at your heart and soul? Brokenness can turn your world upside down. What is He trying to help you get over or get through? He wants you to reap and flourish! Why not try living life differently? Give God a chance to rearrange your broken pieces. I bet you'll be even more beautiful.

My prayer for all is that you won't waste the experiences you've fought through personally or watched your loved ones live through. May you learn and then release what needs to be let go. You can't keep blaming everyone else. You have a responsibility—just as I do—to start owning up and moving forward. For if we don't take care of business, we won't be able to care for ourselves or others when we arrive at the next mountain.

Choose a path or a process to heal so you can get from point A to point Z. I want to do more than just breathe to get by. I want to use the tools God gives me to lead more people into eternity. I don't want anyone to suffer in an eternal hell of fire. I want there to be purpose and meaning between my first breath and my dying breath. May you look at your life, stop trying to please everyone, and start living the way you were meant to live.

It's time we get real and deal with things we keep pushing down or running away from. At the end of the day or race, it all bubbles to the surface or catches up to us. What's holding you back from releasing so you can live the life you were meant to live? Figure it out and release it to get yourself out of the gutter. There's a fabulous life to live in Jesus where peace, comfort, and love prevail!

DECEMBER 24, 2010

127 › Christmas Eve Lost & Found

Michael and I started a new adventure on Wednesday night at 9:40 p.m. We got in my trusty green machine (my Ford Escape) and headed toward Washington State. We were determined to get there in less than thirty hours. I had us drinking our meals most of the way to save time and money, and it worked.

The driving was crazy, but I'm glad we did it to get our minds focused on something else for a change. It was a fun little challenge along the way. We even started on some nitty gritty work in our grieving journey. What has been the most revealing for us through all this? I've said it before—dealing with the relationships in our lives. Things will never be the same. I think it's a positive more than a negative. We want to move forward, not backward.

When we arrived at Michael's sister's house, I had a strange feeling I was forgetting something. Lo and behold, as we were unpacking our essentials, I couldn't find my purse. Everyone looked, but we couldn't find it. I was crushed even more. I had everything in it—and I was unsure of what "everything" meant!

First off, I'd lost my engagement ring last December (never found it); my right ovary and fallopian tube in January (this was not the fault of my mind); and my daughter to death in August. Since I couldn't find our "travel Lily" with a small portion of Lilian's cremains before we left, we brought the mini urn with most of her cremains. I was devastated already about having to bring her urn—but now I had left my purse with Lilian's urn in possibly Wyoming or one of the other five or six states we had passed through.

How dare I? Oh, wait, how could I? Where was it? I bawled in my green machine, disappointed in myself, and realized I am far from being okay. My mental state was revealed—I was crushed. Every little thing I wasn't able to accomplish or figure out was hitting me hard from all directions. I once again felt like a failure.

I sat quietly in the driveway trying to figure out where I went wrong this past year. Why was it continuing to happen? What should I be getting from it all? As I spoke to the Discover card representative to cancel my account, I started crying. Poor lady—she didn't know why I was hurting so much.

If she only knew it was more than just losing the things in my purse—it was everything lost this year. Michael came out to try to get me to go in the house, but I told him I had to sit there a little longer and figure things out. What did I do? I did the best thing possible—I cried and prayed. I prayed that God would have a wonderful person find my purse and not touch anything inside; that their heart would know how miserable I was not knowing where it was; and that they would turn it in or ship it to me and that nothing would go wrong.

I also had words with the devil to tell him to leave me alone. Though he was turning my world upside down once again, he was not going to win. I didn't care if everything about me was in that purse—all my accounts and checkbooks, cards, and Lilian's Warrior Princess Foundation employer identification number (EIN) from the government. All of it could be replaced once I figured out what was inside the dang thing. I remembered a gift from my pastor that was in it. I told the devil these were just things—they could all be replaced. I reminded him because he had reminded me that my kids couldn't be replaced. I agreed with him, yet I made sure he understood I would spend eternity with them. He can't take that away from me.

After trying not to have a breakdown, I kept repeating to myself, I trust You, God! I asked a special request of Him that He keep my purse safe and help us find it—no matter how far away it was. I returned to the house.

My brother-in-law, Kyle, went out to the car one more time. He looked in all the cracks and hidey holes. PRAISE THE LORD—an early Christmas miracle—he found it! When he walked into the house and down the stairs to me, all I could do was hold my face with my hands and cry happy, joyous tears of praise. God had placed it under my seat. We had looked multiple times and found nothing—until I prayed and then Kyle found it.

I know this much to be true—I have no choice but to start slowing down, breathing more, and letting God lead as I have talked about over and over and over again. This was a great wake-up call to get it more together by slowing down and living in each moment—steering clear of the scattered brain, which is a result of grieving and much more. I know I've been doing way too much, which this incident verifies in many ways.

This is a longer entry because I wanted to share that story and write about our Christmas Eve and Christmas Day. This would have been the beginning of Lilian Grace's first Christmas extravaganza—our crazy string of holiday adventures we participate in every year. The eve of Christmas Eve would have been spent with Grandma Miller (Michael's mom), waking up that morning, opening presents together, and eating breakfast.

Next, we'd go to my brother's house so her cousins could make their gingerbread creations and open presents together with Grandpa and Grandma Cooper (my parents). Michael and I did get to build a gingerbread house with our niece and nephew last Friday to keep that tradition going. I've been doing that with them for years now.

Then we would have gone to the Cooper side (my dad's family) to get Lilian and her cousins pumped about Santa coming. Santa's route would be on the news, and we might even get my dad to dress like Santa. He used to do that and recruited another family member or two to be reindeer on the roof.

Everyone would overheat in a crowded room including great-grandparents, great-aunts and uncles, aunts and uncles, and cousins, eating Mexican food and opening gifts. Before the gift exchange, I'd make sure we brought back one of my favorite traditions (I'll fill you in further down the entry). We'd go back to Grandpa and Grandma Cooper's to sleep and the next morning, wake up and head to the Poteet's house (my mom's side). There, we'd enjoy her great-grandma's delicious breakfast with the whole family and open gifts. My grandmother makes the best rice you'll ever eat. I'll have to get to the grocery store here to attempt that tradition from afar, since it's one I will miss the most this Christmas!

After visiting the Poteets, we would load up Lilian and head to Tulsa again to see Grandpa and Grandma Whitten (Michael's dad and stepmom) to open presents before carrying on with the rest of the Whittens for more food and gifts. Would this have been how we would have done Christmas? I'm not sure. Michael is a big believer in our little family making our own traditions, but I'm not sure how that will look in the future. What's great is we have time to figure it out.

Though Lilian Grace is gone, Michael and I feel like part of her is here with us as we keep her memory alive by sharing about good times and what we might have done. I know many of you have lost someone dear to you. I hope you figure out a new tradition or ways to incorporate your loved one like we are. We've added a little wreath with five candles representing various aspects in memory of Lilian Grace. I'm including the words we said as we lit each candle; perhaps you can add this to your holiday traditions.

Holiday Memorial: A Guide for Holidays and Special Days

For this ceremony, place five candles around a simple wreath, which you can place on a table or fireplace mantel. Lighting the candles each year can be a ritual that becomes a lasting tradition. We hope this memorial will help you honor your loved one.

> *As we light these five candles in honor of you, we light one for our grief, one for our courage, one for our memories, one for our love, and one for our hope.*
>
> *This candle represents our grief. The pain of losing you is intense. It reminds us of the depth of our love for you.*
>
> *This candle represents our courage—to confront our sorrow, to comfort each other, and to change our lives.*
>
> *This candle is in your memory—the times we laughed, the times we cried, the times we were angry*

with each other, the silly things you did, and the caring and joy you gave us.

This candle is the light of love. As we enter this holiday season, day by day we cherish the special place in our hearts that will always be reserved for you. We thank you for the gift your life brought to each of us.

And this candle is the light of hope. It reminds us of love and memories of you that are ours forever. May the glow of the flame be our source of hopefulness now and forever. We love you.

(Sherry L. Williams)[2]

Another tradition will be the Christmas decorations moving forward that include a pink tree, bulbs in Lily's birthday color, dragonflies, and teardrop ornaments. An important tradition I used to do with my Cooper family was reading about Jesus's birth. I remember when my Grandpa Cooper handed that tradition of reading it over to me. Wow, I couldn't believe he was letting me read it. I was so blessed. I would sit in my great-grandmother Edith Cooper's rocking chair while everyone gathered around to hear the wonderful story. I think that's why I needed a break this year. I'm noticing some of our family traditions are slipping away, and I don't want that. Sometimes we need traditions to stay because the connection is valuable, while others can be released.

For Christmas Eve, I want to read Luke 2 as my family

---

[2] Sherry Williams (2002), Holiday Help: A Guide for Holidays and Special Days.

tradition no matter where we are or who we are with. It reminds me, from a parent's perspective, that God gave the biggest sacrifice. His Son, Jesus Christ, was born in a manger so that we could live for eternity if we so choose. How many of us parents would be willing to sacrifice so much knowing what our child would have to face to get the end result? Now Lilian Grace wasn't Jesus, but she was a missionary sent here to share God's light with all of us. This story of Jesus's birth has an even greater meaning to me this Christmas and the rest to follow. She was a miracle who shouldn't have been conceived according to the fertility world, yet God created her for all of us to know. She will continue to help change the people who hear her story, because God's fingerprints are all over her life!

Jesus's birth was a complete miracle since God placed him in a virgin's womb, and He remains a miracle through His life, death, and resurrection! Read Luke 2 this Christmas with whomever you are with—whether you are with many or by yourself. Remember, we are never alone! May you have a very blessed Christmas and New Year. Jesus is the reason for the season. Love you!

DECEMBER 25, 2010

128 › Christmas Day: Peace on Earth

I'm listening to "Peace on Earth." Peace is the number one thing I want, desire, and need, not just for myself but for everyone I know. Today marks eight months since Lilian Grace first joined us. I've been trying really hard to have a wonderful day. It hasn't been bad—I'm just having a hard time with myself. Of course, this is natural for me and any one of you dealing with the same thing—missing someone so terribly it's hard to breathe sometimes.

I ended up looking at pictures of my sweet baby girl, and I couldn't control the crying. I miss her with such passion and energy. It hurts to such a degree that I can't even type. Dealing with grief is worth the time I got with my daughter. I watch from behind the computer or while wearing sunglasses or with a smile when I see others spending time with their families. It saddens me to know that this Christmas, Lilian isn't here. What saddens me more is people thinking that in a second, it's all going to be okay for me. I am so happy that everyone gets to have their moments—their happiness—but those are not my moments.

I pray for peace and the day I don't shed a sorrowful tear. I pray this too shall pass. Hopefully, I end up on the other side feeling wiser, stronger, and braver. Right now, I feel numb from the brokenness of lost hopes and dreams that ended so abruptly. I know that day will come!

I have shaken things up by changing our plans for the holidays. I'm still hurting, longing, and wanting peace more than ever. Not being with my family is painful, yet I can't pretend like it's a normal Christmas. I want to nod my head like a genie to fast-forward beyond all the struggling, pain, crying, chaos, and turmoil in my heart.

I know time is a great healer—the part between Lilian Grace taking her last breath and me being able to stand again is sometimes unbearable. That's where I'm at now. I feel like I forgot the basics of living. I'll walk one day and crawl the next. I'm in this limbo stage where I battle a million little battles every day with myself and my emotions. I fight to walk, breathe, smile, and laugh—be positive—just be. Occasionally, I figure out how to laugh for a moment, but I'm still crying in the depths of my soul. I give myself a little pat on the back anyway.

Every laugh is beneficial, but it takes energy like trying to hold yourself up. Laughter provides a mental/emotional break from my grief journey. It's like seeing a break in the clouds during a raging storm. I'm blessed God keeps giving me these moments. Being here in Washington State has opened more blue spots in the sky.

Sadly though, the laughter does eventually stop. The break is short, and the rain starts again. I miss Lilian's sweet smile. Her smile was my break from the horrible experiences. Without her smile, I would have crumbled. When her lips curved up, I could breathe and believe it was all going to be just fine.

Lilian's time here was rare and miraculous. I just wish it could have lasted forever—us taking care of her while watching her blossom. As I scan the pictures and comments posted on Facebook, I smile and think of Lilian's smile. Why? Because she lived and fought; we got to be a family and appreciate all the moments we could see as positive; families are closer; babies are more loved than ever before; and people appreciate the gifts God has given them. Her life taught them this.

As I type this entry, God shifts my perspective and helps me see the light and the rainbow above the stormy skies. It makes this mommy smile knowing babies are being loved more than before because of His love. My baby girl's smile reminds me to keep fighting through the in-between stage.

I have moments when I just want to sit on the "road" and not keep moving. I want to let someone else go through it instead of me. I want to be on the other side of the fence. My heavenly Father flashes Lilian's smile before me to remind me she didn't quit. She fought through three months on earth so His light could shine and His purpose play out in her steps on her "road."

I've posted one of my favorite pictures of Lilian's smile caught on camera. As you look at her and think about your own life, don't overlook the patches of light and blue sky above your storm. I wish I could see a month, year, or decade ahead and where I'll be on my walk. For now, I'll remember her glorious smile and hold her dear to my heart so I can keep walking down my road.

Always smiling!

> *To my Warrior Princess,*
>
> *Eight months ago, God lit up a hidden circuit board within me. He enhanced all my senses because of you. He gave me another purpose and reason for living. He gave me you, an angel from above, to teach me, guide me, and give me more than I would have received just sitting on the "road." I have no choice now but to keep walking and choosing which path to take when a fork appears. I love you with all that there is. I miss you with so much emotion. I long for the day I can join you for eternity. I know it's not my time. I know there's a plan. Thank you for picking up your cross so we can all learn to live.*
>
> *Love,*
> *Your Proud Mommy,*
> *Chrissy*

I hope everyone had an amazing Christmas. If it wasn't, I pray it will one day be more amazing than you could ever hope for. For we who have lost, I want us to remember our loved one by talking about them, remembering all the good times, and reviewing all the lessons their life taught us. Share with everyone and be proud God chose you to have them in your life. We got to see up-close how amazing God made them and witness their life firsthand. I'm one blessed mommy to know I have at least three angels flying high who lived out their purpose, no matter how big or small. Be blessed and reminisce about the beauty! Love you all.

Happy birthday, Jesus Christ! Thanks for being born! My favorite Christmas song is "O Holy Night"! It doesn't even need an explanation, for it's perfectly written with beautiful poetry, capturing the joys of the divine birth of Christ. He taught us how to treat and love others while radiating peace.

Side note: As I typed this entry, I kept listening to Chris Rice sing "Come Thou Fount of Every Blessing" more than a dozen times. Each time my heart was filled with blessings and hope for the future. I sing about His grace and mercy as I live post-Lilian! I'm prone to wandering toward the negative, but I know He will get me to a more positive place. I love you all!

DECEMBER 26, 2010

129 › Borrowed Angels

I've been trying to make myself do some things that can reduce stress and get emotions flowing for the journey. I chose to start training for another marathon. Yay—I have missed this more than I thought I would! I've been logging some mileage here and there, but this week I'm on track.

As I was doing a four-mile makeup session this morning, I listened to my old iPod. I'd forgotten what music I had downloaded. There was a message in each song I listened to. It's like God was running with me, giving me one hug after another! I love that thought! Interestingly, I had downloaded the whole album *As I Am* by Kristin Chenoweth. I remember getting obsessed over *Wicked* and wanted more music from the powerful singer-actress.

I wonder what was going on the day I bought her album? It was months ago, yet I was meant to listen to one lovely song today to comfort my hurting soul! As the song played, I immediately started crying. The song was "Borrowed Angels," and Kristin's angelic voice singing the words brought power. I praise God for giving me this great treasure today to comfort me. I hope it comforts you. I can't help but beam a big smile and shed a tear of happiness knowing my daughter's short life keeps reaching out.

I love you all. May we all keep walking and evolving to a stronger, wiser, and healed version of ourselves. This powerful song might help you in your healing process. Lilian's light did shine brighter. Oh, her little life is making all of us brighter. She's touched me more than anything has before in my life. Praise God for people who follow through with His plan. Thanks, Kristin, for deciding to sing this song so God could give it to me today.

I wish I could have borrowed my angel longer, yet I know God's timing is essential. He truly knows what's best for her and us. I hope you feel peace knowing He holds each of us. He's not out to get us but to love and give us what we need—a constant reminder we need on the daily. God has a plan that surpasses all understanding. I'm going to trust Him and let Him help me live it out.

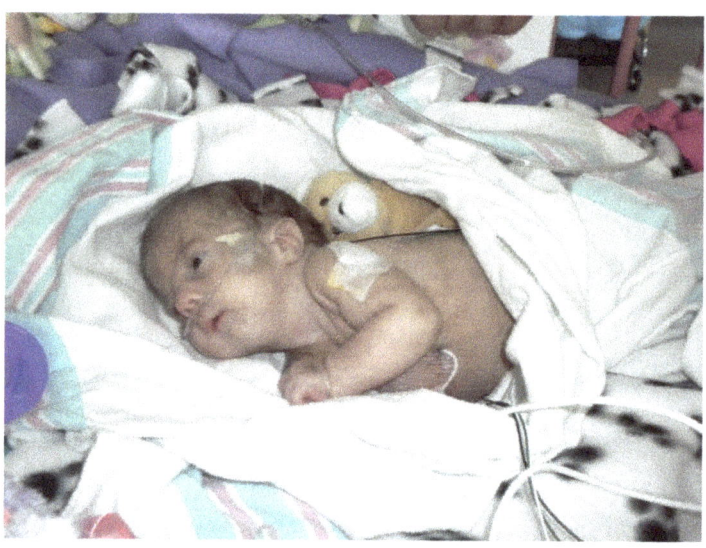

Precious angel of mine

JANUARY 5, 2011

130 › Five-Month Angelversary

The days have marched by one by one. It's now been five months since Lilian Grace earned her glorious angel wings. Time seems to be accelerating faster and faster. It feels like it was just yesterday that I held and loved her with all I had. Two nights before she passed away, Lilian and I got to sleep chest to chest for hours. It was magical in every way possible. I praise God that we got that chance as mother and daughter.

The chance to know we were safe for that moment was all that mattered. After hours of sleeping in the hospital recliner, we woke up when Lilian threw up a significant amount of milk. Anyone who has had a child can relate to that. All I could say was "Where in the heck did you store it?" She just looked at me and smiled her beautiful, angelic smile as if to say, "It happens!"

Last night after chatting with a couple of wonderful ladies who are like mothers to me, I cried for almost four hours. I learned many things, but more importantly, it gave me the chance to recall my calm night of cuddling with Lilian before the storm. Thank You, God, for reminding me of that precious moment.

Feeling her heartbeat so close to mine will always be a favorite memory. If I stop long enough, I can still feel her and the beats near my chest. I can hear her breathing and sometimes a lil roar of a snore from her. I guess I have to admit memories can be miraculous and comforting when we let ourselves finally remember. Praise His perfect plan in making sure I remember the good times more than the bad.

If you have a child, please hold them close to you. Let them fall asleep on your chest. Help them know that by being there, it means you are fully there. Money and things are not what make you a good parent. Time, love, and comfort are what make you a good parent. Being there for them is more important than anything. Praise God when they spell it out for you.

If Lilian Grace hadn't been fussy that night, I would have missed out. If God hadn't tugged at my heart to pick her up, no matter what, and let her be right there close to me, I would have missed giving my daughter exactly what she needed that night. All she needed was for me to love and comfort her even when I was scared out of my mind and didn't know what else to do for her.

Take time to step back, step aside, and feel in your parenting heart what your child or children need. The Holy Spirit is the ultimate wise one to guide us in helping them daily. He knows what's best for us and them. God has really been working on Michael and me through the healing process. I saw a beautiful Scripture that put a huge smile on my face the other day: *"He heals the brokenhearted and binds up their wounds"* (Psalm 147:3). He continues to take care of me no matter what. I'm so in love with my heavenly Father. I am still working on my love for some people in my life, but I know He'll heal those relationships in good time.

I am starting a Bible study this Tuesday night (1.11.11) using the book *Plan B* by Pete Wilson. Even if you don't live here, I'd encourage you to buy the book, read it, and answer the questions in the back of the book. My goal is to make 2011 a year of healing.

I see hundreds of familiar people walking around, hurting. I hope everyone finds their path of healing to wholeness. It's okay to feel and cry while being disappointed—be whatever it makes you be. Let 2011 be the year you give yourself permission to feel it all so you can walk the path you need. I promise you'll find happiness on the other side.

I'm finally to a point with Lilian Grace that I'm proud of our path together. I can rejoice in all of it while embracing her path into heaven. It's a beautiful, courageous story that will live on to inspire and change people. I love you all.

Happy five-month angelversary, Squeaker!

I always feel you from the depths of my heart and dreams. I didn't know I could be so proud of anyone like I am of you. No matter the time frame, you, my sweet little Warrior Princess, taught us all to live and love. I wish I were there to celebrate and witness the spectacular glittery wings that suit you well. I love you deeply . . . I love you to the moon and back and for all eternity. May children get held tighter and loved more because of you.

"I'm Alive" by Celine Dion came up on my playlist, and it made me think of you as I smiled ear to ear with tears flowing down my cheeks. Lilian, you set my heart on fire and gave me a deeper relationship with God. I'm glad I'm alive and sharing all that I can by the grace of God. I love our moments when I feel you near and I see bright lights. God shows me daily He is always near.

Love,
Your Mommy

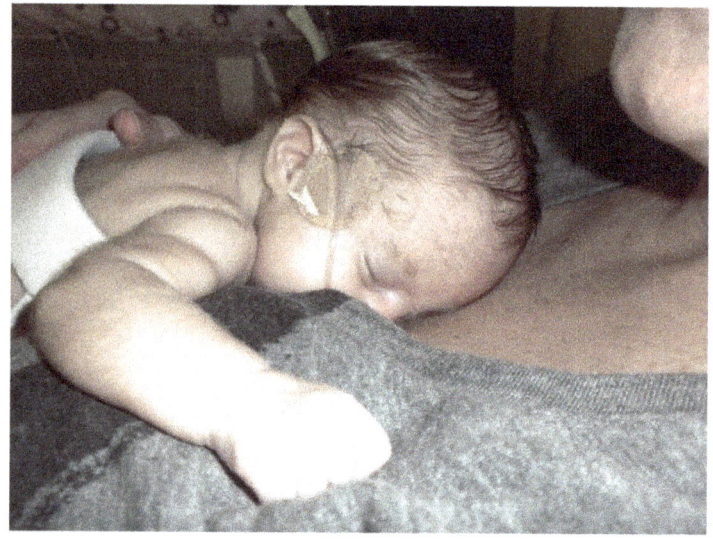

Heart to heart forever

JANUARY 11, 2011

131 › Outside the Society Box

Think outside the "society" box! I want to continue to go beyond the norms. One of my dear trisomy 18 mommies posted the video for "One Last Christmas" by Matthew West. I just finished wiping my last tear after hearing the song. It's based on a true story about a little boy dying. His family and neighbors rallied for this little one to get one last Christmas because he wasn't going to make it. My heart hurts for families who don't even get to spend one holiday with their precious one.

Michael and I were truly blessed to get the time we were given with Lilian Grace. I think that's why I am further along than I thought I'd be at this point. Praise God we thought outside the "society" box as much as we did. Songs and stories like this one are fabulous inspirations in making us cherish the time we get and remind us that it doesn't take much to make a huge impact.

If you are pregnant or your child is alive, focus on each present moment with them, not on the unknown future. I'd like to encourage all families to be like this. I love how God gives us people to encourage us to focus on the positive. This helps us take advantage of time with our angels. We had unconventional moments with her because we didn't care what anyone else thought.

We knew we only had right now. If you know of anyone who is suffering from a disease, sickness, illness, or whatever, you can do something for them. Think of a crazy idea and bring it to life. Create memories! We all, including myself, tend to get caught up in the sands of time slipping through an hourglass.

Trust me, I've cried many tears before, during, and after Lilian Grace's time here. Praise God, He's given me a new perspective. Now I can look back at the chaos and smile. We danced in the fire and swam in the flood that tried to consume us. We came out wiser and more blessed for it.

Yesterday, I went to the doctor to get my ankle checked out. I had an unfortunate encounter with a rock on my Saturday morning run with my RunnersWorld group. I got 2.58 miles into the run before this crazy stumbling block of a rock took me out. As I sat at Lewis corner waiting for my ride, I started laughing. I took some pictures of my opponent (the rock) and myself. Yet as I sat there, I saw a beautiful string of bright sunbeams streaming down in front of me. I imagined Lilian Grace with a slight grin watching me laugh at myself.

I was so worried about getting eight miles in under one and a half hours that I lost sight of the road. I should have seen the rock, but I was focused on the wrong thing. Unfortunately, my running is over for six weeks, which knocks me out of my marathon race for the spring. I'm hoping to be able to run the first annual Warrior Princess Trail Run on Monday, April 25, 2011.

Since I hadn't been to the doctor in a year, I started laughing again when I had to catch him up about the past year. God reminded me of the fires and floods we had faced. Guess what? I am still here—laughing and moving forward with minor hiccups that get in the way. God continues to give us exactly what we need through it all.

Remember to think outside the "society" box and live life out loud. May God keep giving us scenic trails and unconventional ideas to make the most of life. Love you all.

I'm still grateful Lilian's first breath was not her last. We filled that three-and-a-half-month season with memories I will never forget. The last time I held her in my arms, I yearned for more time as I handed her over to the funeral home. Make your moments count by being present and awake. Don't let this fast-paced life or difficult circumstances cause you to lose out.

Choose to make the most of any situation. Avoid getting trapped or frozen by it for too long. There are endless ways to create a memory and celebrate each day of life. We did—by the grace of God.

Injured selfie with my opponent

JANUARY 13, 2011

132 › Set the World on Fire

We praised God by singing, laughing, crying, and remembering Bud Baab—what a day of celebration. He and his family fought his cancer battle for a little over two years—never slowing him or his family down. Their faith grew stronger daily and never wavered. I am deeply grateful God introduced the Baab family to me over five years ago.

They are a major reason why Michael and I stayed positive and praised our heavenly Father through our time with Lilian Grace. I remember us stating that if the Baabs can find joy and happiness through their battle, we can too! Thank you—all of you in the Baab family—for giving us a shining example of God's grace and mercy. Your perseverance paid off over and over and over again. Many have a stronger relationship with our heavenly Father today!

At the celebration, there was a question that popped up—I'm not quoting word for word, but I remember asking myself, "What is my legacy, and what am I doing today to help His kingdom grow?" I want to ask you these questions: Are you kingdom minded? What legacy will you be leaving? Are you giving or taking?

Thank you to Kathi, Whitney, Emilee, Kaesie, Cameron, Kimberlie, McKinzey, and Hudson for sharing this amazing celebration of God's light through your husband and dad. Kathi, I want to be you when I grow up. You are a prime example, along with your husband, of how to be true warriors for God's kingdom.

During the picture slideshow, a beautiful song came on

and caught my heart and ear. I pulled my SoundHound up so I could make sure to see who and what it was. "Set the World on Fire" by Britt Nicole came up on my phone screen. Come to find out, my dear friend Michael (Hartling) had already put it on my iPod. God made sure I heard it.

You know me—I've listened to it more than a dozen times already. It's what I do. I want to set the world on fire by letting God's light shine through. I hope we can all be like that. Just think how full God's kingdom will be!

The lyrics are mesmerizing and true. God's light is the truth. I am nobody, and He is Big! With Him, I can do anything. It's about lining up with Him and letting His plan play out. In His will, the world is set on fire for the good.

JANUARY 18, 2011

133 › Mountains

My lil sister, Kaylee, posted, *"You can make it through anything in life, if you leave it in God's hands"* on my Facebook page yesterday. I remember giving her a Bible and writing those words in the front over two and a half years ago because she was just starting a tiresome climb up her own mountain.

I'm glad she reminded me of it. I love how God brings things full circle for me. She's not the only one who has recalled things I've written. My mom was going through piles of paper and found some interesting things.

I spent money out of my checking account in high school that included the Smokehouse, Wilshire Inn, and Walmart. I could get a chopped brisket sandwich, curly fries, and a drink with my tiger card for $3.25. As much chicken fried rice as I ate, I could have been one with it. Walmart was my haven to buy gifts to brighten my day and that of others.

More importantly, my mom found cards and letters I sent her from my Camp Champion counselor days. My brother was going through his own climb up a mountain, searching for who he was. I remember writing a pretty intense letter, making sure he knew to make the right choices, for they would affect him and those around him. I even signed it MRC (Make Right Choices).

On one card to my mom, I told her to never change, and I meant it. The irony of this one is that no matter what happens, we do change—sometimes for the better and other times not. All these things made me think this morning. I've been wanting a break desperately from this mountain Michael and I have been climbing.

Guess what? We really have been in lighter days. I feel peaceful and understand things more than ever. I've finally been brave enough to work on some relationships that needed attention. I have even taken breaks from groups and obligations.

Right now, I want to praise God for this free time, because I've taken a step back, stopped what I was doing, refreshed, and now I feel reenergized. I know my next mountain could be here any day, so it's time for me to equip and prepare my heart, soul, mind, and body.

Are things perfect right now? No. Am I doing everything right? No. I still have broken relationships and grief, and I'm adjusting to this new life. I'm figuring out what works and what doesn't for my personal business. I still have questions as I figure out how to let go of past hurts. Yet I do know that as long as I give it to God, I can make it through anything! That, my friend, is a peace that will keep on protecting and giving through whatever my days shape up to be.

Observing people (as usual) helps me see what's going on. Every mountain is vastly different. Each person has their own personal terrain. I've seen some climb like champions because God is leading. Others are breaking halfway up the mountain—unsure if they should proceed or turn around. Some just cut their rope and fall back to the bottom because they don't have the strength in and of themselves for the climb. Most people tend to sit at base camp waiting for a sign.

Whatever your mountain is today, God has given you the equipment to climb. Keep your eyes on the Lord and follow Him. He will be your climbing partner through it all because He knows every aspect of the terrain—every turn.

He sees it all.

I'm going to get ready for my next mountain. My ankle injury was a little wake-up call that the devil is not ready to let me be. He's cooking up something rare and spontaneous to bring me down. I'm going to retort by increasing my devotional time. Blaring Christian music to put glorious music into my ears and soul will help me sing when the going gets rough. More prayer time spent talking with God will strengthen me. All this will help me put on the armor of God for upcoming battles.

We all have our own loads we are trying to carry—we are not alone. Actually, this is something people can truly relate to one another about because we each have our unique load(s) depending on the time, season, and our abilities. Here's a prayer for us all:

Dear heavenly Father, I know if we aren't climbing a mountain right now, this is our recovery or preparation time for the next one. We're either climbing; we've made it to the top; we're descending to recovery; or we're hanging out at base camp. I pray You would guide and direct us on our adventures. You know exactly where we are and where we need to be. Please, Lord, send people to us who can guide and direct us here on earth. I pray You reveal the equipment You've given us or will give us. Bring us peace, comfort, and the necessary tools for success. You are our strength! You are our ultimate guide! Thank you, Father, for never leaving us nor forsaking us. We love you with everything and more. In Your forever glorious name. Amen!

Memory Verses 10 & 11

🗡 *"Keep your lives free from the love of money and be content with what you have, because God has said,* **'Never will I leave you; never will I forsake you.'** *So we say with confidence, 'The Lord is my helper; I will not be afraid. What can mere mortals do to me?' Remember your leaders, who spoke the word of God to you. Consider the outcome of their way of life and imitate their faith. Jesus Christ is the same yesterday and today and forever"* (Hebrews 13:5–8, boldface added by author).

🗡 *"Be strong and courageous. Do not be afraid or terrified because of them, for the LORD your God goes with you;* **he will never leave you nor forsake you**" (Deuteronomy 31:6, boldface added by author).

JANUARY 22, 2011

134 › The Climb

I've been meaning to post an excerpt from a dear new friend of mine, Subrenia Jurney. I've mentioned mountains several times, and she told me about her beautiful daughter, Katelyn, signing the "The Climb" by Miley Cyrus. Here is what she sent me:

> *When a person uses American Sign Language (ASL) to sign a song, they change the words to the song into the real meaning of their language. Katelyn continues to amaze me with her translation of the songs that she signs (of course, I'm sure I'm a bit biased lol). Below I have copied in the translation to this song, and I have posted her signing the song (just for you) on my Facebook. When you have a minute, listen (and watch, hehe) while thinking about the meanings Katelyn is signing.*
>
> *Even though this song is not a Christian song, there is a lot that can be gained from it if applied while seeking God's direction and leaning on Him for strength.*
>
> Katelyn's interpretation: *As a Deaf person who has had to jump through hurdles and overcome barriers, I connected with Miley Cyrus's "The Climb" about growth and resilience. It was a good reminder for me to cherish those moments and experiences and not to give up. While the end result is the ultimate goal, it's those steps to get there and the experience (both good and bad) that comes with it that matters the most and what makes a person who*

they are. I chose ASL signs that symbolized barriers and conflict to give that visual demonstration and then showed growth and strength from that throughout the challenges we may face.

To see the video, visit http://youtu.be/1-oE8Dg4BnQ. Katelyn's beautiful interpretation will move you.

The climb itself is a valuable experience, no matter how long it takes or what's on the other side. There are lessons to be learned and glory to be earned in trying to achieve a goal or get through a difficult period. I need to lose the what-ifs and some expectations to get to the other side. I don't want to lose sight of the beauty along the trail or be afraid to fall back a bit to find another way up. What matters is that I don't quit. I must keep the faith, read my map (God's Word), and use the equipment available to me.

There's rich truth in this song. When we get over one mountain, another one looms in the distance. Sometimes, I fall before I can climb again. I fall away from my expectations and what the world might expect of me. Falling can feel like a bad thing, but in the end, it's beneficial. It's when we slow down, seek God, learn from our mistakes, recover, reset, and grow stronger for the next climb.

JANUARY 24, 2011

135 › Inside Out

On Friday, January 21, 2011, I woke up early and knew I was ready to go back to the place where my daughter had two important moments in her life—her first breath on April 25, 2010, and her last one on August 5, 2010. I found myself still nervous as I climbed into the truck because Michael was driving me. The last time he took me there, I was numb from it all. I had to pick up my leftover milk on the first floor of the PICU, which they still had after Lilian Grace flew away with angel's wings weeks before.

Memories flooded in while there, and I remembered the final steps I took with Lilian Grace. I was so numb—I felt nothing at that moment. Presently, I'm feeling everything, and I wasn't sure how I would handle it. All I wanted was to be there for one of my "sisters" and "brothers" (Amy and Michael Hartling) while their lil boy, Jackson, was having surgery. They have been supportive the entire time, through all the emotions—good, bad, and ugly. Their twins and Lilian Grace were born thirteen days apart. I didn't have to be there, but I wanted to be.

As Michael and I got closer to the St. Francis Children's Hospital circle drop-off, I started panicking on the inside, and tears welled up. I took a moment to breathe. More memories poured over me when I realized that his surgery was going to be across the hall from where Lilian Grace had departed from earth. I wondered why in the world this was happening here. They are from Enid, not Tulsa. Why, of all places, was this exact hospital where they were meant to be? Then I realized it was an opportunity for another wound to heal.

I walked through those sliding doors with more tears welling up, knowing God was with me. He was walking me in, and He would stay by my side. Every day He reminds me He will always be with me no matter what turn life takes. Healing is hard, but God is refining me. He's got my back, and I praise His glorious name!

As the elevator opened to the first floor, I felt Lilian's presence in a crazy strong way. I feel her all the time, but this was so much stronger. I stopped in front of the PICU doors to glance down the hallway toward her room. Of course, it was the room straight down the hallway that could be seen from outside the PICU doors—a straight shot.

I'm breathing harder right now as I type this—the tears just won't stop. Hang in there with me, because this is harder to type than I thought it would be. Perhaps this is why I've waited three days to type it.

Back to the moment on the first floor. A mother was trying to keep it together in the lobby area while visiting family or friends. She made the following comment that made me giggle. *"I have to get an update on my Facebook, or I will have a thousand people mad at me or calling my phone. I just can't deal with it right now, so I have no choice. I have to update to protect us."* Wow! I remember feeling everyone's love and the burden of having to update. Some people would get furious if I didn't update. They would think I was mad or didn't care to talk to them, but the truth—the truth was that I was barely holding it together.

Sometimes, I didn't want to have to talk to someone, send a reply, or type an entry. I just wanted to embrace what little time I had left with my daughter because it was a sure thing she wasn't going to be here long. I said a prayer for the mother and her family. Not everyone knows how tough it is until you have been in those shoes—wishing all of it would just go away or you'd wake up from the nightmare. You hope to wake up to a better reality or circumstance—wishing your plans would work out. More than anything, I wanted people to stop being selfish and really think about what we were going through.

As I carried on and looked through those doors to her old room, I knew something was happening. There were several staff members in front of another room taking me back to the day when the staff hovered around our room, waiting to see Lilian Grace's fate—would she fight one more fight, or would she get to fly high and be relieved of suffering? I thank God for all those people who were outside our room. I can't even imagine what it's like for them, knowing they do it often. I pray for those in the PICU when I think of them.

I prayed God would be with the family and staff during whatever was happening to the child. I turned slowly and saw "the hallway"—the route I last took with my daughter in my arms. She had no equipment attached and was wrapped in a blanket, just her body in my arms—no longer here but still my baby girl. I smiled through the tears as I revisited our last walk.

Even though I knew that at the end of it, Lilian would never be in my arms again, I smiled because God was right there comforting us—letting us have that moment with her while she was returning to Him. I held her without worrying if it was going to be good or bad for her. I held her without cords or equipment or anyone in my head telling me what I wasn't doing for them.

As I walked toward the waiting room next to surgery, I composed myself, because today wasn't about me. My "sister" and "brother" were experiencing a piece of what we had gone through. I couldn't go back to the surgery area, because it was a rough day when Lilian Grace had to have her central line put in. I remember taking picture after picture thinking that day was going to be our last with her—that she probably wouldn't wake up.

I knew God would make Jackson's surgery go well—He was there with us all. Being there was a lot harder for Amy and Michael (Hartling)—they had followed my posts about Lilian's journey. They were carrying my load with them into their own journey. It couldn't have been easy having me there because none of us knew how any of us would handle this, considering the past trauma. Lilian Grace's journey was hanging over our heads, but we made it—everything went well.

I ended up taking some breaks from the first floor. I was blessed to see some of my favorite staff members. The newborn intensive care unit (NICU) is an amazing place. If you ever have to be there, know you are in fabulous hands. I even got to see Lilian's doctor, Dr. Gomez, who is a wonderful man. I spent time talking to all of them, and it really meant so much that they all took the time to come see me in the lobby area on the fifth floor. I was just a mother whose child was in heaven—no longer needing their services—but they made me feel like family. I needed it more than I thought I did. I thank you all for making this healing process even more special.

What would my visit be without going to both gift shops? I know, I can't help myself. The only hard part about it was finding the little giraffe Michael had bought Lilian Grace. He had placed it with the items that went with her during the cremation process to make more ashes. I wanted to buy it so he'd have one, so I called him. I didn't realize how hard it would be to hear about the giraffe or for him to drop me off at the hospital. He told me no because it was hers. He didn't need a reminder. We both cried on the phone. Finally, we were breaking through the funk we'd been in to allow more healing. We are beginning again.

We've spent all weekend arguing off and on about other people's problems. We're good at trying to avoid certain levels of healing. We get caught up in stupid things that get in the way, but God is ever so patient by loving us so much that He doesn't let us go stagnant! There are so many wounds to heal—too many! It does feel good when we each get healed—it's just painful as we're going through it.

As I read chapter five today from the *Plan B* Bible study, truths about perspective spoke to me loudly. God focuses on our character, not on how comfortable character development makes us feel. We become the person God wants us to be through our losses, failures, wins, and heartbreaks. It's about being present in our current stage of life and asking God for guidance and strength to survive it and thrive.

Patience is a part of the toolbox—the toolbox that equips me to be the best version of myself. God continues to shape and mold all of us. Does our character contribute to the expansion of God's kingdom? What does your character say about you?

Thanks for hanging in there with me through this lengthy entry. The tears have stopped, and a smile is on my face. Another wound is healed because my Savior is the greatest Healer of all time. I know there are parts of my character that need work, but I trust God will continue to tweak and overhaul! Love you all, and remember He is with us always!

I listened to Hillsong United sing "From the Inside Out"

on repeat as I typed today. I have failed many times in my walk with God. My emotions, thoughts, and actions take turns failing at various moments, trials, and challenges.

This song fills my heart with hope in the promises of God. His strength, grace, glory, and ability will go beyond my weaknesses. I pray He is lifted high. I hope I'll allow Him to rescue me when I've short-changed His training plan. I'm reminding myself that my life should be less about me and more about Him. May He rescue us all from our self-centered bubbles.

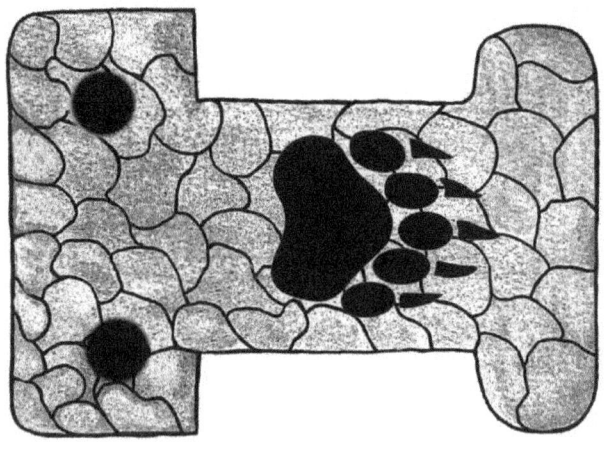

JANUARY 25, 2011

136 › Wonder

The calendar has flipped forward to nine months later. I wonder what Lilian Grace should have been doing by this time as a baby. I looked at the first week of nine months shared by BabyCenter.com to see what they say she'd be doing at this point. Separation anxiety stood out. Interestingly, this matches up to my grief journey. I can relate to needing people to approach me slowly and letting me make the first move. This applies to people interacting with grieving individuals who have lost someone. Take it slow and be normal. I have discovered that I long for normalcy. I miss her all the time, but I keep moving forward.

As I read on, Lilian Grace was ahead of the developmental curve—even being a preemie. She was brave enough to fight, travel, and mesmerize anyone who came near her. She rarely met a stranger! Regarding travel, I don't think that's a problem—she's traveling with angels and our Savior all over the place! Who wouldn't want that? He takes care of her every need. Something really cool is that she's whole and new. She had no problem leaving the body she was born into.

I still can't believe we only have three months until Lilian Grace came into the world a year ago. Bizarre, light speed, limbo, and answered prayers all come to mind when I think back to her birth day. I woke up early this morning since neither Michael nor I could sleep. Our grieving picks up usually between the twenty-first to the sixth of the next month, which could be the culprit stealing our sleep.

Yesterday, I made Lily necklaces with Cindy (Haley), then finally ordered my prints and book using the NILMDTS photos. Tears crept up as I decided what to order while trying not to get lost in the last photos of my sweet angel.

Coming home from Cindy's house, I reminisced about the night before Lilian Grace joined us. I was restless because I didn't know what Lilian's fate would be. I had predicted that night Lilian Grace would be here by ten the next morning. I know the nurses thought I was crazy. Come to find out, at 8:44 a.m., my precious bundle of joy came into the world—just an hour and sixteen minutes off. I had prayed numerous times, asking the Lord to please give us more time by letting her first breath continue to her next. The world and I needed to know her. She had been a miracle since conception! He answered my prayer—we celebrated three monthly birthdays and two additional weeks.

Rolling past me in the operating room, I saw her, and my light board immediately lit up. Everything I knew changed forever in one look. I'd never be the same again. God had a miraculous plan to change many of us by knowing her.

We are changed even more when we know Jesus. In church, we've been going over Jesus's life. We are getting to know Him deeper—falling more madly in love. Just by knowing Him, people's hearts and lives were changed. I only have a taste of experiencing such a miracle—the life of Lilian Grace was lengthened by Jesus. She lights me up a million times over when I think about her. Jesus lights me up bright by knowing Him.

I love you all and pray you can see all the miracles around you daily. If we pay close attention, Jesus is found everywhere as He works all things for good.

Dear precious Tiger Lily,

I know I only called you that when you were acting up and giving us what for, but I have come to love this nickname I gave you. I thought about the times when you were Tiger Lily and realized you were just trying to tell us what you really needed. I am thankful you were verbal in your communication skills at an early stage.

You really get two celebrations a month from my point of view. You have two birthdays: an earthly and a heavenly one. I smile on the twenty-fifth because you lit up my whole being by entering this world nine months ago. God taught me not to take one thing for granted while you were here.

We were on borrowed time—not knowing which second, hour, day, week, or month you'd fly. We knew you weren't going to be here forever, so we lived it up. I thought about what birthday theme we could have for January, and I think it would have been appropriate to do the Wonder Pets this month. Our last name initial W is already on the back of their capes. I feel like you taught us to fly through it all—leading by example.

My crazy self went ahead and bought the three characters—Turtle Tuck; Linny the Guinea Pig; and Ming-Ming Duckling—to remind me to smile even on the bad days. Yes, I'm the one who needs the toys to avoid separation anxiety. Go figure, they really do help in a strange way, as do the additional children's books to share later on.

At one point when I closed my eyes last night, I saw a bright light again. I thought of you with my heavenly Father coming to check on me and give me much-needed comfort. I felt at peace. Thank you.

May people continue to learn from your little story by allowing needed changes to be made in their own lives. My love for you still grows daily. When I see babies of any age, I'm starting to smile again. I pray for each of them to receive the best love, comfort, and guidance from their own families. You've helped make some of their time here much better than it would have been. I remain prouder than ever.

Only three months until you would have turned one on earth. I'm finally getting my act together to plan your special day. Many will come to celebrate God's wonderful ways. We will have a princess and prince birthday party, two runs—the Warrior Princess Fun Run, 1.03 miles, and Warrior Princess Trail Run, 10.3 miles—and release one lantern with messages from many before the night is over.

I can't wait. I love you to the moon and back and for all eternity. I'm trying to be a little more like Tiger Lily so I can communicate better.

Love,
Your Mommy,
Chrissy

PS: The Wonder Pets theme song played while I typed this entry. You helped the world see God by allowing His light to shine brightly through you. He saves the day no matter how big or small—the greatest superhero ever. He's tougher than anything in this world. I appreciate His sacrifices and all-powerful ways.

THE FALL TO THE CLIMB 145

Wonder Pets

FEBRUARY 2, 2011

137 › A Way to Celebrate

I've been working with several of my amazing runner family members to prepare for Lilian's race. It's an extra special day for Michael and me, because race day marks Lilian Grace's one-year birthday. I'm hoping to host this race annually—no matter the size—from now until God says to stop.

Volunteer opportunities will be posted online in the next couple of weeks. I know that not everyone will want to or be capable of running, so there's a way for everyone to get involved to help us celebrate our daughter's life. For those who live out of town and can't make it to the race, we've added a shadow runner option to participate from wherever you live and still get a shirt and custom medal. Pre-information is included here to help start your preparations.

First Annual ~ Warrior Princess Trail Run ~ Monday, April 25, 2011

Start times: 6:00 p.m., 10.3 mile Trail/Road Race and 6:30 p.m., 1.03 mile Fun Run/Walk

Location: Keystone State Park Mountain Bike and Hike Trail (Sand Springs)

Race day registration and packet pick-up: 5:00–5:50 p.m.

The Warrior Princess Trail Run proceeds will benefit babies diagnosed with trisomy 18 and trisomy 13 chromosomal disease and their families by providing assistance, support, and resources needed. The race is in memory of Michael and Chrissy Whitten's daughter, who was diagnosed with trisomy 18 sixteen days into her life.

Lilian Grace Whitten, Warrior Princess, soared above and beyond what was expected of her life. Her first breath was supposed to be her last. She lived 103 glorious days on this earth before earning her wings. God gave us the reason why she was here through the following Scripture: "So that Christ may dwell in your hearts through FAITH. And I pray that you being rooted and established in love, may have power, together with all the Lord's holy people, to grasp how wide and long and high and deep is the LOVE of Christ, and to know this love that surpasses knowledge—that you may be filled to the measure of all the FULLNESS OF GOD" (Ephesians 3:17–19, all caps added by author).

Awards: *Prizes to the overall top three male and female runners (no duplication of awards). ~ Custom finisher medals for all runners. ~ Prize to the best dressed Warrior Prince and Princess.*

Races and Contest:
Warrior Princess Trail/Road Run: 10.3 miles
Warrior Princess Fun Run: 1.03 miles
Shadow Runner Race (from wherever you are)
Warrior Prince and Princess Costume Contest
Entry Fee: *$35 by March 1, 2011, and $40 after March 1, 2011*

Registration: Make checks payable to: **Warrior Princess Foundation, 25 E. Broadway, Sand Springs, OK 74063**

For more information, contact the race director, Chrissy Whitten, at warriorprincessfoundation@hotmail.com[3]

We will have online registration coming ASAP. We are working on getting all other details completed by mid-February. The March 1 deadline is a quick turnaround, but it will help in ordering tech shirts and customized finisher medals.

I didn't realize how much the grieving process would get in my way of planning this special event, but I finally saw a clearing in the storm! God's been helping heal many layers these past few months and more. I look forward to running with you all on the day God changed our lives forever by giving us such a miracle. Lilian Grace faced her obstacles and moved forward, so I challenge you to do the same.

I'd like to encourage you to either start or keep training for the race. I know this will make her birthday easier for many of us by celebrating her Warrior Princess style. Thank you for the continuous support you have given us throughout all this.

If you or your company would like to sponsor the event, there are plenty of opportunities to do so. I'll be posting specifics ASAP. Look at the obstacles you are facing right now, face them head on, and keep moving forward. Love you all!

---

[3] Note from author: This email address is no longer active.

150 Chrissy L. Whitten

FEBRUARY 4, 2011

138 › Snowstorm Enlightenment

Memory Verse 12

🗡 *"God is our refuge and strength, an ever-present help in trouble. Therefore we will not fear, though the earth give way and the mountains fall into the heart of the sea, though its waters roar and foam and the mountains quake with their surging . . . The LORD Almighty is with us" (Psalm 46:1–3, 7).*

Grieving can be understood better by comparing it to the Oklahoma Snowpocalypse of 2011. You know it's coming, but you're not quite sure how it's going to end up. Snow mixed with a thunderstorm can come close to what you're feeling when emotions happen all at once instead of separately. The ridiculous amount of snow represents the emotional and physical dumping you experience during various times of grief.

After you know what the storm has done—just like in grief—you see what's left and at times have a bigger mess than you know what to do with. The piles of snow and ice are obstacles that those grieving face every day. If you have the right climate or attitude, the obstacles melt away, but they don't melt without heat, a.k.a. work!

For instance, Michael shoveled the driveway and back porch for hours. When the sun came out, the driveway was free of ice and snow—a clean slate due to his hard work. It's the same for the grieving process. If you keep trying to shovel what is in the way, eventually it clears the path of what used to be obstacles or roadblocks and creates a cleaner slate.

Since God blessed me with four days off this week, I focused on my anger. For the first time in this part of my grief journey, I let myself be mad. I justified why I needed to be mad by shouting out loud a few times to assure myself I didn't feel guilty. Come to find out, I needed to face the anger. It was healthy to be mad and give all the anger a voice to see what really existed inside.

I will eventually apologize to those I feel I owe an apology to for taking my anger out on them. I let it build up this year and come out through childish decisions like unfriending people on Facebook. Even through my anger, I purposely meant to do it. Why was I mad at them? I thought they would be by my side when I needed them; instead, they were missing—nowhere to be found.

I forgot God didn't intend for everyone to be a part of the battle when Lilian Grace got here. Those who stepped up to the plate were those whom God ordained to support us. I wish I could have stepped back enough to realize this, instead of being selfish myself and getting mad at some people who weren't available or seemed to disappear.

Having been unfriended by at least two family members myself, I know how crappy and unfair it feels—it's not fun at all. I don't understand why and may never get an answer. Though they both have tried to friend me back, I have not accepted yet—it's a trust issue. They unfriended me once, without reason, so they could do it again. I know it's just Facebook, but we can't keep kidding ourselves. It has become an extension of life, like a phone call, letter, or text.

To the ones I unfriended, I will get with you individually soon. I understand that our friendship will never be the same, but you deserve the reason behind it. I'm sorry if this caused you pain. Sadly, I was mad about everything being out of my hands, so I controlled what I could and took it out on friends I haven't heard from.

Back to this horrible weather here—it's a morbid comedy. When we get impatient, wrecks and havoc occur. The comical part is that the ice and snow will eventually melt. It's only temporary. This happens a lot sooner than a heart can heal. As God graciously supplies our daily needs, I continue to admire His fatherly love for His children—all of us.

My wonderful father-in-law found pictures of my husband when he was a little boy for a special birthday weekend I'm planning. Michael, above anyone I know right now, deserves the biggest and best party ever. I've included one of his pictures in this entry that took my breath away. The picture is proof that Lilian Grace looks more like her daddy than I originally thought.

If I have ever seen a baby picture of Michael, I don't recall it. I've been with him for over nine years at this point. Tonight, I got to stare at his baby pictures and appreciate how much Lilian Grace resembles him. I thank God for this moment, because as a mother I got to carry her inside my womb and feel her heartbeat, hiccups, twists, and turns. Ladies, we may have an abundance of symptoms and adversities during pregnancy, but we get to be more intimate with our babies. For Lilian Grace to look like her father gives him an intimate connection with his daughter, like I experienced when she was in my womb.

Since I was extremely happy with the invitation, I had to show Michael. As soon as he saw it, I pointed out how Lilian Grace looked just like him. I informed him that his daddy had searched for his baby pictures for me and sent them to me immediately. The one with him in the wagon was his daddy's favorite. Michael welled up with tears.

I wish I could be like the bulldozer that clears the streets of ice, snow, and havoc. I'd bulldoze all the pain from Michael's heart. I don't think there is one day that Michael and I don't cry. Yes, I'm admitting that tears come often. Thankfully, God gives me lighter ones on some days so I can rest!

The days I fill with distractions like girlfriend time, work, race planning, and Michael's special events have greatly helped. At the end of the day, I do make time to release and let reality settle. Just like with road conditions—you can only go so far until you hit ice. It's best to stay put until things clear up a little more, both on the roads and in your mind.

I've contemplated posting for several days, but it didn't feel right until tonight when I saw Michael's baby pictures. It inspired me to share the above thoughts. I know my life, the grieving process, and the storms will eventually clear up and move out. I always look forward to clear blue skies, flourishing green grass, and warmer temperatures (80 degrees is perfect for me) to enhance the best physical and mental states!

I'm not a fan of freezing temperatures, ice, snow, the grieving process, or messes related to these things. We all grieve in our own ways, but attempting to bury it all down deep isn't healthy. We want to appear whole and normal again, so we disguise our brokenness. You know through my writing that I can't bury my feelings for long.

People who tend to pile things up—like a mountain of snow in a parking lot—procrastinate. Their pile stays around longer than accumulation on the ground. Others think they can drive right through the snow and ice and then find themselves stuck and needing help. Many stay inside, afraid to venture out, which isn't healthy.

However you deal with grief or sorrow, remember that God is always with you—you are never alone. Keep "shoveling" through whatever you face, no matter how you feel. You owe it to yourself to feel all of it and to make forward progress. God keeps teaching me every day like He has for thirty-two-and-a-half years. I'm now owning my feelings more and giving myself breaks.

I praise God for this particular snowstorm because I've had time to catch up on much-needed things for myself, my husband, and our home! Whatever the situation, look up and take a minute before reacting. I need to tattoo this on my brain! Love always, Chrissy.

Proof that Lily looks like her daddy

FEBRUARY 6, 2011

139 › Six-Month Angelversary

Yesterday, Lilian Grace celebrated her six-month angelversary. I decided not to post because I wanted to see if not acknowledging it out loud would make me feel any better. Guess what? It did not. I was experimenting with myself in hopes of finding a way to make grieving better for all of us.

I opened my bedside drawer and found Olivia the Pig dressed in traditional pjs and an unused diaper of Lilian Grace's. "Crazy" comes to mind. Lilian's last nickname was Lil Piglet, so the mini Olivia plush toy is perfect because Lilian Grace looked like she was asleep when I said goodbye until later.

I tend to grab that diaper often and place Lil Olivia Piglet inside it so I can almost feel like I'm patting Lilian Grace on her little hiney. This may be strange, but it's comforting in a twisted way. I have caught myself on other days just grabbing the diaper to stare at it, like it's a mirror into my memories of Lilian Grace. I've even caught myself smelling it because it almost smells like her. During my grieving process, there have been many "crazy" moments. I find myself doing and saying almost anything I think might help. I've heard other grievers do the same.

I am figuring out the keys to being successful in my grieving process. Listed below are the ones I've figured out thus far:

1. Keep remembering and talking about her.
2. Admit it when I don't have it all together.
3. Know that feeling crazy is okay. How I'm dealing with

it might be strange or abnormal to other people. I pray they never have to go through this, but life proves difficult at some point for everyone.

4. My emotions and broken heart need permission to freely cry and speak out as needed. This is healing to my heart and soul.

5. Breathing is like an Olympic game in my life. I hope I can retire one day from the grief events that induce anxiety.

6. God is holding me tighter than He has ever held me before, and I must stay in His arms and hold on for dear life.

7. I'm not alone. There are people who are willing and able to walk this journey with me!

8. I try to tell people what I think I need, but it may not be what they need. I am accepting this reality, but I hope they can accept how I need to do my life right now. I need open lines of communication with them for clarification and to avoid assumptions.

9. Since I am blessed beyond measure, counting the good things in my life and focusing on them helps me stay positive.

10. I can be happy through the tears and sorrow. I'm worthy of happiness and joy!

11. Talking about and doing silly, strange things out of the norm to remember Lilian Grace is part of my journey. It's not crazy or hurting anyone—it's a way to survive.

More could be added, but these top the list for me at the moment. Another month down adds more time separating us from the day Lilian Grace departed. Time quickly slips away, and a weird feeling slips in that I can't seem to put into words. I just know my body, mind, heart, and soul react to a set time frame each month. Our minds are vast and intense with links to numerous things in life. Mine is intertwined with the calendar.

I seem to experience a twisted take on the movie *Groundhog Day*. I'm not stuck on one day but instead on specific days of each month when I experience a spike in emotions and breathing issues. I'm not sure how long this will continue. I think it's strange yet comforting at the same time. Perhaps I'm afraid of what will happen when it stops. What then? I'm not sure, but I'll keep walking to find out.

My bubby called me yesterday out of the blue. I'm not sure if he did it because of the anniversary date, but it meant the world to me. Hearing his voice was exactly what I needed. I didn't share this with him because I just wanted to soak up the moment. I love my bubby more than he will ever know. I love family the same. I especially loved how my family was when growing up before we hit middle school age.

My brother and I were adventurers and explorers. We went everywhere around the neighborhood and beyond. His phone call brought back cherished memories of being outdoors with the sun shining down on us. That time in my life with him has been a tool I use to get through many sad moments. I love how God gives us good memories—an everlasting joy.

During our conversation, my brother asked me how I was doing. I answered, but then I thought about him and everyone else. I asked how he was doing because I know this can't be easy. Do you know what I get that he doesn't? Time to make beautiful memories with a niece or nephew. I know they are not my children, but my niece and nephew are an extension of my brother. They remind me of how Jarrod and I were growing up. It's hilarious yet special to watch them grow up together.

I know for him, losing Lilian Grace is probably like losing a part of me because she was an extension of me. He won't get to watch her grow up or hear her laugh like he and I did growing up. It makes me really sad. I know he has to be hurting because it would be hard if I lost one of his kids. It'd be like losing part of us.

Do you know what I want from people? I want them to talk to me and not suppress what they are feeling. I know more than anyone that we all changed to an extent because of Lilian Grace. We all lost the future we imagined having with her. I want you to share your grief. You add to my journey by sharing your own take on losing Lilian. Just be respectful of other people who are grieving—don't make it all about you. We are all finding our own way through this, so let's support each other.

What makes me mad is when people make themselves the center of attention by grieving in a selfish way. All I want is for them to share in our grieving process. No matter how much I don't want people to feel pain or hurt, we do. We are all grieving, so why hide that fact? Do you know when I ask how you're doing that I already see you are dealing with something? I can see the pain and sorrow mixed with a bundle of other emotions through your eyes. Your eyes give it away every time.

I can't say exactly what is causing that pain and sorrow, but you can't hide it. You can try to hide it with your words, but the eyes will always reveal the truth—no matter what. Please do share, but remember, no one's pain is worse than someone else's. It's pain. It's grieving. It's personal.

If I have to type it a million times in multiple entries, I will—YOU ARE NOT ALONE! Don't be selfish—be selfless. And please be a part of our journey, even if you are grieving for something or someone else. I'm not sure why that needed extra emphasis, but there it is.

"Losing My Way" by Justin Timberlake is a very different song for this entry but for good reasons. I am not on drugs or doing things I shouldn't. The words of this song are very powerful, especially for someone grieving. I know many might agree that you feel you are losing your way. Many times, we search to see, feel, or hear ourselves. We feel like we are in hell because everything is upside down and not what we think it should be. We are continuously searching to see, feel, or hear ourselves and others.

Many times, we all dive into our own "drugs" that interrupt and pull us down. I'm replacing "drugs" in this song with something you or I might be dealing with—such as stacking your schedule; overeating all the foods; spending money you don't have; fighting with everyone who stands in your way; silencing yourself to fit in; or watching ten hours of TV a day. The list could go on. What is the "drug" that distracts you from finding your way? I know during my grief there are several things I let get in my way. I tell myself to stop because I know God has a plan for me. I'm lucky to be living some of that plan out right now without interruptions.

Grief can be a "drug" that doesn't make you feel better but can cause you to lose your way if you don't pay attention. God is my protector and is graciously allowing me to survive this journey. He keeps giving me peace, comfort, and love throughout this whole thing. God keeps revealing Himself and all His wonders to me through people, places, and experiences. I'm one lucky girl!

I hope you can enjoy this song and interpret it for your own life. To answer the question in the song—yes, God and others are out here to help you hear, see, and feel. Praise God that one day the feeling of hell on earth will be over. I look forward to leaving this body and earth to join Him in heaven. Yes—that will be a day of rejoicing! Love you all.

FEBRUARY 9, 2011

140 › Processing & Tears Flowing

My mom surprised me yesterday by driving to visit me in Tulsa. We got to eat lunch and shop together for five fun hours. More importantly, I got to see my mom, whom I love. She knew exactly what I needed to feel better—mother-daughter time.

I know for me, as a griever—I need my life back. I need to feel I'm not this "special" glass figurine, who gets left on a shelf and forgotten. I know life is going to be different now, but I want people around me no matter what my new life looks like.

When my mom and I were in the checkout lane at Ross, she mentioned that my eyes were really blood shot. I told her I'd seen something that made me tear up, which about sums up life most days. The tears range in emotion on a scale from horrid to happy. I never know what switch will be turned on, but the result is always the same—tears flowing. Life goes on, but healing takes forever.

I have decided through all my relationships that there are three realities to life: my reality, your reality, and total reality. My mom and I had some good talks throughout the day. I'm glad my reality is what it is because I've come a long way through life. I wouldn't be me if life hadn't happened the way it has over the last thirty-two-and-a-half years. I will continue to learn, grow, and be shaped into who I'm meant to be—which means I've got many more adventures to go.

Through my down time in this bizarre weather as of late,

I've had hours to process the chapters of my life. I've thought about the total reality of some events. I thank God for the processing time because I'm now grateful for moments I wasn't so grateful for at the time. Lilian Grace was my key to unlocking some of God's lessons and implementing them in my life.

To continue the fabulous day that made my heart happy, I got to teach a one-on-one Pilates session and participate in the *Plan B* Bible study. One of my clients has been rocking out her weight loss by successfully losing over twenty-two inches and eleven real pounds. Praise God for her, because she reminds me that I'm meant to be right where I am—no matter what is or is not working in my mind. I can do this! Thank you for your hard work!

Regarding my Bible study, I love the ladies who are participating in the study with me. I am learning from all of you! Even though plan Bs can feel like plan Zs, God's showing me that plan changes are more about my character development in integrity, growth, spirit, fruit, and tools.

God is teaching me how to be who He made me to be. I pray I don't get in the way like I tend to do. A continuous theme of late is described by the song "Firework" by Katie Perry. No matter the state of your dreams and life, there's a spark inside you waiting to ignite. Show how amazing our heavenly Father made you! We all have a light and gift inside us to share with the world.

Keep searching for the things that ignite you from within so you'll shine His light bright for the world. Reset and discover His original design for you by reading His Word, participating in Bible studies, praying throughout your days, being still before Him, and worshipping His goodness through music. He is ever-present and leading you to what, when, where, why, and how you can be. You are worth everything because He created you! You exist! You are not a mistake! You are a firework—splendid, spectacular, glittery, and bright! Love you all!

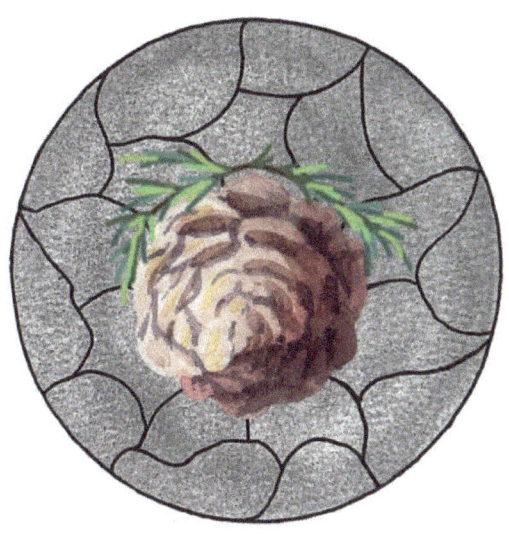

FEBRUARY 15, 2011

141 › Father's Love Letter

I struggled to post this week. I had plenty to say, but I figured it wasn't meant to be read. I never know these days what will come of the journal entries. Should I keep writing? I guess I'll do it when I do it. I've had a busy week with the Women of Faith All Access Conference, Eli Young Band concert, my grandparents' sixtieth wedding anniversary, projects underway, and running my business.

The ice storm really messed up scheduling, working, and everything in between. Everyone seems to be playing catch-up. I'm praying and trusting we can all catch up and make it through whatever we are facing!

With that said, yesterday was a special holiday—Valentine's Day. I was reminded of a Valentine's Day letter I sent many years ago to my family and some friends. I found this letter on the internet, and it took my breath away. Everyone should read this love letter from our heavenly Father. The words make me smile through tears over my past, present, and future.

God is always here. I hope you are encouraged and reassured as the words sink into your spirit. They are all from the Word of God, beautifully weaved into a remarkable letter. Just when I thought I could escape from everything to Nashville, Tennessee, God proposed another plan to heal more layers. Enjoy the letter and remember that I love you all.

Father's Love Letter

My Child,

You may not know me, but I know everything about you.
  (Psalm 139:1)
I know when you sit down and when you rise up. (Psalm 139:2)
I am familiar with all your ways. (Psalm 139:3)
Even the very hairs on your head are numbered.
  (Matthew 10:29–31)
For you were made in My image. (Genesis 1:27)
In me you live and move and have your being. (Acts 17:28)
For you are My offspring. (Acts 17:28)
I knew you even before you were conceived. (Jeremiah 1:4–5)
I chose you when I planned creation. (Ephesians 1:11–12)
You were not a mistake, for all your days are written in My book.
  (Psalm 139:15–16)
I determined the exact time of your birth and where you would live.
  (Acts 17:26)
You are fearfully and wonderfully made. (Psalm 139:14)
I knit you together in your mother's womb. (Psalm 139:13)
And brought you forth on the day you were born. (Psalm 71:6)
I have been misrepresented by those who don't know Me.
  (John 8:41–44)
I am not distant and angry, but am the complete expression of love.
  (1 John 4:16)
And it is My desire to lavish My love on you. (1 John 3:1)
Simply because you are My child and I am your Father.
  (1 John 3:1)
I offer you more than your earthly father ever could.
  (Matthew 7:11)
For I am the perfect Father. (Matthew 5:48)

Every good gift that you receive comes from My hand.
   (James 1:17)
For I am your provider and I meet all your needs.
   (Matthew 6:31–33)
My plan for your future has always been filled with hope.
   (Jeremiah 29:11)
Because I love you with an everlasting love. (Jeremiah 31:3)
My thoughts toward you are countless as the sand on the sea-shore.
   (Psalm 139:17–18)
And I rejoice over you with singing. (Zephaniah 3:17)
I will never stop doing good to you. (Jeremiah 32:40)
For you are My treasured possession. (Exodus 19:5)
I desire to establish you with all My heart and all My soul.
   (Jeremiah 32:41)
And I want to show you great and marvelous things.
   (Jeremiah 33:3)
If you seek Me with all your heart, you will find Me.
   (Deuteronomy 4:29)
Delight in Me and I will give you the desires of your heart.
   (Psalm 37:4)
For it is I who gave you those desires. (Philippians 2:13)
I am able to do more for you than you could possibly imagine.
   (Ephesians 3:20)
For I am your greatest encourager. (2 Thessalonians 2:16–17)
I am also the Father who comforts you in all your troubles.
   (2 Corinthians 1:3–4)
When you are brokenhearted, I am close to you. (Psalm 34:18)
As a shepherd carries a lamb, I have carried you close to My heart.
   (Isaiah 40:11)
One day, I will wipe away every tear from your eyes.
   (Revelation 21:3–4)
And I'll take away all the pain you have suffered on this earth.
   (Revelation 21:3–4)

I am your Father, and I love you even as I love my Son, Jesus.
(John 17:23)
For in Jesus, My love for you is revealed. (John 17:26)
He is the exact representation of My being. (Hebrews 1:3)
He came to demonstrate that I am for you, not against you.
(Romans 8:31)
And to tell you that I am not counting your sins.
(2 Corinthians 5:18–19)
Jesus died so that you and I could be reconciled.
(2 Corinthians 5:18–19)
His death was the ultimate expression of My love for you.
(1 John 4:10)
I gave up everything I loved that I might gain your love.
(Romans 8:31–32)
If you receive the gift of My Son Jesus, you receive me.
(1 John 2:23)
And nothing will ever separate you from my love again.
(Romans 8:38–39)
Come home and I'll throw the biggest party heaven has ever seen.
(Luke 15:7)
I have always been Father, and will always be Father.
(Ephesians 3:14–15)
My question is . . . Will you be my child? (John 1:12–13)
I am waiting for you. (Luke 15:11–32)

Love,
Your Dad
Almighty God [4]

---

[4] "Father's Love Letter," Father Heart Communications, (1999), accessed 2011, www.FathersLoveLetter.com.

FEBRUARY 22, 2011

142 › Fresh Eyes, No Blinders

If my tears from today could have been gathered and stored, they would fill a kids swimming pool from Walmart. I usually don't start crying this early, yet today's tears weren't all about Lilian Grace. They've been more about my broken and hurt heart over relationships in my life.

I have experienced more game playing than I care to be a part of. I've been a crybaby about stupid stuff—and more importantly, about real life. Not only that, but I keep searching for my blinders that Lilian Grace took from me. All I come up with are fresh eyes that can't seem to get away from seeing the raw truth about everything and everybody as it is right now.

I observe people whom I'd love to be like and others whom I don't want to be like. Life is tricky in grief—it keeps going while people around me live normally. Their circumstances and choices play out. Their poor decisions often hurt me, and then I'm stuck on damage control duty. At the end of the day, God graciously puts life in my lap to deal with—no matter how far I try to run from it all.

If I could sew together everyone's broken heart, I would do it in a heartbeat. If it meant I had to spend hours laboring to make enough money to pay to fix it all, I would sign up and participate as soon as I heard about it. If I could read a million books to help me know how to make it happen, I'd start reading until I couldn't see straight.

What have I discovered? When I remove whatever or whomever I'm blaming and truly decide to let it go, life gets better. At the end of the day, week, month, year, decade, and beyond, the most important thing is to deal with who I am, not who someone else is. If I'm not happy and haven't dealt with myself, then it'll never get better.

You can only blame others for so long until you wake up and realize you've got work to do on yourself. No matter what we go through, we must continue to deal with and work on what is needed to grow personally. I know more individuals trapped in circumstances, gutters—whatever you want to call it—than I ever remember seeing before.

I'm crying today and choosing to trust God continuously—no matter who is around me or what I see. I've decided to keep working on myself and all the issues within. I need to stop trying to fix everyone else's issues. It's time we all face our own issues. "Let go and let God."

My tears, along with learning and adjusting, will continue despite how much I would love to wave my white flag. I hate the gutter and being trapped in circumstances. It doesn't make me or anyone else prettier or more handsome when we are stuck. Praying for us and loving you all!

FEBRUARY 24, 2011

143 › I Will Carry You

Memory Verse 13

"May the God of hope fill you with all joy and peace as you trust in him, so that you may overflow with hope by the power of the Holy Spirit" (Romans 15:13).

When God placed a beautiful angel in my life ten months ago at 8:44 a.m., April 25, 2010, He released my trapped emotions, feelings, and fears. What do those look like? They take on different faces and masks, but presently I'm feeling an abundance of anger toward many in my life.

Why? I continue to set the bar high with expectations that cannot be reached by a normal human being. I've carried anger since middle school when my mom got deathly sick. I felt helpless and unequipped for what the future would hold. Would my mom even survive at sixty-something pounds?

I was so young to have to face life without my mom. I remember trying to be extra tough to support my family. My mom almost died in the hospital from bleeding out. These days, I can't seem to turn the emotions off. I go back to the younger version of myself who thought she had everyone fooled with her tough-as-nails persona. Deep inside, I was scared and didn't think we would make it through all of it.

I remember my mom telling me about going through the dying experience, and all she could see was pictures of us kids as babies—her babies—flashing before her. She knew she had to fight so we wouldn't be without her. I appreciate her ability to fight, especially knowing she's still enduring pain daily caused by Crohn's disease.

I don't ever forget she is in pain daily, and I constantly think about her strength. I know how much she loves us kids through whatever she faces each day. I appreciate her and can only imagine how hard being in pain 24/7 is. Thank you, Mom, for fighting and never giving up. I hope you see how much you've accomplished by fighting to stay here so we don't have to know what it's like to be without a mother.

In dealing with my emotions, I wish, hope, and pray for each of us to find happiness despite our broken hearts. Our brokenness, over time, gets healed as long as we are willing to be healed. I wanted you to know where I've been mentally this week so you'll understand my present challenges.

I asked Michael if Laureate Psychiatric Clinic was covered on our insurance plan because I thought I might need to go there if I couldn't calm down or control my emotions. My anger toward some people has been so intense. I thought the only solution at the time was people passing on to heaven. I know that sounds horrible. It's hard when I want to fix things or people, and solutions do not come quickly. We are all stubborn human beings. I'm the "Queen of the Stubborn People," which I may dress as for Thanksgiving (inside joke from my ladies Bible study).

Truthfully, I don't want anyone to die. I just want us to die to our hang-ups and stubborn nature. I want us to stop the game playing and let reality set in. I want us all to stop throwing stones at one another. Life is naturally full of drama, so why hold on to things that just weigh us down and make us look ugly and ridiculous?

I thought I couldn't cry any more this week, but I was wrong. Wednesday at two o'clock, I started throwing up in both areas of my body—sorry for the TMI. I was miserable for more than twenty-four hours. I felt like I might have C. diff again, like I did exactly a year ago. I've lost five to six pounds this week. It could have been food poisoning, a stomach bug, or a complete meltdown of my mind, body, and soul.

I'm not sure, but I know I felt horrible, and being sick made my life come to a halt. I can't stand not being able to do anything. I took three showers to feel better. I even put a pallet on the bathroom floor because I was tired of rushing to the ceramic throne. The cold tile felt soothing. During one of my showers, I bawled as hard as I possibly could. I even sat on the cold tile floor and let the water pour over me while I pretended to rock my baby girl back and forth.

At that moment, I suddenly felt comfort and peace. I wanted more than anything for Lilian Grace to be right there at that very moment. I know she's in a better place, but my heart can't help but ache for her. The truth of the matter is that Michael and I have been continuously trying to conceive another miracle with no result. Each month of unsuccessful tries makes it harder, yet I still trust God.

I keep reminding myself that He knows exactly what we need. I will give Him all my emotions.

🕯️ *Dear Lord, please take these burdens from me. Forgive my anger when I lash out, cuss, and pass judgment. Grieving, sickness, and battles do not give me the right to be horrible and unjust to anyone. Thank you, Lord, for this horrible week of one bad storm after another. I needed the cleanse and reality check. I still have a long way to go, but I'm giving it all to you. I beg You to take it—be in full control, instead of me!*

Sorry for the length of this entry, but I thank you for

hanging in there with me if you're still reading. Always trust God. Stop running. When we fail to deal with life head on, we cause so many things to happen or not happen. I love you all. You are worth the effort to be your best self—who He created you to be.

The gorgeous song "I Will Carry You" by Selah explains our grief beautifully since losing our baby girl. We had big dreams and plans for our little family. Now I'm barely hanging on, waiting for relief and healing.

I know God has bigger plans—a beautiful story that will unfold to reveal His love, grace, and mercy while He carries us through it all. I wanted our story to include Lilian Grace physically being with Michael and me, yet it's not how God authored our lives. He chose me to carry her for a short time, he allowed us and others to meet her, and as a result, we will love her for eternity. Our heavenly Father now gets to hold her and watch her grow up in heaven. I praise Him for choosing me to be a part of Lilian's story.

Lilian Grace,

I will carry you just as our heavenly Father carries each of us. I love you with my entire being. I smile, thinking about the day I'll join you in heaven to catch up for all eternity along with your two other siblings I never was lucky enough to meet. You, Warrior Princess, took my blinders and fought so I could grow and live to be a better version of myself. I hope I don't disappoint you as I try to go wherever our heavenly Father leads—just as you did so faithfully. You could have let your first breath be your last, but you said bring it on by giving me 103 days. You gave me everything a mommy could ever hope for—a baby girl to love with all my heart and guidance in becoming who God intends me to be.

Love,
Your Mommy

MARCH 5, 2011

144 › Seven-Month Angelversary

Seventh heaven is this month's angelversary for Lilian Grace. When I think of her, I close my eyes and picture a perfectly designed angel with beautiful glittery wings spread wide and a bright shining halo hovering over her head. Seven months have added up since Lily earned her wings.

Her daddy, Michael, turned thirty yesterday, so we're celebrating his life here on earth and hers in heaven. I can't believe I've known her daddy for almost ten years now—incredible. I know this is nothing compared to the time we'll spend together as a family in eternity.

Last Wednesday, I spent time at Hallmark trying to pick out birthday cards for Michael. Since Lilian Grace can't be here on earth for his birthday, I decided to get a card for him from his daughter. I bawled in Hallmark as I tried to read all the cards. It seemed like forever as I read one after another trying to find the perfect one to fit our situation. I finally found the perfect one I think Lilian Grace would have chosen if she'd been the right age to do so.

Furthermore, there was the cutest lil plush pig (a little bigger than a golf ball) that I couldn't resist buying along with a guardian angel car clip that reads, "Dad's Guardian Angel." I gave them to Michael at 3:38 a.m., the time he came into this world exactly thirty years ago. I couldn't help myself. He deserves to have his little girl here for his birthday, so I felt like this was as close as I could get.

I'd like to think she was watching us at 3:38 a.m., smiling

and giggling at the gifts that were dubbed from her. It puts a huge grin on my face thinking about it. Michael and I cried happy tears together because we felt like she was there with us—Lilian Grace is always in our hearts. We know she is rocking it out loud with our heavenly Father just as she did here on earth.

The past two weeks have been rough, but God has been working on me and in my life. My next chapters and rollercoasters are going to be crazy and adventurous. Even though they might take my breath away, I'm buckled up—continuing to adjust to and enjoy whatever comes my way.

Last night, I know Lilian Grace got to see some of our family and friends celebrate a wonderful man—her daddy, Michael Dale. I'm so blessed to call him my husband and best friend. From above, Lily is proud to call him her daddy. Keep us always in your prayers as we navigate life celebrations without her.

Continue to pray for trisomy 18 families and their babies. March is Trisomy 18 Awareness Month. Many of these babies fight to live another day. I'm so amazed by them all. They keep my life and abilities in perspective. I don't want to waste a single gift God gave me.

This month, I will be introducing some of Lilian Grace's earthly and heavenly buddies to you. As you read their stories, please remember to lift them, their families, and the medical staff up in prayer. They need an abundance of peace, comfort, and unconditional love.

Happy seven-month angelversary, Lil Angel!

You have taught us all that GOD IS BIG! He keeps knocking our socks off, blowing our minds, and captivating our hearts. You have played a part in changing attitudes and paths. Thank you for continuously reminding Mommy to keep trusting God no matter what. I miss you more than ever and look forward to the day I get to hold you again. I love you to the moon and back and for all eternity! A million hugs and kisses sent your way!

Love,
Your Proud Mommy,
Chrissy

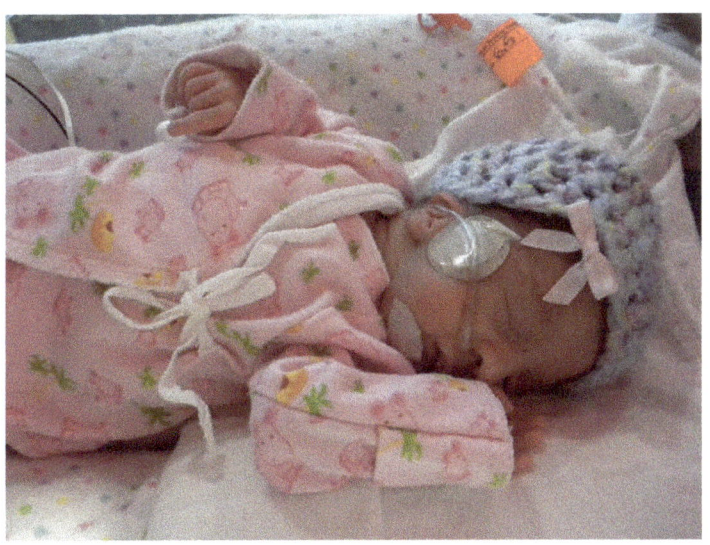

Lil Angel of Mine

Race logo

MARCH 7, 2011

145 › Challenge Yourself

Memory Verse 14

⚔ *"And let us consider how we may spur one another on toward love and good deeds, not giving up meeting together, as some are in the habit of doing, but encouraging one another—and all the more as you see the Day approaching" (Hebrews 10:24–25).*

I wanted to give everyone a friendly reminder to register for the Warrior Princess Trail Run. I need to order shirts and medals by March 16 if possible, so the deadline to guarantee you a shirt and medal is March 15, 2011.

For those who cannot attend one of the races on Monday, April 25, 2011, you can register as a shadow runner. This way you can still participate without having to be there physically. All you do is decide to run a certain distance close to the date and send me your time and distance when you complete it. You will get a shirt and medal when you do so.

Registrations will still be taken after March 15, but you may have to wait to get your shirt and medal—possibly until after race day. I look forward to seeing you all either as a runner, shadow runner, walker, onlooker, or supporter, whether present or afar on Lilian's birthday. It means the world to us when others share our story and register and participate and help us raise money to help other trisomy 18 or 13 families.

The above Scripture reminds us that we are better

together than alone. We are to meet together and not give up. You, our supporters, have really encouraged us on our journey.

There are two ways to register: Send me an email at warriorprincessfoundation@hotmail.com, and I will email you a registration form to mail in.[5] Or . . . You can go online to register at www.getmeregistered.com/warriorprincess.[6]

Thanks, everyone, for your continued support. It will be here before you know it! Remember to challenge yourself every day! You are capable of more than you think.

Lots of love your way from this proud momma! Below are three other ways you can challenge yourself at any time in memory of Lilian Grace or a loved one you have in mind:

1. 103 crunches, sit-ups, or burpees.
2. Pray for twenty-five individuals who are currently battling in their journey.
3. Work out or do a project for 103 minutes (one hour and forty-three minutes) with breaks as needed.

---

[5] Note from author: This email address is no longer active.
[6] Note from author: This registration link is no longer active.

MARCH 11, 2011

146 › Race On

I'm getting very excited about the Warrior Princess Trail Run! I had a meeting with Brian Hoover at RunnersWorld of Tulsa today. He, Kathy (Hoover), Sandra (Wright), and Ken (Childress) have been amazing in getting me going in the right direction. I don't think a lot of people realize what happens behind the scenes of a race. I'm here to tell you, it's a lot!

Here are the volunteer needs for the race. I know some of you want to be a part but can't run. Here's your chance! Just look over the list and send me an email at warriorprincessfoundation@hotmail.com with how you would like to help.[7] Remember that this Tuesday, March 15, 2011, is the deadline for a guaranteed shirt and medal on race day. This also helps me to be able to get shirts and medals at a cheaper cost when I can order larger quantities. Don't forget, you can be a shadow runner if you can't be there. Thank you to those who have already registered—it means so much. Love you all!

---

[7] Note from author: This email address is no longer active.

> **Volunteers Needed:**
> Race Packets Organization: Saturday, April 16, 2011
> Need helpers putting shirts and race numbers together for racers
>
> **Race Day: Monday, April 25, 2011**
> Registration table (2–4 people)
> Packet pick-up table (2–4 people)
> Aide station 1 (2–4 people)
> Aide station 2 (2–4 people)
> Race start/finish aid station (2–4 people)
> Fundraising table to sell T-shirts, cookbooks, and necklaces (3 people)
> Race timing with Brian Hoover (3 people)
> Set-up (2 people)
> Tear down (2 people)
> Jug and table placement (need muscles) (3–4 people)
> Medal hangers to hand out medals at the end of the race to finishers (2–3 people)
> Standby crew in case we forgot something (?)

We may have some other volunteer needs come up. I'll keep you informed. We don't have much longer until Lilian Grace's first birthday. Though she will be looking down on us, I know she'll be happy to see us coming together in her memory. I can't thank you all enough, so be prepared to see it on here many times. Love, love, and more love out to you all. Please make sure to share this with your friends, coworkers, and family! My heart can't thank you all enough for your support. To register for the race, go to www.getmeregistered.com/warriorprincess.[8]

PS: If you are unable to register this far in advance, you will still be able to register later, but you won't be guaran-

---

[8] Note from author: This registration link is no longer active.

teed a shirt and medal on race day. I'll order some extra shirts, but I saw that a lot of people were registering for the St. Patrick's 5K today and weren't getting the shirt size they wanted because they were sold out of them. Plan ahead if you can.

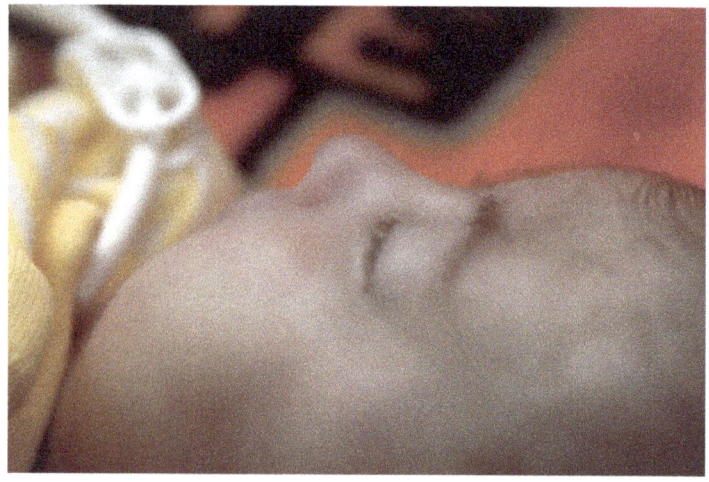

Always on my mind and in my heart

MARCH 13, 2011

147 › Two Trains

Emotions—they come quickly. When I hear the news of another trisomy 18 baby earning his or her wings, my emotions explode to another level. I feel like I owe many of my trisomy 18 mommies an apology because I have been at arm's length due to the hardship of watching their babies grow. I'm not mad or jealous that they get to be with their babies. I praise God for their moments and gift of time, but it seems to make the hole Lilian left even bigger and more sorrowful.

I remember Lilian Grace's fight when I witness babies suffering. I'm thankful when they have good days, but I know how hard they fight for a good day. Trisomy 18 families and babies are hardcore. They don't overlook the little things—things most parents might take for granted—because each moment is amazing for parents of these special borrowed angels.

Through my grieving, I've had to go numb to protect myself from more heartache. Just like anyone who has been married, then divorced; birthed a child and lost them; climbed the career ladder only to get fired; or who shared years with a partner but lost them unexpectedly—my life changed in an instant. I never wanted to be a creative thinker who writes my own ending, nor did I sign up for this.

When your world suddenly changes, you have to take time to prepare yourself to navigate your new reality in order to survive. Sadly, several trisomy 18 babies I know passed away recently. I haven't been able to write about them. Although my closer trisomy 18 friends keep me strong, today I'm feeling crushed by news of a baby who just earned her wings. She reminds me of Lilian Grace.

Emalee Graycen Whaley joined our heavenly Father and Lilian Grace. As I read the messages on her mommy's Facebook page, I wept. Reading the updates from Angel, Emalee's mommy, was like going through Lilian's death all over again. Just when we thought we were getting somewhere, Lilian Grace crashed. Emalee seemed to do the same thing.

It's scary, because I was hoping Angel would never have to experience the loss of her little girl. I know Emalee fought so hard. She lived almost three times longer than Lilian Grace. I ask that you pour many prayers over Emalee's family, friends, and the people who knew her story. Pray God's kingdom grows because of her touching story. I pray Emalee's life is not wasted. I know Angel's and Adam's hearts have broken—pray for their healing journey.

Kris (Ramsay), a new friend, and I were talking yesterday about grief. We came up with the best example for how to explain it. I think Kris said a friend had mentioned grief being like two trains traveling parallel. In one train, there's happiness and life in the present. The other contains my grief, my broken heart, and emptiness, where I'm continually missing Lilian Grace.

There's not one day that goes by that I don't think of Lilian Grace. It's like she was just here yesterday. More and more I relate to and understand a lady named Granny who lost her little girl in 1938. She said similar words—even after seventy-three years had passed since her little girl earned her wings, she still felt like it happened yesterday. Wow, strangely, I find comfort in that. The biggest comfort is in knowing I won't ever forget Lilian Grace—she will continue to be alive in my thoughts, heart, and soul for eternity as I continue to do things in memory of her.

The Whaley family is all the way in Ohio. I have been blessed to communicate with Angel off and on these past eight months or so. I'd love to leave a message to her and others grieving.

Angel and grieving individuals,

I don't know what you are feeling. I only know how I feel in my own grief. Keep walking, especially when you want to quit every single day. There will be times you pinch yourself so hard because you are convinced this is a nightmare and you'd like to wake up. Hang on tight to God! He's the only one who will not let you down. Without Him, I probably wouldn't be here.

You'll feel numb for a long time. I wish I would have listened when the doctor told me not to make any drastic life changes or decisions for a whole year. Things I decided on abruptly, though they have been wonderful, have worn me down. Remember to breathe, because there will be days you want to forget to do so because the hurt and pain is so great. It's scary.

People laugh because I always talk about breathing. I'm not kidding! It's hard some days even for the strongest warriors to breathe. Grief has many facets. The hardest thing about losing someone, something, or anything big is that your blinders get ripped away from you.

What I mean by that is you see the world and life through a fresh set of eyes. On some days, you'll want the blinders back, because certain things are painfully clear. Loss reveals people for who they are and aren't. My biggest struggle has been trying to accept people for who they really are. All these years, I've tried to make them way better than they are. I still have expectations, but I'm more realistic about some relationships now.

I pray for you as you grieve. Remember as you keep walking through it that there's no skipping, going around, stopping, or U-turning—only moving through it. Let yourself feel. Don't let everyone else try to tell you how to be, deal, or do. If they truly knew how hard this walk is, they wouldn't try to make you just get over it. They would understand there's a process that must be followed to heal your wounds and broken heart.

You will never be the same again. Praying, praying, and praying as I trust God to carry you through it. On most days, I repeat over and over, "I trust You, God! I trust You, God! I trust You, God!"

Love from a mother walking her own grief path,
Chrissy

PS: Emalee, please give my baby girl, Lilian Grace, the biggest hug and kiss on the cheek from her mommy, daddy, family, and friends. We miss her and love her!

MARCH 21, 2011

148 › Speed

Ten days feels like forever since I've shared. I've been at full speed with Lilian Grace's memorial race, trying to make sure all things are working out. I give it up to my running buddies who put on races all the time. There's endless work to be done, from special requests to bizarre moments. I've questioned myself often about putting this on.

We've got a great start on numbers for the race with fifty-six individuals already registered. You are a huge help! My brain has been all over the place. If you have not heard back from me by text, email, or Facebook message, please send another email to our foundation email. It has been very stressful trying to keep up with all the locations for messages.

It feels like my grief is accelerating, like God opened a floodgate to get me moving. I wasn't prepared for all the processing while planning this event. I guess when grieving, we can't predict what the day is going to bring. I've been crying often but remembering they are healing tears—at least, I hope.

Please remember the families who have recently lost their babies. The grieving process starts with numbness. The real processing begins when they least expect it. I still can't believe that in a few days we will be a month away from Lilian Grace's one-year birthday anniversary—it's bittersweet. Pray for Michael, me, and our family and friends who are processing this time of year. We are all traveling our own grief journey.

Shelley (Davis), one of my dear friends from back in the day, posted this wonderful Facebook post that was timely and much needed: *"When the foundations are shaking and you wish you could hide, remember that God is still in control. His power is not diminished by any turn of events. Nothing happens without His knowledge and permission. When you feel like running away—run to God. He will restore justice and goodness on the earth in His good time."*

I may not understand all of God's timing, but I do know that I trust Him when it all comes down to it. He sees the big picture when I can't even see a piece. I hope each of you are scaling your mountains, allowing God to fuel you with strength and perseverance.

Here's a picture taken after Lilian's bath time—one of the coolest moments I witnessed between her and her father. I've been struggling with some relationships lately due to fighting for who Michael and I are to Lilian Grace now. I'm trying to step back and own our truth. Though heaven and earth separate us, Lilian Grace will always be our daughter. I need to rest in the truth that we were chosen to be her parents, no one else.

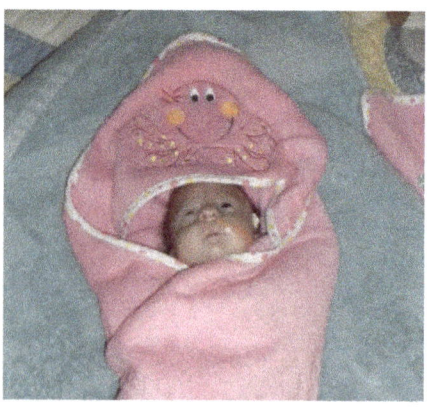

Snug, clean, and relaxed

MARCH 25, 2011

149 › Eleven-Month Birthday Anniversary

Tumbling through the numbness and some newfound information I have to live with has me crashing down and feeling burdened. Also, I was warned that the closer we got to Lilian's birth and death dates, the harder our grieving journey would be. They weren't kidding. Her absence magnifies as we approach her first birthday.

No matter the goodness happening in life, nothing makes missing her any easier. In exactly a month, it will have been one year since God blessed the world with Lilian Grace Whitten. I prayed that my baby girl's first breath would not be her last.

In fact, at this time last year, I prayed more than I'd ever prayed. I spoke verse after verse out loud, trusting that somehow we'd come this far. Surely, I'd get to know my baby girl, even if for mere seconds, and see her and watch her move. It would have to be enough.

It's crazy how the doctors gave us no hope, yet we experienced three months with Lilian—the greatest miracle, a blessing from God. The miracles didn't stop with her. I keep seeing them all the time. I wish Lilian Grace were getting into everything, crawling, walking, and trying to say dadda and momma. Remembering her sweet squeaks, I know her voice would have been angelic.

Eleven months later, I'm left with only memories of the glorious 103 days I got with our baby girl. I never thought I'd be wishing and sending her a happy eleven-month birthday all the way to heaven. No parent deserves this. We all take much for granted. Me included, except when Lilian Grace was here. With her, I was fully present in each moment because I wasn't promised any more seconds, minutes, or hours. Each second, minute, hour, day, and week was a bonus round—a reminder that anything is possible.

Last week's episode of *Private Practice* was hard to watch. Michael and I watched through tears, relating to the moral of the story—parenting doesn't have a time limit. Whether a child is here for a second or for eighty years, you are always and forever a parent. A quote from the episode made me happy and brought tears: *"Parenting is more than onesies and bassinets. It's a lifelong commitment, no matter how long or short that life is."*

I want to thank those who have been here through all the craziness and miracles. I appreciate those who haven't tried relating to us. You've been exceptional about being here for us. The only way someone can relate is if they've lost a child to death. I don't want that for anyone.

Sometimes in our grieving journey, we have to be alone with God. Other times, we need someone to simply listen. God has given us friends and acquaintances who have sadly lost their children to death. Naturally, we've bonded with them through our shared experiences. They remind us of what we've all learned from God and our babies.

I included this information because numerous people have told me they don't know what to do for us or what we need. We need individuals to stop fighting us; others to stop asking us to just get over it; and some to love us unconditionally when we don't know what we are saying, doing, or needing.

I struggle daily—like I'm trying to sort through a huge

pile of bricks that have crashed down on me. I argue with God when He tries to glue pieces of my heart back together because I don't like the new positioning. Ultimately, I trust Him to make me stronger by shaping my heart better than it was before Lilian.

All I'm asking people around me to do is try! Try to learn from mistakes; to become a better version of yourself; to let go of how it's always been; and to not accept people as they are when you know they're not in a good place. I need more people than just myself trying to work on things. If I would have given up before Lilian Grace was born, we wouldn't have cherished memories with her. She wouldn't have had the fight, stubbornness, and determination in her blood. It matters that she existed.

> *Lilian Grace,*
>
> *My precious lil one! Today marks what would have been your eleven-month birthday. Time keeps ticking as the calendar pages turn. I keep loving you more and more though. I know you are in the best of hands. I long to hold, hug, and be near you. I wish you a very happy eleven-month birthday with your angel friends. Make sure to dance and sing today, because it's a reminder that you taught us all to live for today with no guarantees of tomorrow. I love you to the moon and back and for all eternity!*
>
> *Love,*
> *Your proud and loving momma,*
> *Chrissy*

APRIL 5, 2011

150 › Eight-Month Angelversary

For the first time in the last eight months, on the fifth of the month, I didn't wake up at three in the morning to relive Lilian Grace's crash. I even talked this morning about feeling really good and wondered if my memories were slipping away.

Why did I wonder? Grief is unpredictable. Just when I think I have it figured out, I am further from knowing how it's going to go. I've been trying to protect myself and others from negativity. I still have to come out of the shadows when I don't feel like it. I just want to hide so my brokenness and load don't mess up someone else.

Life seems funny to me at times in how God sets it up. He doesn't want us to hide. He wants us to keep processing all of life while moving forward. I'm trying to process and move forward, even if it makes others uncomfortable. It's a positive thing. I may not do it how people think I should, but then again, they have no clue what this is like. We all process differently, which I'm trying to be mindful of when being there for others.

As the day progressed, I hadn't forgotten or ignored what this day meant, no matter how powerful my positive attitude. The brain, heart, and soul don't forget. Even when I beg to forget, I can't. I have to admit that by staying present, I do keep processing and moving—willingly or not.

When I got to work, I realized my fitness studio dream may not play out how I originally intended. I have to make some adjustments to my dream, but I'm enjoying those who come workout. I adjusted my dream of seeing Lilian Grace grow up when it was demolished by her death. It was a huge dream! My dream now consists of angel wings and fluffy clouds, knowing she's in better hands.

The reality is she's in a good place. She doesn't have to deal with the bad like we do every day—struggling to survive a life that is always coming at us and never stops. The one thing that keeps me going is His promise of eternal life with Him and all my children.

I have cried off and on ever since 12:50 p.m. A coffee mug that was my Mother's Day present from Lilian broke, which sent my tears and pain going full throttle again. It's a silly mug, but seeing it break opened the emotional flood gates. When I got home, I got a phone call from the Tulsa County Health Department wanting to do our interview about Lilian Grace and her death. Wow! Really? Today—of all days? There are so many other days in a month. Can't they see her death (angel) date is today, so why choose today to call?

It's not their fault! They are just doing their job. It's just crazy how horrible the timing is. Today, I'm choosing to feel and cry over and over as I try to process and move forward! There's life, and it keeps coming! I want to be ready for whatever comes in the next hour, day, week, month, and year. I shouldn't be shocked anymore because I couldn't make this stuff up if I tried.

> *Lilian Grace,*
>
> *Happy eight-month angelversary, Lil Mermaid! Mommy is going to keep swimming in this deep ocean of life. I may cry enough tears to fill an ocean, but it's going to be okay. I hope you know that I would do anything to hold you for one more second. I'd do it all again, no matter the amount of time. I love you with everything that I am. I am truly blessed because of you. You have some new baby angels with you today. Please give them a huge hug and kiss from their families. They miss them greatly. Party it up and show them all what a beautiful Warrior Princess you are.*
>
> *Love,*
> *Mommy*

Note: Please pray for Michael, me, our families, and anyone touched by Lilian Grace. April 25, 2011, is getting closer, and it will not be easy. Our grief continues and at times grows. I can't believe it's coming up on a year since God blessed us with our baby girl—the beginning of our fight and path to August 5, 2011, her one-year angelversary. It is going to be a tough road this year. I've been warned by many parents who have lost their children that the two dates, birth and death, are incredibly painful but also joyful. Please remember us all. Love you.

APRIL 9, 2011

151 › The Next Miracle

It seems that at thirty-two years old, I've learned way more than I should know. I've seen, experienced, grieved, and lived. What about now? I'm still standing tall but with a broken and heavy heart. My heavenly Father continues to repair me. As I look back at thirty-two years, I start laughing through the tears.

If today were my last day, I would rejoice knowing I have lived life to the fullest. At times, I was completely worn out due to my inability to say no. I don't know all the answers to life's questions, but I do know that living is the way to go. The darkness will come—oh so often and swiftly. But we must remember we have access to the greatest light source to help us conquer it.

I was going to wait to share our miraculous news with the rest of the world, but today God played "In My Life" by Bette Midler for me as I walked down a baby aisle. For the first time in six weeks, I let myself feel excitement. I've been extremely scared and anxious. But I'm still standing, and there is a sliver of light in the darkness shining through.

God has blessed Michael and me with another miracle. I took three pregnancy tests to verify I am pregnant! It was an amazing birthday gift for Michael the night before his thirtieth birthday. For the past six weeks, I've been grieving more than previously. Each doctor appointment has been difficult for me. I've broken down talking to my amazing doctor who delivered Lilian Grace. She has been phenomenal in helping me through each breakdown. She simply lets me cry and get it all out, acting like it's a normal part of the process.

I truly am blessed. I don't know that my anxieties and fears will go away. I can assure you that no matter what I experience, I will trust God all the way—come what may. He was so gracious and powerful throughout our journey with Lilian Grace. I won't ever see Him differently nor will I change my perspective. I love my view of, idea of, and my focus on Him. He has never and will never forsake me.

This pregnancy, Michael and I are doing things differently. I won't be sharing every detail. I want Michael to have privileged information this go round because he sacrificed by allowing me to share our whole story about Lilian Grace. I appreciate you all giving us privacy as you continue to lift us up in much-needed prayers. Michael is very excited. For the first time in months, he's not crumbling. I love watching him be giddy and smiling—in love with the idea that he gets to have another child.

I, on the other hand, became the crumbly one. Seeing "The Who" on the ultrasound for the first time caused memories of Lilian's time on earth to flash through my mind. I have proven I am able to process the good, the bad, and the ugly. I want to be as whole as I can when this miracle comes into our lives. They deserve everything, especially strong parents like Lilian Grace knew!

I want to talk to everyone today. Yes, everyone! I have watched many of you face hard journeys—some are brand new and others have been on a long road. I want you to know that you are strong enough to get through it when your strength comes from God. He is going to give you EVERYTHING you need, no matter how the journey ends up. He loves us that much; He will make sure we're taken care of. No, the journey may not end how we want it to end.

Don't miss the blessings He provides in it all—especially among the fire, smoke, and ash.

I know it's hard to come to terms with life and how unfair it seems sometimes. Regardless of your choices, God provides when you let Him. He's the only reason I'm still standing and breathing after experiencing the hardest thing I have ever faced. He has taught me a million lessons as well as given me a billion blessings. I don't always look at it the right way, but I do eventually get there.

I love you all! I'm excited to see what this journey brings. I have an amazing husband who puts up with all that I am—no matter what! God knew I couldn't have done this with anyone else. I praise His name on high as I thank Him a billion times over to infinity for everything He is, has done, and will do. "The Who" is our next miracle and blessing. I'm praying for the most normal pregnancy, delivery, and life. I want my baby to get to be grand and special in whatever God has in store for their life and journey. And no matter how abnormal Lilian Grace's life became, she will always be the greatest gift I could have ever asked for.

May you all find peace, rest, and strength in God for whatever journey you are facing. We all have our journeys, and you are the only one who knows what all yours entails. God bless you all as you fight, battle, and successfully make your way through it.

Lilian Grace,

    I'm excited you can be an extra guardian angel for your sibling. I wish a million times over that you could be here to experience them with us. We know that you have a better seat than we ever will. Please visit your little sibling regularly because your daddy and I are not perfect. We will make mistakes, but we will always try our hardest. You deserve so much credit for what kind of parents we've become. A diaper change will never be taken for granted. An opportunity to hold them will not be lost. A moment to experience with them will be fully seized.

    I thought about you and me the other day. I wish I could have taken you to the store. I would have given anything to have that moment with you. To see your eyes light up with every new thing you saw would have been another precious gift. All the firsts with your sibling will be extra special though, because I know you will be there in spirit to experience them with us. I love you to the moon and back and for all eternity.

    God's timing is crazy, but He's amazing for giving us this gift. Mommy has cried a lot lately. There are two kinds of tears flowing simultaneously—tears of missing you as I remember all the good, bad, and crazy times and tears of joy that you are safely in heaven and for the new baby growing inside my womb. Both sets of tears keep me moving, growing, and preparing for what's to come. Thank you for doing God's work so that I can finally see!

Love,
Your Mommy Who Thanks You So Much

APRIL 18, 2011

152 › Warrior Princess Trail Run

Only one week to go until the Warrior Princess Trail Run! It's not too late to register. You can still do so in the following ways:

1. Online registrations available until April 23, 2011. Visit www.getmeregistered.com/warriorprincess to register today.[9]

2. Go to RunnersWorld of Tulsa, 4329 South Peoria Tulsa, OK 74105. Cash or check (make checks payable to Warrior Princess Foundation).

3. Race day at the Keystone State Park Mountain Bike & Hike Trail (Sand Springs) at 5:00–5:50 p.m.

I've attached a photo of the tech shirts. We have 109 left. Register now to make sure you get the shirt size you want. First come, first paid gets what's left. Here are the sizes as of 11:11 a.m. on Monday, April 18, 2011:

XS–12
S–13
M–32
L–36
XL–14
XXL–1
XXXL–1

---

[9] Note from author: This registration link is no longer active.

Red race shirts—front and back

Race packets can be picked up at RunnersWorld of Tulsa during the following hours: Monday–Saturday from 10:00 a.m.–6:00 p.m. and Thursday from 10:00 a.m.–7:30 p.m. FYI—I ordered 200 finisher medals!

If you can't be there on race day, you can still participate as a shadow runner. Just complete whatever distance you decide and report the time/distance to me by the end of the day on Monday, April 25, 2011. If you are out of state, I can mail your stuff to you. Thanks to all who have registered!

I can't believe Monday marks a year since Lilian Grace came into our lives. My, oh my, how much we have experienced since that time. This event symbolizes the race of life. We'll be running on unknown trails and over or around obstacles such as roots, rocks, branches, terrain, elevations, and wildlife. I can't ask for a better simulation of the emotional roller-coaster ride, obstacles, and challenges we encounter in our personal life races.

> **First Annual Warrior Princess Trail Run Details**
> Monday, April 25, 2011
>
> 6:00 p.m.: 10.3 mile Trail/Road Race
> 5.5 miles of trail and the rest on paved road
> three aid stations
>
> 6:30 p.m.: 1.03 mile Fun Run/Walk
> Keystone State Park Mountain Bike & Hike Trail
> (Sand Springs)
>
> Race Day registration and packet pick-up
> from 5:00–5:50 p.m.

The Warrior Princess Trail Run proceeds will benefit babies diagnosed with T18 and T13 chromosomal disease and their families by providing assistance, support, and resources as needed. The race is in memory of our daughter, who was diagnosed with T18 sixteen days into her life.

Sharing this from our promotional materials:

> *Lilian Grace Whitten, Warrior Princess, soared above and beyond what was expected of her life. Her first breath was supposed to be her last. She lived 103 glorious days on this earth before earning her wings. God gave us the reason why she was here through the following Scripture: "So that Christ may dwell in your hearts through FAITH. And I pray that you, being rooted and established in love, may have power, together with all the Lord's holy people, to grasp how wide and long and high and deep is the LOVE of Christ, and to know this love that surpasses knowledge—that you may be filled to the measure of all the FULLNESS OF GOD" (Ephesians 3:17–19, all caps added by author).*

God's plan is unfolding along our beautiful journey as we grieve and heal. His fullness is in all the tiny details that truly are taking us all in a positive direction no matter our circumstances and attitudes. God is Big!

Lily's bunny supporting her race

APRIL 22, 2011

153 › Glory in the Cross

Only days to go before we all lace up our shoes and hit the trail or pavement. Thank you to those who have signed up already. I am ready for it to all come together and happen. I even have a special sky lantern we will light when it's all over. If you can't run, you can still come out and support the daring runners.

Remember that you have until Sunday to submit an online entry. We will take registrations at the race from 5:00–5:50 p.m. The 10.3-mile race starts at 6:00 p.m. and the 1.03-mile fun run/walk starts at 6:30 p.m. There are only eighty-five shirts left!

My nerves are increasing as the race date approaches. Can you believe God made it so that I would be exactly twelve weeks pregnant on Lilian's first birthday anniversary? I wish she could be here to share in this next miracle. I have been very sick, but we are trying to get that under control. Perhaps when the race and birthday are over, my nerves and emotions will settle down.

I am learning the many facets of being a race director. I totally give it up to my buddies who do this kind of thing all the time. I have greater respect for you all. I definitely didn't know I'd be pregnant when taking on this giant endeavor. I'm going to keep believing God knows what's best, even though at times I wish I could see myself as He does. Then again, perhaps I don't want that!

Many of us have been struggling with an overload of cares, problems, sorrows, and joys. I pray God keeps giving us exactly what we need. I'm working on the "unloading on Him" technique, but I still struggle, like many, in doing so. We are only human, and I'm reminded of it daily.

God graciously made Easter and my daughter's first birthday celebration without her coincide closely on the calendar. I'm taking it as a reminder that He loves me more than I will ever know or understand. I sacrificed for only a short time when it came to my daughter and our journey with her. God had to watch His Son suffer much more than we ever will so that you and I could have a chance at eternal life with Him. Now that's what I call the greatest parent for all eternity. I don't know one of us who could make the same sacrifice that He did so long ago.

I'm praising God today that His plan is grander than mine or yours will ever be. I love His details, even though I get a little anxious at times about how uncomfortable they make me. If you are feeling uncomfortable, hold on tight as He works everything for good. I love you all. Enjoy the fact God thought we—yes, you and me—were worthy enough to sacrifice His Son to save us. Wow! He takes my breath away!

I read the lyrics to "I Will Glory in the Cross" by Dottie Rambo after hearing it with one of my good friends during her father's celebration of life last week. I remember when Pat Mattherly would sing and sign this song with her family—it brings chills and tears every time.

The song paints the picture of the old rugged cross as it points us to His suffering and the promises that His cross brings to each of us. As we glory in the cross and benefit from His grace and mercy, I recognize there's nothing I've done to earn or gain this privilege. He died in my place—for my sin. It lifts my spirit as I marvel at His sacrifice, knowing all I had to do was accept Him as my Savior.

I imagine myself at His feet now and for all eternity, and I find great comfort in knowing He loved me before I even existed. My weeping and sorrow are earthly and not permanent. Praise God for reminding me that I am worthy and His child!

APRIL 24, 2011

154 › Keep Fighting

Oh, how I love the rain and thunder! Today we celebrate that death has no hold on us because Jesus sacrificed Himself. My emotions have been overwhelming the past two weeks as I think about everything that has happened in my life thus far.

I am blessed to have a heavenly Father who will never let me down, even when I'm far from deserving. Without Him, I would be nothing. I get chills and shivers as I think about the day they went to that tomb and saw no body was there. Talk about increasing your faith by the sight of it all.

Not only have I been thinking about Jesus's sacrifices, I've been thinking about my own life. Nelle Swindell, one of my earthly angels, passed away a week ago this past Friday. I was blessed to have such a saint show me how to persevere through anything the devil throws at us. She was my aunt and uncle's neighbor, my yearbook coordinator, English teacher, mentor, and best friend.

She and I connected when it came to the battlefield. I hope I scare the devil half as much as she did when I awake each morning. I know the enemy hated to see her fight, because she never gave up. She reminds me of Jesus and Job—two examples of humans who never gave up, no matter what the devil hit them with.

I hope to carry on the legacy that God shaped in her seventy-plus years to show that the devil can't win the war. Yes, we will lose some battles, but the important thing is to get back up by the grace of God and allow Him to rejuvenate and mold us into better warriors. This life will pass, but eternity is forever.

I hope whatever you are facing this very minute that you remember to face it head on while placing trust in God to get through it—fighting like the warrior prince or princess you are meant to be. People who lived when Christ walked the earth and met Him were so blessed! If I could go back in time, I would love to hear Jesus teach and see Him perform miracles. How amazing would it be to overhear Him talking to His heavenly Father in the garden?

Today, I feel like it's all going to be better than okay. I have many more battles to fight, but I'm reassured that I will never, ever be alone. God will be right here—fighting for me as long as I get out of the way. Praise Him on high this Easter Sunday.

APRIL 24, 2011

155 › Details

Important information for Warrior Princess Trail runners: First off, Michael and I want to personally thank everyone for supporting our daughter's race on her special first birthday anniversary. The time leading up to this has been extremely emotional. I wish Lilian Grace could be here to do the race with us, but I know she'll be watching from the best seat! As we tackle our own goals and obstacles in life, face everything like a true warrior prince or princess by trusting God to always provide. Here is some helpful information for race day.[10]

> **Location:**
> The race site is located where Hwy 151 (the Hwy that Keystone Dam is on) intersects OLD Hwy 51. We will have balloons flying at the stop sign where you will turn. The race site is between the Keystone Dam and Keystone State Park/Pier 51 entrance.
>
> To see the area where we will be, go to this webpage: http://www.okearthbike.com/MAP%20OF%20KEYSTONE.pdf

---

[10] Note from author: The "okearthbike" website address is no longer accessible.

Packet Pick-up & Registration:
From 5:00–5:50 p.m., you will be able to pick up your race packets if you have not done so by now. If you know of anyone who needs to register for either race, please advise them to come during this time.

Parking:
Please try to arrive before 6:00 p.m. to accommodate the creative parking that will take place. The gravel parking lot will mark the area of the start/finish for both races, so limited parking will be available in that area. We will have to park along the old Hwy 51 road. I would suggest carpooling if you can.

Costume Contest:
Don't forget we are having a contest for the Best Dressed Warrior Prince and Princess. Get creative and tasteful. I've been hearing about some of your costumes, and I'm excited to see them!

10.3 Miles Trail/Road Race Important Details:
- Think about bringing the following items: **headlight/flashlight** (just in case you go long and it gets dark); **water bottle** (if it's hot, we will have extra water at aid stations—but you may need more water at various times); and **cell phone** (just in case you get off the path and can't find your way. The course is very thoroughly marked).
- **Rocky obstacles:** The trail part of the race is very rocky in places, so please be advised to pay extra attention to your path. Praying for an injury-free race. There will be flat and smooth parts, but there are many rocky sections to challenge you.

- **Creek crossings:** With all the rain we've gotten, the creek may cause you to have a wetter race. Be careful when crossing over wet rocks and streams.
- **Mud:** Be advised that you probably are going to get muddy. It might slow you down a little, but you should be okay.
- **Tree trunks/Limbs:** Make sure to check for trees that have grown over the path. Ken and I weren't strong enough with our superpowers to get them out of the way. We've hung long pink tape to help you with this. Just be careful.
- The race is 5 miles of trail and 5.3 miles of road. There are some bail out points on the trail section if it becomes necessary to shorten your race, but you should be sure that you are taking a route that will get you back to the finish.
- **Ken Childress** is going to be our sag runner, which means he will be the last racer. If you need to bail out of the trail portion, it would be best to call him so he can make sure you take the best route back to the start/finish area.
- We have marked the trail every hundred steps or so with pink tape. There is yellow caution tape at the trail intersections that should not be crossed. This is to keep you on the right path.
- If you are a speed racer, know that the 1.03-mile fun run/walk will be happening along the Old Hwy 51 road where you will end up after halfway. Those runners have a turnaround way before you do. You will be running 2.65 miles down Old Hwy 51 before turning around at your last aid station on the road (past the railroad tracks).

- There will be three aid stations along your 10.3-mile race.
- We have angel trophies for the overall top three males and females! Once we get the top three in for both male and female, we will do a quick awards ceremony. Every runner will get a Warrior Princess crown medal!
- After reading this, you are free to move down to the 1.03-mile fun run/walk if you'd like. I, Chrissy, was going to do the 10.3 miles but decided to switch. Just let us know before the race at the registration table so we can adjust our timing system.

1.03 Mile Fun Run/Walk:
- We will walk/run down one-half mile along Old Hwy 51, which is a downhill descent. Turn around to climb back up the hill. It should be a short and sweet adventure for all of us.
- Even though your race starts at 6:30, please be advised to get there early. Both races will have the start gun go off at exactly 6:00 and 6:30 with no delays.
- Once you cross the finish line, you should receive a Warrior Princess crown medal for participating.
- Once the fun run/race is completed, you are free to leave. Please be aware that there will be 10.3-mile runners along the Old Hwy 51 road. Yes, some people will be that fast to reach that point.

Sky Lantern Lighting:
When it gets dark, we will hold a ceremony to light a sky lantern in memory of Lilian Grace and another mini one for our new miracle "The Who." You are welcome to come and hang out to watch this occur. Please do not feel obligated to stay. We know it's a Monday night, and people have to work the next day. If you do decide to stay, I'd suggest you bring lawn chairs to sit in and hang out.

Thank you again for joining us on this special day. It makes our hearts full of joy and love knowing that you'll be with us on this bittersweet day. Lilian Grace was an amazing Warrior Princess.

We love you,
Michael, Chrissy, Lilian Grace, and "The Who"

Making the most of Lily's first birthday anniversary

APRIL 25, 2011

156 › First Birthday Anniversary

Happy birthday to my dear Lilian Grace! May I someday get to be with you to celebrate in person! I can't believe it's officially Lilian Grace's first birthday anniversary. A year ago, at 8:44 a.m., God blessed us with a miracle who would change thousands of lives just by being here. She knew how to tug at your heart. God's light shone bright in her, teaching me and giving me a new perspective. I didn't have a choice in it all, but I praise God for all that's happened.

I'd do it all again if needed just to spend another second with her. She has forever impacted my spirit and being. I wouldn't be who I am today if God hadn't sent us on this journey with our little Warrior Princess. A year—what usually happens in a year anyway?

In our case, I couldn't even begin to write it all down. I do know that I will never forget this ride. Even though some friends were MIA this past year, God provided people who loved on us abundantly. They have surrounded us and are helping carry us through. I have never been more blessed than I have in this past year. Has it been easy? Not ever! The only reason I keep moving is God! I couldn't do anything without Him. I sometimes think God is a little crazy—okay, a lot of the time. I wonder what in the world He is thinking. He graciously gives me gifts every day though. And they're like the best presents ever!

Tonight, all the planning, craziness, and everything came together. The storms didn't stop us from putting on the Warrior Princess Trail Run. Oh no, the storms couldn't stop us from making Lilian's time here on earth extra special. I saw almost a hundred people tonight come out and rock either the 1.03-mile fun run/walk or the 10.3-mile trail/road run. Everyone was incredible. Each runner/walker faced the challenges and didn't stop.

The volunteers, family, friends, and runners were phenomenal in being a part of something bigger than us. Tonight, we celebrated God's love and encouragement. Words are hard to find, but I do know Michael and I would not have survived Lilian's first birthday anniversary without you all—even those who supported us from afar. You will never know how much this meant to us. You showed us that you care, and we felt your love through it all.

The race was fabulous—even better than I expected. I learned from the experience and will make minor adjustments. This race will be an annual event for at least five years! Not only do Michael and I need this but so do others who either know our story or have similar stories. We are all in this together to process life and continue living.

Lighting up the night sky with lanterns made me laugh and cry. It was a perfect example of what life was like with Lilian Grace. We knew it was going to work out, but we didn't know exactly how. For example, tonight, a lantern floated up toward the sky for a bit before getting caught on electrical wires. Just when we thought it wouldn't go anywhere, it flew free before coming down. Wow! It gave me chills. Lilian Grace didn't have a working system, yet she took her first breath and millions more in 103 days, even when she wasn't supposed to have the ability to do so.

I cannot thank everyone enough, especially Runner's World of Tulsa (Brian and Kathy Hoover), Trail Zombie (Ken Childress), Old School Bagel Cafe (Bill Ford), and all the volunteers and participants. Thank you for making this a huge success. You saved Michael and me by giving us an amazing race in memory of Lilian Grace on a day when it was going to be hard to celebrate without her. Praise God for that and every single thing! We love you all!

Ready for release

Lilian Grace—the ultimate Warrior Princess,

My love for you is bigger than anyone can fathom. This morning I wanted to curl up and never leave my bed. I didn't know if I would make it through one hour of today. All I could picture was you eating your first birthday smash cake—yet you aren't here.

I know heaven is way better than this place, but there is so much we won't get to experience with you. I will cherish the moments we did get. I praise God for how much He is using you and our story to expand His kingdom. I hope for the day we will all dance on the streets of gold together.

I hope you got to peek through heaven's floors or windows to see just how many people love you and support us all. I hope you got to be with each runner, and I hope they are blessed for participating and challenging themselves. May the smile on your face be as huge and gorgeous as I remember seeing here on earth.

I'll never stop missing you. I'll always love you to the moon and back and for all eternity. Your birthday bash was legendary—just like you, our Warrior Princess. I thank God for choosing us to be your parents. I wouldn't want it any other way. Happy first birthday, baby girl! Someday, I'll celebrate with you in a mansion on the hillside!

Your Proud Mommy,
Chrissy

MAY 5, 2011

157 › Nine-Month Angelversary

Yesterday was a rough day for me. I found myself watching the Nick Jr. channel for hours like Lilian Grace and I did at home in our living room. Our place was made into a true castle where many things would happen throughout the day. The crazy educator in me planned several learning hours to include the following:

- ★ Music therapy—pretend time to play instruments and sing;
- ★ Physical activity;
- ★ Dance hour with Mommy;
- ★ Morning and afternoon nap time;
- ★ Kids TV programs for learning;
- ★ Lilian's personal play;
- ★ Feeding;
- ★ Medicine shifts;
- ★ More fun, spontaneous moments.

Needless to say, we completely filled our time that God granted us. Today, well, it isn't as bad as yesterday. The date, May 5, 2011, marks nine months since Lilian Grace was in my arms. The previous day, May 4, 2011, was tougher, as it marked the anniversary of our last day when my daughter smiled and moved her precious self in every single way.

I charged my old phone and discovered wonderful pictures of Lilian Grace in the memory files. They were hard to relive. The last three photos prove she was here mentally, physically, and spiritually. That time was so challenging. Losing a child never leaves you. Seeing her innocent, smiling face during the calm before the storm made it crazy how she drastically declined hours later. That perfect moment can never be revisited again, but I hope to have more perfect moments when we meet again in heaven.

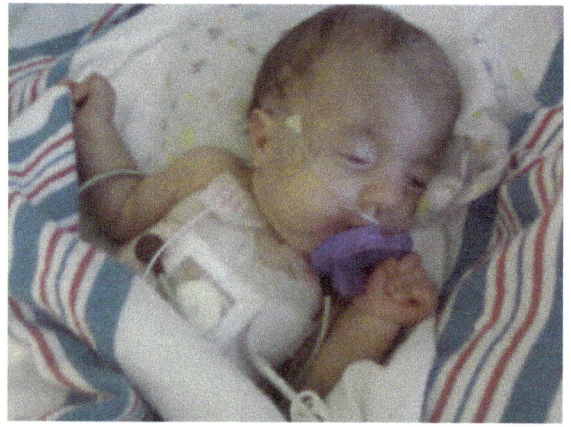

Exhausted, but alive!

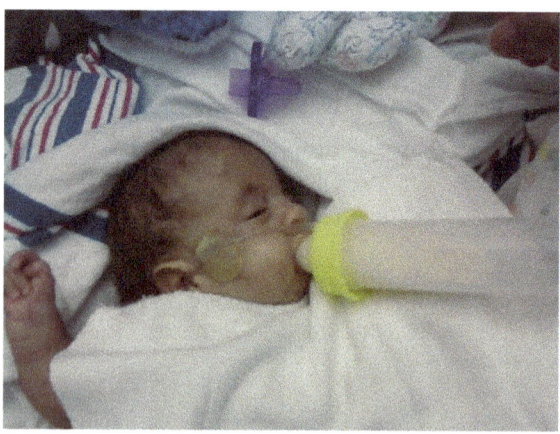

Milk coma

I praise God because He's taught me how to grieve actively and process grief aggressively. How do I know it's working? I made it through a doctor appointment last Friday without having a mental or emotional breakdown for the first time in nine weeks. Yes, for the first time, which is progress—a small victory!

Michael, "The Who," and I had to be at Dr. Blake's on Tuesday. That was the first time I'd seen her since two days before Lilian Grace was born. I woke up knowing I was not in a good place this week. I warned Michael it was probably going to get ugly. I couldn't force myself to adjust my attitude or control my emotions. This is how I feel more often than not. I'm still trying to adjust to it all. A control freak doesn't like knowing she doesn't have control over something.

The appointment lasted longer than expected because "The Who" is always active like their big sister was. The difference between the two children is that Lilian Grace loved to move her arms and legs while rolling, and "The Who" loves to be a jumping bean. Perhaps this is why I've been so much sicker with this pregnancy, because "The Who" thinks he or she is on a trampoline inside of me. At least I know this one is mine!

Seeing my baby-to-be helped me tremendously at the appointment. We made it through the first testing to see if they have Downs Syndrome or any other trisomy chromosomal disorder. They measured the back of the neck, and it seemed normal. The blood test will come back next week to verify. Yes, a normal result was a surprise but welcomed. I was tickled to hear "normal" but know it's just the beginning. With Lilian, our dreams weren't crushed until about twenty weeks gestation. We thought everything was going perfectly minus the surgery I had for the removal of a cyst and partial hysterectomy, plus getting C. diff.

Next, we'll have the big anatomy measurements and such in five to six weeks. Please lift us up in your prayers. This was the test when we found out Lilian had problems. The weeks that followed were hard. We received bad news at each appointment. We never got a break until she was born alive and survived her first breath against all odds.

I do want to say something about all the doctors, nurses, assistants, and techs who work at doctors' offices or hospitals. They have such a hard job mentally, emotionally, physically, spiritually, and so forth. They truly are gifted by God to work in a field where so much can happen—good, bad, or indifferent. I praise God for Dr. Blake. She had to give us a magnitude of bad news about Lilian Grace. I pray every day that God is with her and the others. I pray this pregnancy will be healing for all of us. In this next miracle, I pray for normal-like vanilla ice cream, as Dr. Razdan said, so we get to spend a lifetime learning and growing with this child.

Amid my wounds and brokenness, I pray we accept the healing. Lilian Grace was here to turn us all upside down so we could live upside right. May this next baby's mission be successful!

Though I did great at this appointment, we were all holding our breath and continue to do so. It's not easy to go down a tragic path, yet there's beauty in it. I may be sick—that's putting it mildly—but I am praising God for adding to our family. I won't ever stop until God says it is finished, despite what anyone says to me. The suffering is worth it all! I think Lilian Grace can communicate with her sibling already, because we feel her here with us. I hope she's teaching them how to be a fighter like herself—to never give up until God calls him/her home!

When I was looking at "The Who's" ultrasound pictures, I frantically wanted to find Lilian's but couldn't. They were in a chest with all the things she wore. I cried tears mixed with joy and pain and disappointment in myself. Perhaps this is what my tears will always be made of, but I'm okay with that. Without the hard times, I can't appreciate the good ones. We're never promised rainbows and sunshine!

My prayer for everyone I've been blessed to meet, talk to, walk alongside, and grow with is for everyone's wounds and gashes to heal. I still struggle with some relationships in my life because I am not meant to fix them. Surprising for me to say? Nope, it's a reminder to myself that each of us must work on ourselves with our heavenly Father. We've all been hurt, have hurt others, and everything in between—we all need healing. Isn't it time to look in the mirror and start working on ourselves? No one on this earth can fix us nor can we fix each other. Reconciliation has to start within us first!

We can be there for one another, but we're not the HEALER. There is only one HEALER—GOD! I'm not saying it's fun or a quick fix by any means. When you continue to work with Him, though, it gets easier. If you don't care enough to do it for yourself, then do it for those who would love to have a relationship with you. It's sad when Satan separates family members or friends.

Today, I'm all over the place, but God is graciously working on me. When I just want to be left alone to watch Nick Jr., God works through the shows I watch. The ones I used to watch with Lilian were great affirmations. Yes, He used kids shows. He never gives up, even if we try to! He always meets us where we are. Love you all.

The picture below, taken on August 4, 2010, makes me want to jump into the picture, scoop her up, and never let her go!

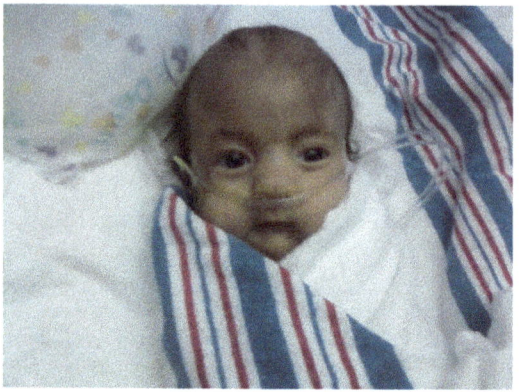

The calm before the storm

Lilian Grace—my Lil Angel,

Nine months have come and gone as you remain in my thoughts, prayers, and heart. I held your lil monkey and imagined you were here in my arms. Tears flowed as the flood gates opened. I think about our crazy days here at home and laugh because I thought those days were so hard. I would take them all back a million times worse just to hold you and love you here on earth. A mom can still imagine.

I know heaven is exactly where you are meant to be, but the human side of me has a hard time accepting this truth. I watch all the other mommies who have angels just like you, and I feel a strange comfort knowing I'm not crazy. People keep wanting to know how I really am, but I can't tell the full story. I'm scared of how uncertain it feels to adjust and carry on each day. This is more true of days I asked God to let me join you because the pain was so great.

I'm getting better because I know you are being taken care of. I know God has me here for many reasons. When my mission is complete, then, sweet baby girl, I'll get to join you! I'm good with it. I just have to give it all to our heavenly Father so I don't lose sight.

I hope you are having a gorgeous nine-month angelversay celebration today. I think I will go buy a slice of delicious cake in celebration of you and your time with our heavenly Father. I watched some of our favorite shows, including the Wonder Pets. They were fabulous. I even saw Ollie the Bunny, which reminded me of your huge rabbit Daddy would lay you on! Thank you for fighting to give me those amazing memories. I'm getting better at remembering the good times more than the not-so-fun ones.

I love you to the moon and back and for all eternity.

Love,
Your Mommy,
Chrissy

PS: Can you ask God to stop my sickness so Mommy doesn't throw up so much? That would save my sanity!

MAY 8, 2011

158 › Mother's Day

Hang in there with me this morning. I'm including words inspired by a song and two poems and writing. This will be a little longer than some entries. I appreciate your reading this on such a special day. Three of my children are not with me, but they are in the arms of Jesus. This proud momma is happy to know they will be with me for eternity though. I've never met two of them. One I carried for weeks until miscarrying on week eleven or twelve in 2006. The next one came and left in early 2009. I didn't even know I was pregnant, but we had to do a counseling session with our doctor after confirming I'd had a second miscarriage. We were blessed to meet our third baby—precious, angelic Lilian Grace Whitten.

Each baby scarred me yet made me stronger than I could ever fathom. Lilian Grace had the most impact—not to downplay the others. Meeting her, holding her, observing her character traits, and watching her every move made losing her hurt even more. Taking care of a child is the hardest job you'll ever have in life. There are days you wonder how you will make it through, but God walks us through it with grace when we trust Him.

For months now, I've been dreading Mother's Day. I didn't know if today would be the breaking point when I would snap and unleash what's buried inside. Doing holidays differently since Lilian earned her wings helped.

I hope my family knows, even if I'm not in their presence, I still love them immensely. One day things will smooth out for me. One day I will be stronger and breathe easier. Life will never be as it was because I see with new eyes and feel more deeply now. A mother who has lost her baby after holding and caring for them (even if for a minute) climbs to a strange, lonely place. Her viewpoint is drastically different, and it takes time to adjust to a new plateau.

One thing I can say with confidence is that things are going to get better. They are already better for me. God's been right here the whole time, in whatever my waves look like. I know it will make me stronger. Many of you have lost loved ones or experienced major life changes. Remember, it is going to pass and make you stronger—just fall into the arms of Jesus! "Stronger" by Mandisa played while I typed this entry. There's a reminder throughout the lyrics to keep holding on a bit longer because God cares about us and what we go through.

As we hoped for just a shred of good news about Lilian Grace, I could feel God holding on to us. Our journey with her was meant to make us stronger. I know He will make good come out of it all. I have to surf the waves that threaten to take me under. I'm Chrissy—holding on to God for dear life as He gently helps me balance on my board. He will complete the work He started in me. Trust the process. It will get better. Keep your eyes on Him and lean into His strength and faithfulness.

Two poems stole my heart this morning as God nudged me to type this Mother's Day journal entry. Last year, I was blessed to hold my baby girl—finally having one of my children with me on Mother's Day. It was a hard Mother's Day last year because I knew my time with Lilian wouldn't last long. God gave me a miracle in the time I got with her, though, which was blissful.

I won't forget the blessings God gave me through the crashing waves that have come and gone in my life. Today, on Mother's Day, I'm dressing up and looking pretty for my angels and "The Who." I'm stronger because God is my strength! Today, I'm going to church with my head held high, knowing God loves me unconditionally and chose me to be the mother of these special babies. Not everyone is built for this journey. He's given me peace and understanding that it's an honor to be chosen. When I think of all the scars on my heart, I'm proud I was chosen among a small number of individuals to live this out!

The first poem I recommend is for mothers who have lost their children, either inside the womb or years later. It's "What Makes A Mother" by Jennifer Wasik. Please find it online and enjoy reading it.[11]

The second poem, "Bless Our Mothers: A Mother's Day Prayer" by Joanna Fuchs, is a prayer for all mothers.[12] I love you all. May everyone remember how hard motherhood is daily, but it is such a worthy and honorable job. For those who get it right, thank you for your sacrifice and example—you are soaring.

Happy Mother's Day! Hold on to the memories you've lived, enjoy the ones you are making, and look forward to the ones to come. I love you all. God is Big as He has always been. I praise Him for all eternity as I look forward to the day I meet Him in person!

---

[11] Jennifer Wasik, "What Makes a Mother," http://community.babycentre.co.uk/post/a280045/what_makes_a_mother_a_poem_for_those_whove_lost.

[12] Joanna Fuchs, "Bless Our Mothers: A Mother's Day Prayer," https://www.poemsource.com/mothers-day-poems.html.

Lilian Grace and my other two angels,

I am a better person because of each of you. I love you to the moon and back and for all eternity! I'm blowing a million kisses your way and sending just as many hugs. I'm one lucky mommy! Thank you!

Love,
Your (Getting Peace at Last) Mommy,
Chrissy

MAY 15, 2011

159 › It Is Well

After weeks of battling nausea and contributing food in reverse order to the white throne, I find myself trying to keep my sanity. Many of you are wondering how it's going. Well, you don't have to imagine what it feels like—just think of the above never stopping twenty-four hours a day. I find that I can be going through my day looking better and feeling a little more human. All of a sudden, the ugly stick hits me, and I look like death warmed over while feeling as if I might lose everything inside my stomach.

I know it's not a pretty picture, but it's the result of any of the following: hormone overload, "The Who" jumping around, nasty smells, or grief. Sadly, the grief of a thousand things expands from our past and present, hitting us like that ugly stick. I'm getting better at dealing with grief when it tries to consume me. Knowing and recognizing it are important tactics in surviving the moments that take my breath away. I try to face those moments as they bubble up so that I can keep moving.

Trying to juggle too many things in the brain and heart can trigger grief during the day. I'm just glad God takes the best care of me as He gives me more of what I need in the nick of time. It does hurt, but He makes it better.

I've been listening to "It Is Well" by Mary Mary tonight and found comfort. My grief, brokenness, and pain are not going to go away. There are times it can take over, and I forget I need to keep still and let God work it out. He is so good about reminding me that He never goes away! He works everything for the good of His kingdom, so my grief is not wasted. That's so reassuring to my soul and makes it all worth it and well within me.

No matter who, what, when, where, how, or why you find your heart and spirit broken, don't forget to keep working toward it being well within you. Do the work! It's hard to process brokenness but worth the outcome on the other side.

Whatever turn your journey takes, I pray you come to a place where it is indeed well with your soul. I pray you feel His presence and know He is making it all for the good. No matter what storm or level of extreme conditions come your way, rest and remain in Him. He always gets us to where we need to be. I'm experiencing that every day!

I'm not always excited about the journey. Trust me—I'd rather not be sick twenty-four hours a day, but I know this, too, shall pass. I look forward to adding another miracle to our family. I have no clue how "The Who" will turn out, but I'm starting to smile more and feel unexplainable excitement about what will happen. Also, I am starting to have wonderful daydreams about holding this precious child from God and getting to do the simplest tasks with praise and gratitude!

I hope and pray our journey with "The Who" is a long one. May they live a long life as Michael and I experience all the craziness and joy they will bring to us. I know God brought me to this road, and He will get me through it. I love all His promises. Life has happiness and, sadly, hurts. Through the good, bad, and indifferent, one thing remains the same—God. He is the Vine! Praise God for whatever comes our way while we remain in Him!

It is well with my soul as long as I stay connected to God. Without Him, I can do nothing. My successes depend on my ability to continuously lean and trust; He is my vine to bear fruit and grow.

Memory Verse 15

🗡 *"I am the vine; you are the branches. If you remain in me and I in you, you will bear much fruit; apart from me you can do nothing"* (John 15:5).

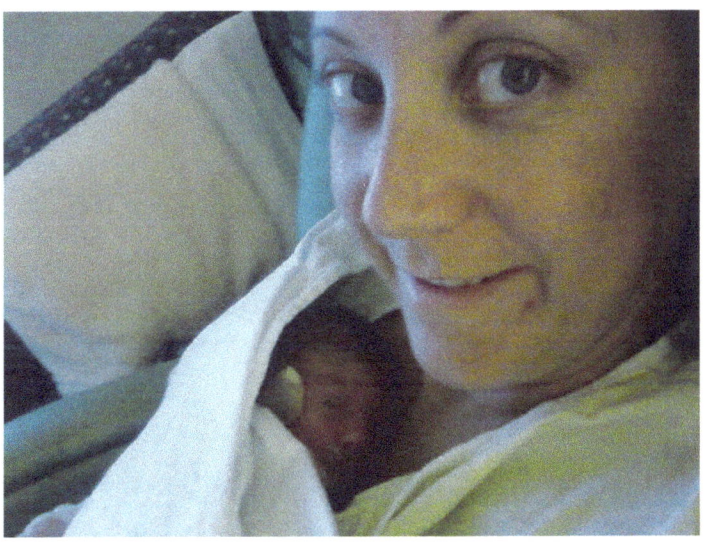

Peek-a-boo—I see a miracle in you!

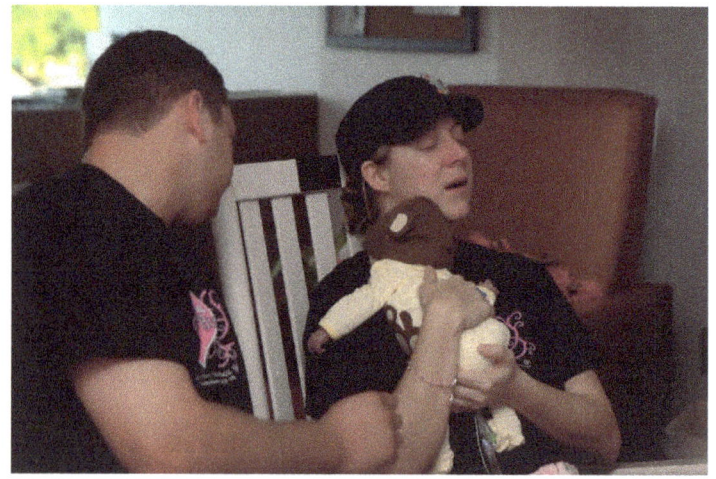

Just breathe

MAY 17, 2011

160 › Never Wave My Flag

I just listened to "Never Wave My Flag" by Mary Mary—my anthem right now. I'm literally out of breath, getting crazy dancing, shouting, and singing as this song plays. You can't help but get pumped up and excited after hearing Mary Mary sing this empowering song. Today, more than ever, I needed this song to play in my ear!

Today was my interview with the Tulsa County Health Department about Lilian's case. They investigate every death to help families in the county dealing with similar experiences and try to prevent future happenings. In my head, I imagined this huge ordeal that might weigh me down when having to answer questions. It wasn't anything like I thought. I made it through the almost two-hour interview, and the interviewer was very patient with me. I got to talk about Lilian Grace, which made this mommy's heart happy.

I feel like this was another step in the grieving process. I can do this! While I'm doing it, I can continue to help others by sharing God's love and light. I'm glad the interview has come and gone. In July, they'll finally review her medical records and such. I have until then to open the closet in Lilian's room and dig through paperwork to provide more information for their investigation. Until then, I chose to start organizing pictures and getting all the picture books completed for Lilian Grace using Shutterfly.

We had a doctor appointment today, and things seem to be moving forward. I'm not as afraid and feel more relaxed. I know God continues to give me what I need through it all.

The interviewer today made me feel very good about how I've been grieving. The feedback she gave me was very positive. I feel like the broken pieces of my heart are fewer because of the way God's been helping me through the grieving journey. I'm not feeling so empty.

It takes so much work to actively grieve, but it's worth the happiness and healing that comes after all of it. As I looked through hundreds of pictures of Lilian Grace, I let the tears roll tonight. The videos seem to get me more than anything else. The tears were very healthy. I do miss her abundantly, especially when I see her interacting with us or hearing her little squeaks. We don't have many videos, but the ones we do have play a special role in keeping memories alive. She was incredible and breathtaking. I'm so lucky to have had time with her.

Even when talking about our journey in the interview, I smiled from ear to ear. We had a jam-packed journey that will never be forgotten. I will not wave my flag anytime soon! We got hit in the face daily. We encountered one obstacle after another but didn't wave our flags!

Whatever your reason for grieving, don't let someone tell you to forget it or to stop talking about the one you've lost. You will know if someone doesn't want to hear about it. Find people who are happy to listen. Remember the goodness you experienced beforehand, during, and after. That has helped me along the path toward healing! Oh, healing sounds like the perfect antidote—I'm up for it!

This mommy had a full day today processing things, but I'm better for it. I needed to cry more and release some pent-up tears. I wonder where my crazy life story will take me next? I can't say it is boring after recounting our journey today with the health department. I just laugh because I know the devil has tried many times to finish me off—to finish us off. I praise God for stepping in and conquering!

Well, I am going to put on that full armor of God daily and never wave my flag. Will you join me?

Just hold on

MAY 18, 2011

161 › Destiny in Purpose

Praise God, I have amazing news! Before I share, I'd like to focus on two great songs that explain a good portion of my journey, "Destined" by Avalon and "Said and Done" by Michael Boggs. Avalon and Michael Boggs tie for providing the perfect words to express my joy over the wisdom of God's providence and His purpose for my life. God has been phenomenally patient with me, and I feel like the past thirty-three years (in less than two months) have brought me where He wants me to be. The music in my life is sweeter and more beautiful now than ever.

Every time I've questioned, God answered in ways you can't imagine. In my weakest moments God suddenly gave me strength. He provides the armor I need for each battle. His greatness and light are evident all around me. I love Him with all that I am and beyond. I adore His magnificence and holiness. I am blessed to worship Him with my heart, soul, and life.

I've been fortunate to have some free time. I've taken advantage of every minute, trying not to waste it. When it comes to Lilian Grace, I don't regret anything about her. I do regret holding on to my people-pleasing habits. I could have saved myself a lot of grief by letting go of things and people's approval. I'm thankful my husband was patient and overlooked what I lacked at the time.

I pray people will see God weaving and writing through my life. He is Truth and Light. May He keep shining brightly through my grief and happiness. I hope when all is said and done that He will say to me, "Well done, good and faithful servant." Not that I'm perfect, but that I did the best I could with what I faced.

Okay, the amazing news is finding out yesterday by letter that the Warrior Princess Foundation is officially a 501(c)(3) Public Charity under the 509(a)(2) Internal Revenue Service Code. Contributions to the Warrior Princess Foundation are deductible under section 170 of the Code. We are qualified to receive tax-deductible bequests, devises, transfers, or gifts under sections 2055, 2106, or 2522 of the Code.

Hallelujah! Praise God! After eight months plus of sheer effort and moments of doubt, we are official. I feel like Lilian Grace's legacy/mission/life can live on and help other trisomy 18 and 13 families in their journey. There's endless work to be done, but I couldn't be more excited as her mommy for the opportunity to keep sharing her story, journey, and mission.

I won't ever get paid by the foundation, which is wonderful because mothers don't get paid to do their jobs. I know I will always be her mommy no matter what, but now I get to do something tangible for her again—a more active role. This makes my heart happy. May God continue to guide me on my journey. I want nothing more than for people to see my Father's love.

MAY 31, 2011

162 › Project Details

Well, I survived some crazy moments the past couple of weeks, and I'm still not waving my flag! God continues to be gracious taking care of me. I broke down through lullaby songs, a wedding shower, Lilian's thirteen-month birthday anniversary, a state conference, and Memorial Day weekend, but I kept my composure during my niece's dance recital. I can't believe my lil Lilian Grace was all dressed up a year ago in her colorful dragonfly dress with shades looking like Lady Gaga—G-rated, of course. Life keeps happening, and we keep living.

Michael and I got much-needed husband and wife time these past few days. I have to admit I wasn't thinking this weekend would turn out as nice as it did since Michael and I weren't communicating well. Thankfully, we adjusted. We watched movies at home and at the theater, played miniature golf, and completed projects. God knows how to get us reconnected. Ever feel disconnected? I get that way every now and then. I'm learning to slow down some so I don't miss out on opportunities to connect with those around me.

Since today is Memorial Day, I thought I'd honor my daughter by giving you all overdue updates on all the projects we are starting, doing, or trying to finish up. Sorry for the length, but it's worth sharing! We continue to miss Lilian Grace, but we know she and God improved our lives by rewiring us and giving us a higher view of life. Hope you all have enjoyed your weekend and remembered those you've lost. Thanks to all the men, women, and their families who sacrificed so we can enjoy our lives safely. We are blessed as a nation!

We appreciate those who have generously participated in projects regarding Lilian Grace and the Warrior Princess Foundation. I'd like to sell our remaining inventory, so if you or someone you know would like to support us in one of the following ways, please let me know.

- **Lilian Grace Memorial Necklaces for $40/necklace:** This necklace represents all 103 days of life through birthstones of each day for each month, plus the angel wing charm to represent her earning her wings—only eleven necklaces left!
- **"God Be Big" T-shirts:** We sold these shirts while Lilian Grace was here! It's the signature shirt that reminds us to keep trusting in Him. Ephesians 3:17–19 is on the back, reminding us why we are on this journey—only three large shirts left for $15.00.
- *Timmy's Tasty Treats II–To Topple Trisomy 18*: This cookbook contains shared recipes from trisomy 18 families, including a couple from Lilian's great-great grandma Cooper and great Nan West. We teamed up with a trisomy 18 family from New York on this project. It has some great recipes—only thirty-seven cookbooks left for $30 (includes shipping)!
- **Women of Faith Conference in Oklahoma City, OK, November 11–12, 2011:** The foundation doesn't get any of the money from this project, but this one is in memory of Lilian Grace. Sybil and I have teamed up to get 103 women to attend the conference to celebrate Lilian's beautiful life by refueling for future battles. I'm in charge of selling fifty tickets and have already sold

five! If I can get all fifty sold by July 1, 2011, all ticket holders are eligible to get a complimentary Women of Faith 2010 worship CD. Tickets are $89. When you buy a ticket, you are entered into a drawing for a free ticket! I will not be organizing the trip to OKC but encourage women to get together and enjoy. Sign up today!

- **The Warrior Princess Trail Run Inaugural Race** was held on April 25, 2011, in celebration of Lilian's first birthday anniversary and the race we and other trisomy 18 and 13 families ran or currently run every day! I'm excited we will be able to raise money through sponsorships now that we are tax deductible! For those who didn't get to participate, you still can! We have the following tech shirts left to sell for $20/shirt—there are forty-nine left (XS–6, S–3, M–19, L–21).

I'm also offering two specials for those who would still like to run. Since we have the shadow runner option and medals left over, I want to give you more time to participate so you can snag a medal! June was a rough month for us because Lilian technically died and came back to life in the wee hours of the night. You have from now until June 15, 2011, to run whatever distance and time you'd like. I have seventy-two race medals and forty-nine shirts left. It will be first come, first served. Here are the two specials:

> 1. Tech shirt (only the shirt sizes left are available) and finisher medal: $40
>
> 2. No shirt, but finisher medal only: $25

As of today, we have made only $363.05 because we weren't officially a 501(c)(3) until recently. I'm excited that this number will be a drop in the bucket after next year's efforts because we can now accept sponsorships for the race! YAY! I learned from doing and gained a better understanding of race logistics. Here's a breakdown of expenses and income to help anyone who would like to put on a fundraising race event:

Total Expenses: $4,205.40
- Tech Shirts: $2,284.47
- Medals: $935.60
- TATUR Timing & Set-up: $397.98
- Closing Ceremony, Sky Lantern: $31.85
- At Your Service, Porta Potties (one donated of two): $125.00
- Trophies & Awards: $61.29
- USATF Oklahoma, Liability Insurance & Sanction: $125.00
- Race Registrations & Packet Supplies: $88.97
- Postage: $20.15
- Food & Race Supplies: $135.09

Total Income: $4,568.45
- Race Registrations: $3,855.00
- Personal Donations: $384.71
- Extra Shirt Sales: $328.74

I want to make sure you all know who officially registered for the first annual race in both the 10.3 mile trail/road race and 1.03 mile fun run/walk. We had 115 registered runners/walkers.

10.3 Mile Runners—35 Runners

Kari Williams	Rafael Santiago	Sandra Wright
Wes Hollander	Tasha Todd	Teresa Ellington
Deon Bean	Stormy Phillips	Nick Klenovich
Tom Robinson	Randy Ellis	Matt Hancock
Paula Lee	Caroline Glenn	Taylor Sartin
Arnold Begay	Joyce Beasley	Kathy Hoover
Joshua Brazeal	Karrie Garriot	Jason Beasley
Dana Childress	Bob Hauge	Darryl Stillson
Cole Graves	Ken Childress	Callie Ortiz
Aaron Ochoa	Candice Brown	Charlz Childress
Bronda Gray	Jennifer Blair	Caroline Luelf
Pat McCracken	Cassy Russell	

1.03 Mile Runners/Walkers—54 Runners/Walkers

Chrissy Whitten	Janese Whitten	Kaylee Cooper
Susan Michaels	Susan Westmoreland	Crystal Borelli
Kristen Cooper	Bobby Michaels	Kris Ramsay
Ellysiana Staley	Caleb Cooper	Paula McCracken
Melissa Carder	Kim Arnold	Cali Cooper
Tiffanie Barto	Alicia Harrison	Addison Arnold
Chris Hubbard	Sharon Whitten	Lindsay Howard
Jessica Going	Lisa Hubbard	Brittany Downing
Amy Hartling	Jarrod Cooper	Lauren Hubbard
Ryan Hubbard	Mitch Drummond	Janie Hooker
Kim Christy	Rachel Foley	Kandice Bentley
Sheryl Klenovich	Leslie Ball	Teresa Allen
Shanna Santiago	Michael Whitten	Alex Christy
Derek England	Pamela Estes	Sereita Cooper
Sandra Burton	Rick Haynes	Stephanie Dooley

JoAnn Poteet	Chuck Burton	Ellen Agronis
Brooke Henderson	Chris Cooper	Athena Harrison
Robin Haynes	Debbie Cooper	Karen Marquis

Shadow Runners—27 Runners

Bill Ford	Scott Parmley	Ryan Rapp
Tammy Whitten	Sheila Ford	Cindy Metcalf
Jenni Hawkins	Shannon Hester	Allison Orr
Monty Whitten	Susan Hamil	Veda Hester
Cassandra Clark	Jessica Mills	Brooke Hunt
Micah Mitchell	Brad Johnson	Justin Mills
Cheryl Morgan	Robin Miller	Marsha G. Johnson
Subrenia Jurney	Shirley Owensby	Margaret Miller
Katie Parmley	Tiffany Myers	Don Gillam

Thanks again for continuing to support us. Please pass on this important information so others know and can participate! God has blessed me more than I can ever relay to you all. I wake up and think about all the blessings as I continue to praise God for letting me live out this journey, despite what it might look like at the time!

I am proud to announce that Subrenia Jurney will be joining me for next year's race as our volunteer director. She will oversee our volunteers for the second annual Warrior Princess Trail Run set for Wednesday, April 25, 2012!

A sneak peek into next year's theme: On Lilian's second-month birthday, she was the most precious Tinker Bell I've ever seen. Our color will be green, and we will have a fairy costume contest. Men, you are never too manly to get your fairy wear on—you can make yourself as good-looking and magical as ever! Lilian's favorite Disney movies were *Tinker*

Bell and *Tinker Bell and the Lost Treasure*!

I want to make sure everyone has plenty of time to plan for next year's race. It will be here before we know it! We might add another race with a length of 10.3K. This is not official, but we are throwing around the idea.

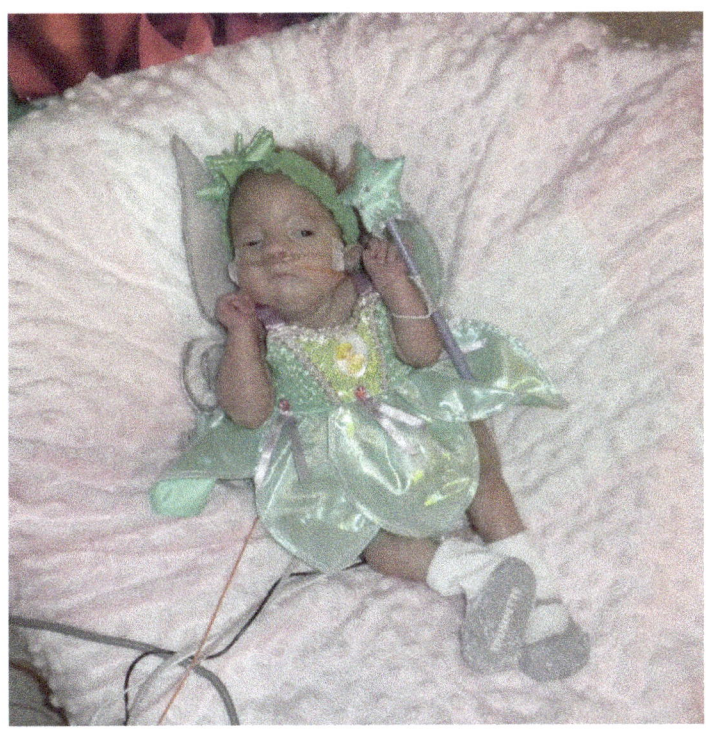

Forever magical

JUNE 4, 2011

163 › Tenth-Month Angelversary

Tomorrow marks ten months since my world crumbled—my baby celebrates ten whole months of being with Jesus. Tears keep coming. The other night I thought I could handle going into the closet where almost everything of Lilian's rests. My intention wasn't to clean up but to find a piece of paper with all her nicknames from us and many of you.

I found myself digging through boxes and containers as more tears streamed down my face. I have deep pockets in my heart where buckets of tears wait to pour out, yet I'm restrained by fear. I'm not ready to release them yet. The tears I do allow take so much out of me. Even with God's energy, I still get worn out because I'm human.

I unpacked all the clothes she never wore. I can recall most of the people who gifted each piece of clothing. Their smiling faces conveyed joy and hope, and the dreams they shared with us for Lilian Grace gave us peace, especially considering our long journey to get Lilian here. Sadly, she never got to live out those dreams or wear most of the clothes, but she's living out God's dreams for her, which is a blessing to share with each of you.

I can barely breathe when thinking about her living out God's dreams for her. More tears fall, but I need to breathe and get through this post. Apparently, God needed me to process another layer. The bucket holding these emotions is spilling, and I can't stop it despite my desperate attempts. One great thing about giving your life to God—He is with you through grief and will lighten your load.

It feels like the pace of life is picking up. Sometimes I wonder if I can keep up while grieving and healing, but God keeps affirming He'll help me through it. Just when I think I'll take back the reins of my life, God reminds me they are in His hands. His plans and dreams for me supersede mine.

God—I'm breathing—You are truly breathtaking and fulfilling! You teach me something every day, no matter my mood, ability, personality, or character, because You love me. Another bucket spills with the mere thought of You—no words or expressions do You justice. All I can do is keep stepping aside to let You do what You do. My heart aches and rejoices simultaneously, which is the craziest and wackiest feeling I've ever known.

These parallel feelings cannot be experienced unless someone is walking with God through grief. As tomorrow comes and goes, I know He will be with me. He's been with me from the day He made me in my mother's womb to the day He received Lilian Grace back into His loving arms and beyond to this point. Nobody can give me the peace my heavenly Father gives me. He has never once let me down.

"The Who" has been quiet in my tummy. I've been paranoid because I felt like I ripped my stomach on the inside when I twisted too quickly. This past week felt like an eternity. I have more time between doctor appointments now. You would think I'd welcome more time between appointments, but anxiety has kicked in. Whoa! I know now why God made Lilian's appointments so close together and provided multiple doctors to care for me. I still don't know when doctor appointments are scheduled. Michael keeps track and gets me there. This helps my anxiety. It works for us, but the time is dragging by this time around.

Finally, the last couple of nights "The Who" became active again, which reassured my spirit and made me feel better. Sometime in the next two weeks, I will go to Dr. Blake for our big scan. It was during this ultrasound when we found out Lilian Grace had problems, which began our spiral. If you have asked me how the baby is doing, I probably wasn't gracious in my response because I don't know. Up until twenty weeks gestation with Lilian, we thought we had a healthy baby with no problems, until we were crushed by her diagnosis. So that's why I've been quieter than usual. I'm trying to manage my grief and anxiety, but it's hard.

Please say extra prayers for us with this big test coming up. I pray God prepares us to be who this child needs us to be. Of course, I pray for health—just as I did for Lilian Grace. I'm also praying God will prepare us for whatever is coming.

My song today tipped another bucket of tears. "He Is with You" by Mandisa is perfect for all of us who are going through grief and change. She sure can stir a spirit with her soulful gift. The song brings to mind everyone who has written me. I hope you look it up and listen. Her music will bring you strength and peace. Praying this for each of us!

Ecclesiastes 3 comes to mind as I hear the words being sung. There is truly a time for everything. I may weep more than I want, but joy comes in the morning. He is with us in all things, especially when we take our final breath. A mustard seed of faith is all you need to allow God to be Big in your life! I know I need to release my strongholds so I don't interrupt His progress with me. Many people have lovingly reminded me that He is right here, battling for me—that reminder is much appreciated.

Lilian Grace, my roly poly,

My tears pour out today because I have another level of healing to do. I will be with some of our family tomorrow and wanted to make sure I did some processing early to ensure they get me smiling more than crumbling on the floor. I tell you this because I am still moving forward by doing the hard things—letting God empty out all those buckets of tears in my heart to breathe and live.

I miss you tremendously and with a desire I cannot describe. I seem to feel you more these days and am unsure if you've really been coming around, but it's a sweet thought and feeling none-the-less. I had a crazy thought that you moved my hair out of my face and stroked my face. Regardless of if it was you or not, it was a wonderful feeling.

I know you've been continuing to give your brother or sister lessons in the womb. There are so many things they do that remind me of you. I can't wait to meet them. I hope they have your big, gorgeous eyes and character. I hope they get to live out God's dreams and desires just like you did, sweetheart. It makes me happy to keep seeing your mission change people.

I hope you have an amazing celebration tomorrow as you celebrate ten months of finishing your journey here on earth and beginning your life there, whole and healed with God. We will be celebrating a cousin's birthday, so hopefully I'll get some cake. Deep down, I will be celebrating your milestone of ten months in heaven and praising God for showing me, without a doubt, the reasons why you were here for such a short time.

I love you to the moon and back and for all eternity. May we do some great things with your Warrior Princess Foundation. I hope you are excited like me to see your mission live on. God made it possible!

Love,
Mommy

JUNE 7, 2011

164 › Returning Love

God woke me up early today. I didn't really want to get up, but I needed to watch a movie that's been around for weeks now. I just didn't feel like watching it until seven thirty this morning. I caved in, got up, threw up (side effects of rising too early), heated up breakfast, and decided it was finally time to watch *Fireproof*.

God and His timing! The past few months, despite my grief over losing Lilian Grace, the broken pieces in my heart and soul have been slowly healing. My love for other people, even myself at times, is harder to regain. I've tried talking to a select few about it all but find I come up empty. I really don't know how to get the feelings out. I know that's hard to believe for some of you, but it's true.

I'm aware the issues I had with people, even myself, are deeply rooted. The issues weren't tied to Lilian Grace's time and what happened; they have taken place over the course of many years. God let her life shed light on the brokenness and lack of love in some relationships—and the issues were uprooted. My respect and desire to keep fighting for these relationships had been diminishing, and then my grief journey made it impossible.

Truthfully, it's harder to deal with some people because of two major things. First, I'm tired and have decided it may be time to move on. Secondly, I see with another set of eyes, unable to live in denial. *Fireproof* may be about a marriage, but I can apply it to all my relationships. Eighty percent of my struggle with most relationships is having no respect or getting no respect. I have to admit, I often see love as a feeling instead of thinking about the unconditional aspect. It doesn't just exist because I say it does—it takes work!

Love is the key to all my relationships. When there is a lack of love, it's hard to continue a relationship—especially when it feels like love is one-way. I can admit I know where I fail in my relationships and where I do not. I've lost friendships because it was time to move on without them. An unhealthy relationship can only be healed when both parties see where they have fallen short. Some of my relationships have been one-way for years. Because I don't have the energy to keep reaching out, those relationships have been lost.

Friendships that have soared are a two-way street. There's no jealousy—only two people wishing the best for the other party. Love reigns in those relationships because somehow, we get it. We practice give and take, which is beautiful to experience.

What am I going to do now? I'm going to do the forty-day challenge using *The Love Dare* with not only my marriage but all my relationships. It may take me a few forty-day trips with some people, but I'm tired of fighting and struggling. I'm exhausted from battling hate in my heart. I didn't know it could be this strong until I lost my daughter. I will be taking inventory of all my relationships to gain a deeper understanding of myself and others. More importantly, I want unconditional love in every relationship. I miss that part of me and recognize that God has been trying everything to get my attention lately to resolve or dissolve the issues.

It's like thirty-two years of junk tumbled on me and now I have to sort through it. The relationships that were hard to maintain broke while I was trying to process and survive

Lilian Grace's death. I just couldn't do it. Some people have been amazing and overwhelmingly patient with me. Others sadly have not, instead displaying selfishness, jealousy, and more.

Ten months and two days later, it's time for love to win and to get rid of any hate in my heart. I miss the Chrissy who gave people a million chances because love ruled. There is a difference between people who run over you and those who just don't know any better. Hopefully, God will teach me how to conquer all in love.

Let me make it clear—this will be hard. It will take energy magnified to the nth power, but I need to let God do major healing. What's funny and brilliant at the same time is that I already had *The Love Dare* book, card set, and *Fireproof* movie before Lilian Grace got here. God set me up for success with these resources I didn't want to access at the time. I've got about four shots at the forty day challenge before "The Who" arrives. Today, I will begin with patience for day one.

I'd like to encourage any of you who feel bitterness, resentment, hate, or loneliness to do this challenge with me. Even if you have gone through a divorce or lost a partner to death, place yourself and anyone else in this challenge. You don't have to be married to do this love dare—I'm extending it to all my relationships. It's time to start walking my talk!

Love you all. "While I'm Waiting" by John Waller is a song from the *Fireproof* soundtrack and contains an important reminder for this kind of endeavor. While I'm waiting for healing and love to return to my relationships, I will move forward and work with the tools He's provided! I'll worship Him through it all as I wait patiently for Him to move. I'll serve and worship Him through my waiting. I hope I'm ready when He calls me to move.

JUNE 8, 2011

165 › Blessings

Warning: I've bawled more than usual typing this one. You may need Kleenex for this entry as well—you've been forewarned.

The Love Dare: Days 1 & 2

📜 Another day of healing took place as I started *The Love Dare*, which is exactly what I need right now. Today I focused on making an unexpected gesture like an act of kindness and saying nothing negative to my spouse or any other person. I've had to watch myself to keep from speaking negatively or joking about certain individuals. On day two, I find myself needing more work—perhaps more than expected—in certain relationships.

I decided to look up blessings today and found a magnificent song called "Blessings" by Laura Story. I've heard it before, but today I focused on the words. As I sat here and listened, tears poured out. Listen to her sing this creative song. It's a true blessing in and of itself!

My prayer life has magnified through our journey. All the trials and mountains have become blessings from God! It's not always been easy to think of our trials this way. The more my heavenly Father teaches me, the easier it is to see them as beautiful blessings. I'm starting to see that even my broken relationships can be a blessing. When it's meant for me to work on these relationships, I and the other person both have the opportunity for a piece of our character to be transformed and healed. I'm excited, despite being scared or bitter, for the transition, transformation, relief, and release of all that weighs me down.

It gives me hope that I don't have to stay in the gutter of negativity, sadness, or brokenness. I've lived there too long while sadly accepting that others are resting there as well. Relationships take hard work, but I know it's worth seeing each one whole and solid! It's time I started giving grace and mercy with God's help to the people in my life.

Furthermore, I have more miraculous news about "The Who." We had our big scan yesterday. My blood pressure was high. I owned that I need more of God. Our dreams could be altered in a moment, and I wasn't sure what my reaction would be. Michael and I talked and prayed about it beforehand. We were in a place where we knew God would give us exactly what we needed despite the outcome Dr. Blake gave us. Still, even with this attitude, my fears wanted to creep in and take over. I'm signed up for whatever the journey looks like. Sometimes before you climb a mountain, you second-guess yourself.

Michael got to be there for some of the measuring. Just seeing "The Who" on the ultrasound monitor was breathtaking. The tech, who was an angel, was fabulous in every way as we went from one measurement to another. I could identify huge differences between this baby and Lilian Grace. Through these measurements, God showed us this baby is healthy in every way at this point.

As I noticed each difference, I bawled, not only for this current child, because they appeared to be whole and perfectly made, but for the overwhelming awe of knowing that Lilian Grace, with everything wrong in her systems, rocked out 103 days. I'm more amazed at her and God than before. My heavenly Father proved to me, the doctors, and everyone that He made no mistakes with Lilian Grace. He made sure she could live to the exact day she was meant to live so that we could learn, grow, change, and be who He intended us to be.

The brain, the heart—Lilian battled many odds against her with all the defects, and our next child showing perfection took my emotions on a ride. I couldn't stop crying and trying to breathe. All I know is that Lilian Grace can now run circles around any of us. She never let what she had or lacked get in her way of living out her purpose here on earth. God taught her not to let limitations, her prognosis, or anything stop her from living out her mission for Him. I sit here in awe and silence, trying to fathom it all. How many of us let ourselves get in His way?

As Dr. Blake reassured us that "The Who" is one of the healthiest babies they've seen in a long time, I rejoiced and praised God on high as tears fell. I'm still processing and praising—trying to wrap my mind, heart, and soul around it. My joy is truly indescribable at this point. God gives me more grace and mercy than I deserve. I have no idea what the future holds, but I will rest in His plan. I am buckled up to live it out through curves, dips, or whatever comes at me!

God continues to be bigger than I imagined. Thank you all for the prayers. Even my umbilical cord has all the parts working this time. How incredible! I will praise His name forever through the good, bad, and everyday of life! Please continue to be with us as we progress through a normal pregnancy, and pray it continues to be this way. If it doesn't, pray He will get Michael and me to where we need to be. Love you all!

JUNE 9, 2011

166 › Works in Progress

I don't think we realize how we talk until we stop and listen to ourselves. I've learned more than I care to in the past three days. My words are not all positive and fun like I want them to be. My random act of kindness was not well thought out. I did not intend to create more work for my husband when I started a project he wanted done. Let's just say we both got a good laugh out of it. Being pregnant really puts a limit on what I can do and causes me to move at a snail's pace when trying to finish what I started. I need to keep in mind how my projects affect Michael and myself! For those who are joining me in this challenge, remember to process and hash out the random act of kindness before acting.

God keeps blessing me this week by working out much-needed goals and objectives in my business and pregnancy. I've been trying to be more laid back and let God work things out for His good, even with minor details that keep me on my toes. I'll let Him work and continue to show up and be Big. This makes me happy!

The Love Dare: Day 3

Unfortunately, I still have work to do—training myself to ignore negative thoughts about people; thinking about who I will choose next for a random act of kindness; and spending money on someone—something I'm fabulous at doing. Getting back to doing things for others is overdue—including buying gifts for them—and it makes my heart overflow with happiness. I wish it didn't, but it does. It shouldn't be therapeutic, but buying things is my jam.

Now on to other things. Not too long ago, I created a list of projects I wanted/needed to accomplish before "The Who" arrives. I've not marked off many items yet, but there are several "works in progress," so to speak. How many of us let our "projects" or circumstances weigh us down and prevent us from being who we should or doing what we should? I think many of us can admit there are too many things getting in our way.

I pray we all start weeding out, processing, and marking off projects to lighten our load to make forward progress. The lighter our load, the better we can hear God leading us to the next marker on our journey with Him. Here's a verse from today's reading: *"Do nothing out of selfish ambition or vain conceit. Rather, in humility value others above yourselves"* (Philippians 2:3).

This is easy to say but not easily done. We all have our agendas and want what we want. I've seen this in many (including myself) during Lilian's time when people put what they wanted in front of what she needed. I always tried to think of her first, but I know my selfishness got in the way on occasion.

God help us all to be selfless, instead of selfish!

JUNE 10, 2011

167 › Healing Stick

As I start the day, I'm feeling a little better about myself. I've been holding my tongue and paying attention to how some people treat me. No names will be shared. This challenge is for me to hopefully help others. It's interesting to stop and observe not only my own feelings but what someone else's deal could be.

What am I finding out? We are all broken in our own way. I wish God would give me a healing stick so I could tap each person I meet and poof—they're healed! Getting to a better place personally and experiencing how rich and positive relationships and community can be—it's such a wonderful thought. Just imagining all the people I know being whole, happy, and worthy—incredible! There would be less arguing and fighting for sure.

The Love Dare: Day 4

Today's challenge is pretty simple. You'll have to read *The Love Dare* to find out for yourself, but let's just say it's a lot easier than trying to refrain from negative reactions, thoughts, et cetera. Check on someone you haven't spoken to in a while. It will bless you both!

On the health side of things, my sinus infection and thyroiditis are getting in my way. It's challenging and starting to wear on me. I've been taking Children's Liquid Benadryl at night, but I went ahead and took a second dose early this morning. It's hard to stay positive and energetic when my body feels the complete opposite.

Hopefully, this will run its course. I am grateful I'm not throwing up these days. In fact, it's been almost eighteen weeks since I've thrown up! Praise God! I guess we all trade one thing for another, but it keeps life interesting.

I do ask for more prayers regarding our trisomy 18 and 13 families and their precious children. There are quite a few who've had multiple bacterial infections and so forth. My heart aches for them all. It's never easy having to watch your child suffer with pain. Pray for God to heal them. I know that when any child gets an infection or other sickness, it's not fun. These special babies have a harder time—a small infection can lead to life-threatening situations, even death. Pray God gives the families comfort as He provides. I know their lack of sleep cannot be good. Keep in mind those who are struggling with decision making. Pray God will reassure them and lead them to good choices for their child.

With Lilian Grace, we went with the plan of doing stuff for her until it became doing stuff to her. It was the best plan for us. I can stand here today having no regrets in regard to her care, and that's the priceless benefit of that plan. Love you all! Till tomorrow!

JUNE 11, 2011

168 › Sarcasm & Irritation

My schedule's been crazy, going from one thing to the next. I'm just now reading day five's dare. Note to self and anyone participating: read the book in the morning! God provides important information to help you be more successful throughout your day during this process, and I missed out.

The Love Dare: Day 5

📜 Today's verse comes from Proverbs 27:14: *"If anyone loudly blesses their neighbor early in the morning, it will be taken as a curse."* I discovered—actually, I was reminded—that my sarcasm is worse when I am in an uncomfortable setting or when I try to get back at someone who has hurt me somehow. I'm not proud of this, but I'm finding the root of my struggle. I wish I would have read day five this morning because I would have been more aware of myself. No, I shouldn't need a book to make me aware, but it would have woken me up and helped in the way I spoke to various people.

My sarcastic tendencies need curbing, which may be a long road. In today's dare, I had to ask my spouse to tell me three things that cause him to be uncomfortable or irritated with me. Gulp—drum roll please! Yes, I'm going to share.

1. My overcommenting on anything.
2. My worrying—sometimes not trusting things will really be okay.
3. I share too much about my bathroom experiences.

Okay, these could have been worse. I'm not going to lie;

I held my breath as he thought about them. I can look back and see why my husband was frustrated when one or all of the above occurred. On the third one, my tomboy ways seep out from time to time—perhaps way more than they should. These three things are manageable.

What are three things that annoy your spouse, children, friends, or whomever? Think about it. I'm sure there are a few. I can think of several that annoy me about myself. I can agree on the second one with my husband in that I do worry more than I should.

About my health: My sinus infection and thyroiditis have moved into my chest. I pray this goes away ASAP, as well as for the throwing up to pass (it's back). I'd rather be nauseous than have difficulty breathing. I feel like someone is trying to smother me. Hope everyone who is sick gets well ASAP—feeling bad is not a fun thing! Love you all!

JUNE 12, 2011

169 › Adding Margin

My cold has officially moved into my chest. Sharing love and positivity while not feeling up to par is hard. Thank God today was church day. I love my church family. I will be napping all afternoon because it completely wore me out.

The Love Dare: Day 6

Today's dare is about making a list of ways to add margin to my schedule. One of my biggest challenges is that I love to be around people and doing things. I need to start spreading out my social time and adding more time with my hubby—not forgetting the dreaded to-do list that needs to be accomplished.

My stress levels and health suffer when I try to cram too much into a day. I've tried working on this for years but still struggle. Since I'm not feeling well, I've had to cancel things. Now I just need to give my body the rest it needs to heal.

Are you a person who is stressed all the time? Consider your schedule first and see if you are giving yourself enough time to recuperate and be ready for what comes your way. Sometimes our attitudes and reactions to others are due to our lack of time or energy.

Lil Sophee is going through heart failure right now. I haven't heard any updates, but she needs our prayers ASAP. Her mom is Summer Fuller. Pray God gives them wisdom, strength, comfort, and whatever else they possibly need.

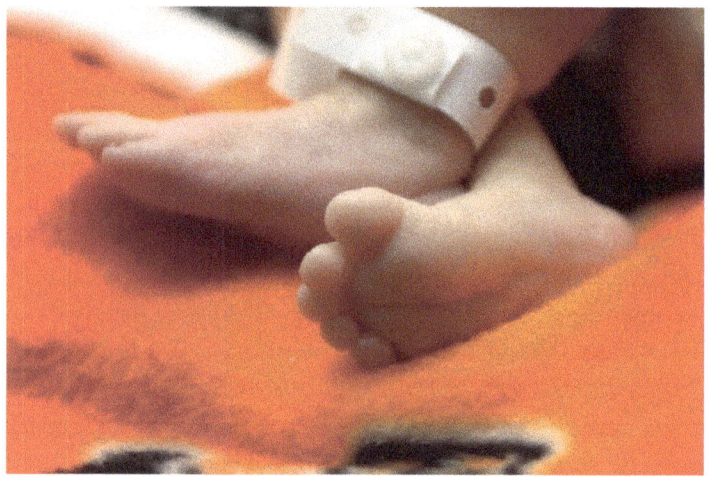

Tiny feet, impactful footprints

JUNE 13, 2011

170 › Sickness Amid Grief

After deciding that being stubborn is not the way to go, I went to urgent care yesterday afternoon. I thought I was wasting my money going, but God used a lady at the Walmart register to give me wisdom. She told me that the medicine I was purchasing would not help my symptoms. I took it as a sign I needed to see a doctor.

Well, I ended up having a fever and acknowledging that it was a mistake to downplay my sickness. When you have been sick for years, it's easy to do this. I have strep, as does Michael—darn sickness! I should have gone Saturday when I suspected things had gotten worse. Oh well, I already feel ten times better after three pills from the Z-pack! Praying for one hundred percent recovery as soon as possible for me and my husband.

In sadder news, lil Sophee earned her wings. Each time one of our trisomy 18 or trisomy 13 babies pass away, my heart breaks and rewinds back to the beginning of our grieving journey. I wish I could take that away from the other parents. It's not an easy journey—not even close. I pray for her family as they start down a new road without her.

Strep is not a big deal when compared to losing a child. I'll get over strep within days, but losing a child is a lifelong struggle. Relief will come when Jesus calls me home. I know this may sound morbid, but I've accepted it. I know I need to actively grieve, yet my daughter dying took pieces of me I'll never get back.

The Love Dare: Day 7

As far as day seven goes for *The Love Dare*, my failure and need for growth stand out. We all have sinned and carry past hurts and trauma. In reviewing old posts, I see I've talked a lot about this subject. It's nice to see it mentioned in another book.

My dare is to write two different lists: positive and negative things about my spouse. I am going to write several of these lists to help me with other relationships in my life too. I'm even going to write one for myself. Yes, when I stop and listen to myself, I sometimes find I am my own worst enemy. Take some time to write your own lists.

Here's a poem one of my friends, Brianne (Paxton's mom), put on a grieving mother's page. It's beautiful.

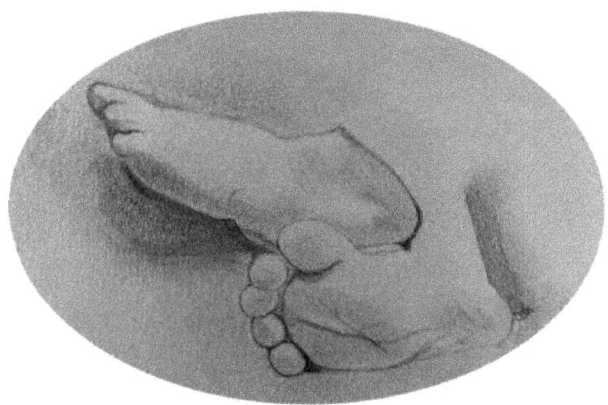

Tiny Footprints

These are my footprints,
so perfect and so small.
These tiny footprints,
never touched the ground at all.

Not one tiny footprint,
for now I have wings.
These tiny footprints were meant
for other things.

You will hear my tiny footprints,
in the patter of the rain.
Gentle drops like angel's tears,
of joy and not from pain.

You will see my tiny footprints,
in each butterflies' lazy dance.
I'll let you know I'm with you,
if you just give me the chance.

You will see my tiny footprints,
in the rustle of the leaves.
I will whisper names into the wind,
and call each one that grieves.

Most of all, these tiny footprints,
are found on mommy's heart.
'Cause even though I'm gone now,
we'll NEVER truly part.

(Tamara Barker)

JUNE 14, 2011

171 › Bad Days

Let's talk about having a jazzed up day that gets the blood pressure super pumped yet is not the good kind of jazzed. Thus far, this is the day I've had—
- Late to work by a few minutes;
- Stopped working out with clients because I started getting sick;
- Continuous vomiting until I got medicine refilled;
- The pharmacy could only give me twenty-four pills due to the insurance denying it, though my prescription was for ninety;
- After three hours of dealing with the pharmacy, doctor's office, and insurance, I'm enrolled in a high-risk program and hoping they can give me the full ninety pills each month until I do not need them;
- By the way, these pills are the only thing keeping me human and able to function and the only solution at this time to prevent and/or stop vomiting;
- Broke a bowl with leftover dip and cut my foot while I was on hold with insurance;
- Clients had to cancel today;
- Ate lunch, which got cold, while being on the phone for two hours with insurance, and my stomach isn't liking it too well if all the grumbling is any indication; and
- Let's see—yep, that covers this day thus far, and I'm hoping sleep will come sooner rather than later so I can start a fresh, new day.

As far as day eight goes, I'm going to have to do it tonight. It involves too much thinking for me at the moment. I'll include a two-for-one deal tomorrow. Just remember that if you're having a bad day, reach out to your prayer warriors and ask them to start praying. A couple of mine were hard at work when I realized I was not in a good place today. Their prayers have been felt, and I thank God for them! There's a verse that helps explain how powerful our prayers are for ourselves and others on the battlefield.

Memory Verse 16

🗡 "This is the confidence we have in approaching God: that if we ask anything according to his will, he hears us. And if we know that he hears us—whatever we ask—we know that we have what we asked of him" (1 John 5:14–15).

Hoping you all are having a much better day than I am and sending love your way! Be a prayer warrior for others. I couldn't battle as strong without their prayers.

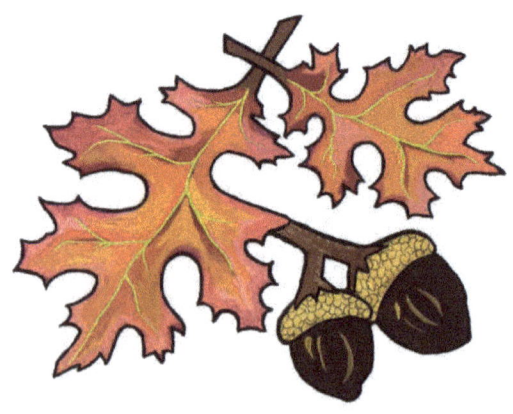

JUNE 18, 2011

172 › Quietly Processing

I've kept myself off here for a few days because I've been quietly processing. It's strange how our emotions can control us and keep us preoccupied. Words again escape me in trying to describe or pinpoint what has been happening this week.

If I could find the words to write, I fear the judgment in them would wreak havoc. Therefore, I think quietly processing my emotions and reactions of late is the best course of action. Ever go through anything like this? Sometimes it's good not to say anything at all. I felt like you should know I'm still processing.

Regardless of your circumstances, each day is full of obligations and opportunities to process life. A million things can happen in a day. A driver cutting us off, someone giving us a dirty look, or a reaction to our behavior or words can all fire up emotions and create experiences we need to step away from and process. If we don't process, it can alter our emotions and affect our attitude and reactions to others and life.

When I said earlier that my words might be judgmental, I mean that I've been harsh on myself and others for how we have acted or reacted. Yes, I'm getting bitter again about past situations and even about new ones. This is not my idea of progress, although this time I caught myself in the act. Thank God, He has woken me up. Perhaps I can prevent more hurt by being aware. How aware are you of yourself and what you are doing on a daily basis?

Anyway, God woke me up, and I'm typing at five in the morning and hoping I'm making sense. Pain on my right side from the old hernia surgery reared up a fight with me this week. Yesterday, it about defeated me, but I refuse to wave my flag. God has me in His all-powerful hands. To be clear—I will suffer through whatever comes with each pregnancy to meet the children God has made and will make in my womb. I'm not caving in to pain.

If God chose me for this path, then I will consider this pain to be training for what lies ahead. I'll continue to step aside and let His will be done despite struggling and losing small battles. God has my life! I will succeed only when He is in the lead!

Now for *The Love Dare* challenge—here's a quick wrap-up for days eight through twelve to catch up those interested!

The Love Dare: Day 8

📜 Tuesday, June 14, 2011: This day, as you read from the previous journal entry, was not as fun. I can now report the day got better; my emotions needed some maintenance. I did do what the book suggested and focused on my hubby's positive attributes. This made our date on Wednesday one of the best in a long time. Michael wasn't the reason I had a bad day on Tuesday, but he was the reason the next few days were a whole lot better. God really has given me a man I can love and who loves me unconditionally. I detected that when things weren't going well, I needed to shift my perspective to make the day better.

The Love Dare: Day 9

📜 Wednesday, June 15, 2011: I was supposed to greet my

spouse today with a smile and enthusiasm, plus differently than before. Well, I thought about Michael's previous comments regarding me dressing up for other things and not him. So, for a spontaneous date night with my hubby, I got dolled up and felt as sexy as this pregnant body could feel! When he got home from work, I was completely ready and surprised him. It was a very precious gift to see his reaction. I know the importance of doing this and not taking him for granted. It was a fabulous date. We spoiled ourselves with Mahogany Steakhouse—a heavenly meal! Dating is a must to keep our relationship strong. I am completely in love with him and grateful that prioritizing is finally paying off for my marriage!

Greeting people positively—even those I currently struggle with—is something I need to work on. I have tried it with a couple of people, and it's paying off. I feel like my attitude toward some people is finally tipping to the positive side. Yay—it's about time!

The Love Dare: Day 10

Thursday, June 16, 2011: Day ten is rich in discussion about unconditional love and how choosing it helps a relationship last longer. I wish I could spell out all the mini lessons within each daily lesson.

Today, I got to do something special by encouraging my hubby to play golf because he loves to do it. It was easy, especially since God decided I need to spend some quality time with others. I got to eat dinner with my girls from The Phoenix Experience Bible Study Group—I love my fellow Christian sisters.

My hubby got to play more golf—guilt free—enjoying it all without any worry about what I was doing. This in and of itself was a gift he appreciated. I think it's important for spouses, friends, and family to have their separate time—but not too much time and dependent upon the activity! A couple of us got to see a free concert at Rhema Bible Church, which included my all-time favorite artist from this past year, Kari Jobe. The praise and worship was incredible. The charismatic crowd was almost too much for this soul, but it was fun. Hearing Kari sing the songs I sang in the shower, the car, or in the hospital—even to Lilian Grace—triggered tears, causing buckets to pour from within.

I've mentioned several of her songs in my previous entries, but during one of the songs, I found myself feeling like a professional singer—though I am not. Belting out the words with her, I let raw emotions loose as the band played and Kari sang. Unknowingly, I needed this concert for another layer of healing. It reminded me God is really for me and helping me see who He is!

At the end of the concert, I made a wonderful connection between Lilian Grace and "The Who." Both of my babies got to hear Kari Jobe's angelic voice live in the womb—totally God. He orchestrated two beautiful moments so my babies and I could worship Him together with the same artist. He coordinates down to the details! I can't wait to share with "The Who" later in life all they have in common with their sister. That's important!

The Love Dare: Day 11

Friday, June 17, 2011: In all our relationships, we need to remember that how we treat other people affects us. Our reactions and actions toward each person bear consequences. If we realized we were attacking ourselves when we attack others, would we do it? Perhaps it would make us think twice before lashing out. Our relationships would be better for it!

I did do a small act of kindness for Michael and a couple of others. It was nice! And then I needed some downtime. I took a "me" moment in the afternoon and watched four episodes from a favorite series of mine. It was guilt-free and wonderful. I think "me" time is a must (especially for those who put everyone else ahead of themselves), but it's not something that should get in the way of life. It's meant to happen but in moderation. I say this because it's tempting to take too much "me" time, which can be hurtful to others.

The Love Dare: Day 12

Today—well, I just got done reading today's dare. I can see why God woke me up early to catch me up. Today is about demonstrating love by willingly choosing to give in to an area of disagreement between you and your spouse. It affirms a few decisions we made this week. Even this morning when I was determined to go through whatever each pregnancy brings me, I know it's right since we both desire to have children. No, it's not an easy path by any means. To some it may sound like a horror movie at times because of our journey and my health scares—but growing our family is important to us. I am putting my hubby's preferences first, which is a nice change from my own.

This week *The Love Dare* has been about prioritizing and putting my spouse first, which has been helpful. I'm even looking at some of my other relationships to see how I can apply this to make them better. I love this verse from today: *"The wisdom that is from above is first pure, then peaceable, gentle, willing to yield"* (James 3:17 NKJV). Now that really is the best love advice from the Bible, as the book suggests!

From all of this, I hope you see that life is worth living.

If you are bored, you may not be living life to the fullest. If your life is in turmoil, roll up those sleeves and get to work on the areas that are most in need of repair and attention. I love that you all continue to read the words I type.

Before Michael left early for his first of two golf tournaments today, he asked if I was okay because I was working on another CaringBridge post. I love that he gets it when God wakes me up at a crazy hour. He understands I am brain dumping on my phone when God says it's time. He is present and aware of what's going on. He knows my tail end would not be up at five in the morning for the fun of it, especially during pregnancy! Michael will be the first to say he's only read a few of my CaringBridge posts. I do hope when this all gets published that he will read it and appreciate how far God has brought us. I never thought I'd still be typing on here, but God's not done with this journal project yet.

Enjoy this amazing Saturday! I've been typing this entry for almost three hours now, which is not unheard of for me and my entries. I never feel like I've been working that long though. Time doesn't exist when He's got me in the zone. Thanks for hanging in there with me. Be blessed and take time to inventory the blessings He has bestowed upon you today, even if you feel like it's not a good day!

JUNE 19, 2011

173 › Father's Day

Father's Day—wasn't it just yesterday? Nope, it's already been a year. I want to say one thing about my own father before reflecting on my husband. My daddy taught me how to stay when the going gets the hardest it can ever get. Without his example, I wouldn't be who I am today nor as successful. I thank God for giving me such a fabulous and amazing daddy. I love my daddy so much. I may not get to talk to him every day, but I think of him almost every day.

Thanks, Dad, for being the example I needed to get me through the hardest battles of my life thus far. You have also shown me how to be a hard worker, a goofball, and exactly who I am. Thank you! Thank you! Thank you!

My husband's turn. I could not ask for a better daddy for my children. I know Lilian Grace was completely enthralled by him. He captivated her, and there are many beautiful pictures of him and her. I love staring at the two of them in those moments we captured. I was blessed to be a spectator of their relationship. Together they took my breath away. I wish Lilian Grace could be here with Michael this Father's Day, but I know our heavenly Father is using her for a higher purpose.

No other man could fill my husband's shoes. Like military comrades, we've bonded on battlefield after battlefield over the past ten years, fighting side by side. He has my back, and I have his. More importantly, no other man could be the man my husband has been and will be for our family.

When he signed up on our wedding day, I knew he was clueless about what he was getting into. God made him really special—an amazing husband and father to take care of me and our children. Unless a man has lost a child, he will never know how much strength it takes a father to keep stepping forward. I'm blessed that he does this daily.

Michael is courageous and worthy—a true warrior created by God. He is the kind of man, husband, and father who could run circles around other men. I pray God continues to guide and direct him all the days of his life. I know Lilian celebrates how special her earthly daddy is. Please look up a poem titled "A Real Father" by Joanna Fuchs. It's perfect for Lilian or any child to give to their father.

I hope each of you enjoys this special day dedicated to honoring our fathers. You may be without yours now, but know that on the day you were born, he was one proud daddy. If you had an absentee father, know there is a man named Jesus who loves you so much he died for you. And we can't forget our heavenly Father—without Him, we would be nothing. I praise my heavenly Father on high! No words can ever describe how glorious He is and how thankful I am to be His daughter.

No matter what your day looks like today, your heavenly Father is holding you, walking beside you, and leading you through it. He loves us unconditionally and teaches us how to be better than we are. Love to all the amazing Christian men in my life.

PS: This photo is one of many showing Lilian Grace and her daddy sharing an incredible moment. It looks like she's whispering a secret straight from God or giving her daddy some major props—either possibility puts a huge smile on my face, as well as her daddy's! This may beat their bath time photo for most precious. I'm eternally grateful and happy knowing my daughter has an amazing daddy on earth and in heaven.

I can't wait till "The Who" meets Michael. I know Lilian Grace has already been whispering to her sibling about him. "The Who" will not be disappointed. Their daddy will show so much unconditional love—goosebumps! Is it October or November yet? The thought of it all leads this wife and mother to believe everything is going to be all right—come what may—for God designed my life and gives me everything I need to live each day! PRAISES!

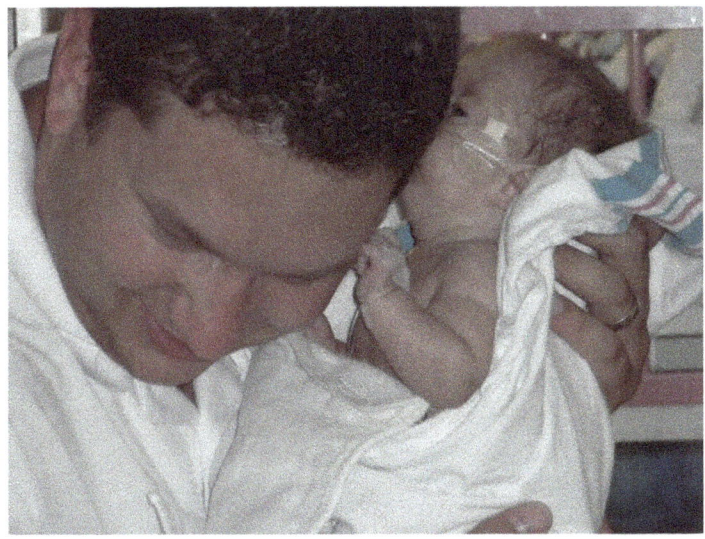

Sweet whispers

Finally taking time for me

JUNE 29, 2011

174 › Fighting Rules & Priorities

A week has zoomed by overloaded with activities. *The Love Dare* challenge has been working despite crazy minor hiccups and not-so-fun moments of disagreement.

The Love Dare: Day 13

Sunday, June 19, 2011: I figured Michael wasn't ready for today's dare, so I decided to write out my own rules in regard to disagreements.
1. *I will stop talking and listen more before responding to Michael.*
2. *I will think about my own issues and trauma before reacting or responding to him.*
3. *I will watch my tone and remember to keep bitterness and anger at bay.*

These seem simple, yet they are not—especially when I am passionate about something. I will be practicing these frequently for the rest of my life. How do you fight with those in your life? I know in the past couple years I have been way too passionate and angry while arguing with family members (I'm not referring to Michael). Here's to hoping the fighting fades away!

The Love Dare: Day 14

Monday, June 20, 2011: I read this Love Dare on my way to Eureka Springs, Arkansas. My college girlfriends and I finally got together for a girls trip after years of waiting. We had a wonderful spa experience. I will admit I'm the worst at relaxing, but I really am getting the hang of it. I had a fabulous ninety-minute massage and a deluxe pedicure. It's important to take care of myself. It helps my mood and makes me a more pleasant person to be around!

The opening paragraph really hit me in today's reading about leading and not following your heart. Your feelings and emotions should not be in charge of the direction you go. Too many of us let our hearts lead, which can lead to false and ever-changing decisions, situations, and mistakes. I want to love my husband every day, even on days when he makes it hard to like him.

The Love Dare: Day 15

Tuesday, June 21, 2011: Today was about honor! There are two sections in the book that are worth reading. Check it out at the library or buy a copy! Reading these entries will grab your attention and make you think. The first one is true for any relationship. It's about honoring others by respecting them and esteeming them highly in the way you treat them.

The second one is for married couples. It made me rethink some things I do on a daily basis. It's about giving your spouse more commitment than you give anyone else. As far as my commitments, Michael takes a back seat a lot of the time. I've been trying to make him number one recently, but it's hard.

I'm starting to value his opinions before others' unless I agree with others. It's tough to give and take, but with me intentionally taking his opinion into consideration more often, he plays a bigger role in my life.

The Love Dare: Day 16

Wednesday, June 22, 2011: Today was about trying to change our spouse or others. We spend much of our time trying to change everyone instead of accepting them for who they are. I've worked on this one for many years. I do accept people for who they are, but if our points of view are on opposite ends of the spectrum, I limit my time with them. This doesn't mean I love them any less. It just means we have different morals and values. I enjoy this stuff, and they enjoy that stuff. It's okay to be different.

Today's *Love Dare* is focused on prayer. I believe in the power of prayer, especially when you and God are lined up right. He provides so much for me and others in my life. I find myself praying for the littlest things, like for my cooks to be blessed and make the best burger. I prayed for safety on our girls trip, that we'd make wonderful memories, and especially that we would receive the best massages and pedicures. God made it amazing! Now I'll be praying for God to move in areas of my husband's life and others' and for our relationships. It's extremely important to hand it all to God because we are far from perfect. No relationship is either.

Tomorrow I'll post days seventeen through twenty-one. I hope you are enjoying these recaps. I love you all!

Lily's legacy at work

JUNE 30, 2011

175 › Processing Wins

Just when I think I'll write another entry, a random distraction pops up and takes priority. We all tend to lose focus of what we're trying to accomplish while time slips away quickly. When I last posted, I had planned to post the next day, but here I am almost a week later. Wow—it just doesn't seem possible. Here are highlights from days seventeen to twenty for *The Love Dare* and miscellaneous adventures.

The Love Dare: Day 17

Thursday, June 23, 2011: This is more of a private dare for today. It's about protecting what your spouse tells you. I decided I'd pull a Scripture from the reading that reminds us that God knows every detail of who we are—secrets and all—even things we don't know about ourselves yet. And yet, He still loves us deeply. *"You know when I sit and when I rise; you perceive my thoughts from afar. You discern my going out and my lying down; you are familiar with all my ways. Before a word is on my tongue you, Lord, know it completely"* *(Psalm 139:2–4).*

The Love Dare: Day 18

Friday, June 24, 2011: I've been cooking again! I know it's something that should happen fairly often, but I had a brain block about it. I have to admit, Michael is a way better cook than I am. I think he could open up a restaurant and be wonderful at it. On the other hand, I'm impatient about trying to get everything going at the same time—a challenge with my ADHD! I am starting to learn to meal prep and such, so we shall see how long this lasts. I am having fun though. Is there something keeping you from being adventurous? Are you stuck in a rut with your daily chores? I'm learning to make special moments with my hubby and others by slowing down and seeing what makes them tick. Try it! It gets interesting!

Fourteen months mark another one of Lilian's monthly birthday anniversaries. I wish she could have been here to celebrate and experience the tremendous day her daddy and I had at the Waggles for Wyatt Golf Tournament Fundraiser. I had a blast with my sweetheart. I just can't thank God enough for giving me such a magnificent man to call mine. What better way to celebrate our daughter than together—both laughing and talking while helping another trisomy family! He got to play golf, and I got a tan—a wonderful, effortless compromise! He was a good sport about letting me take pictures. I think we entertained the other two team members who were part of our scramble. I did not touch the golf clubs, but maybe I will one day.

We finally got to meet lil Wyatt (a baby with trisomy 16q chromosomal disorder) along with his parents, Josh and Jackie (Griffith), and other family members. This couple is just as incredible and super as the other ones I've met who are or have been on a similar journey. I thank God for giving me opportunities like this to be surrounded by His people. I just love the energy they have.

What's cool is that the Warrior Princess Foundation finally got to help out a family! This is hopefully just a small beginning. I look forward to watching the foundation grow and be able to help in larger ways to reduce the financial burden this special journey creates for families.

The Love Dare: Day 19

📜 Saturday, June 25, 2011: Today's love dare focused on unconditional love from within us—impossible for us alone, yet through God we can come close to having unconditional love for others. These verses from the book are great:

"Love comes from God" (1 John 4:7).

"Apart from me [Jesus] you can do nothing" (John 15:5).

"If you remain in me [Jesus] and my words remain in you, ask whatever you wish, and it will be done for you" (John 15:7).

"Now to him who is able to do immeasurably more than all we ask or imagine, according to his power that is at work within us" (Ephesians 3:20).

The takeaway is we cannot love others on our own. When we are right with God, His unconditional love flows through us, which sounds pretty good to me. God, please love on others through me!

The Love Dare: Day 20

📜 Sunday, June 26, 2011: Halfway point—I'm still cooking and loving it. The only problem is I need to cut recipes in half. It's okay to eat leftovers once, but after a few times this momma and hubby need a change-up! Michael and I continued to hang out today. We always have a good time shopping together because we both love seeing how creative people can be.

Today was a big step for us both. We went to Buy Buy Baby, and we are totally in love with that store. It was heartwarming to watch Michael get excited again over baby stuff, especially the high dollar, super cool, engineered gadgets. It was a relief to confirm we are on the right track and God is healing us one scar at a time. Praise His name forevermore!

As far as today's dare goes, it focuses on getting yourself right with God and knowing Jesus sacrificed everything so we can live. It's a dare to take God at His word and place our trust in Him. When we are right with Him, everything else in life starts falling into place. I'm not saying life won't change for better or for worse. I'm saying that with Him in the center, you'll be able to conquer whatever hits you!

Powerful in every way!

The Love Dare: Day 21

Monday, June 27, 2011: This has to be one of my favorite readings from *The Love Dare*! We do need God every single day—round the clock. My weapon in surviving everything thus far in my life is God. Some things sidetrack or sideline me temporarily, but I ultimately remember that I need Him. When I am in sync with God, I can make it through anything by leaning on and trusting Him!

I can't help but use the verses from today's reading. I wish I could tattoo them on my heart to remember that He is who and what we need in every trial we encounter.

"Do not be anxious about anything, but in every situation, by prayer and petition, with thanksgiving, present your requests to God. And the peace of God, which transcends all

understanding, will guard your hearts and your minds in Christ Jesus" (Philippians 4:6–7).

"I know what it is to be in need, and I know what it is to have plenty. I have learned the secret of being content in any and every situation, whether well fed or hungry, whether living in plenty or in want. I can do all this through him who gives me strength" (Philippians 4:12–13).

"And my God will meet all your needs according to the riches of his glory in Christ Jesus" (Philippians 4:19).

"Take delight in the LORD, and he will give you the desires of your heart" (Psalm 37:4).

Have you tried to find someone who can fulfill all your needs? Have you failed? Stop looking—God is the only One who can completely satisfy! Praying you are allowing God to guide your life in every way! You are loved and treasured by Him always!

Blowing bubbles can cause change.

JULY 1, 2011

176 › Be the Change

The best feeling involves letting go of anxiety and catching up on things you want to accomplish! Yesterday, I did it—I caught up, and I hope it stays that way. Here are the *Love Dare* challenges I haven't posted yet. I hope you are enjoying these entries and growing. If you haven't started *The Love Dare*, I highly recommend it and encourage you to participate.

We all get stuck complaining about how things need to change, but we neglect the idea that change starts with us. When we do the work, things start to change for the better. When we are happy and content with ourselves, people will want that for themselves as well. It's a great fire to start in our relationships—the fire of happiness and contentment.

The Love Dare: Day 22

Tuesday, June 28, 2011: Today is my parents' thirty-sixth wedding anniversary, and yesterday was my daddy's fifty-fifth birthday. I have watched my parents go through many trials, tribulations, and victories. The last few years have been rough on all of us, but I remember growing up and learning that you fight alongside your family to survive whatever comes your way. You don't run away! You stay and face it together—doing whatever you can to make the most of the situation.

Today's *Love Dare* deals with loving your mate (or anyone else in your life) without expecting love in return.

Talk about a tough one to live out. There's a section at the end that got me thinking more about my broken relationships that need closure. The writer encourages you to give undeserved love because Jesus gives it to us all the time.

Gulp. This made me stop and take a deep breath, swallowing hard while heartache set in, because I know this is not how I am in several of my relationships. *The Love Dare* is helping me search, find, and conquer those dark spots in my heart. Do we publicly display our gratefulness to God for loving us? Just a question to ponder. I know I have a long way to go on that.

The Love Dare: Day 23

Tonight, Michael and I gathered with my immediate family—my brother, sister-in-law, niece, nephew, and sister—to celebrate my daddy's birthday. I prayed that our time together would be blessed. Like I said before, in the the last few years, or even more, there have been countless crazy moments, heartaches, and joys. We were hit hard year after year. Life turned upside down and became unpredict-able, making it hard to adjust.

For the first time in a long time, I am happy to share that I feel we've come full circle—stronger, better, happier, and changed. It took time; we couldn't speed through it.

I thoroughly enjoyed watching my daddy stand before us and share his emotions and thoughts with all us kids and grandkids. It brings happy tears knowing we will survive as long as God is our center. Nothing or no one will ever be perfect, but I'm proud to say we are strong! Praise God to infinity for all the healing! I look forward to my other relationships being the best they can be through God!

Today's love dare is about removing anything that

makes it hard for relationships to be healthy. I'm getting better at adjusting and changing my priorities and schedule, but I still have moments of overload. Earlier today, I caught up with some important people in my life via the phone. It is important to make time for those you love.

God couldn't have given my daddy a better present than time spent blowing up fireworks with his little family unit. It was magical and exceeded my expectations. I love how God works!

The Love Dare: Day 24

Thursday, June 30, 2011: Today's dare is about lust. This is the area that bothers me the most. Poor Michael has to deal with my insecurity—thinking he could snap one day and end up having an affair. I've tried to work on this over the years, but sometimes I still worry, even though he's never given me reason not to trust him.

Early in our marriage and throughout, I've been aware that either of us are capable of falling prey to chemistry we might have with someone else. Admittedly, I've had a few friendships that needed boundaries because something could have happened if I had been willing at the time. Thank God for always making sure I have an escape or out when temptation comes calling.

I've always been the type to love people quickly. I genuinely love people. I'm an open book, so I tend to bond with people quickly. This is okay with female friends, but when it's a male (for me)—not so good. I've been honest with Michael when I am attracted to a gentleman so he knows to pay attention. I've gotten smarter about screening and protecting current and future friendships with the opposite sex.

Since no one is perfect, I try not to speak of my marriage in a bad way nor spend any alone time with the opposite sex. It's good protection. I always want to remember that I am not above sinning. I'm careful to stay away from situations where sin is a temptation. I see all around me how destructive lust and sinning is—the damage is permanent and hurtful for those involved. I hope all of us allow God to guide our steps away from anything destructive.

The Love Dare: Day 25

Friday, July 1, 2011: July! Really, July? I can't seem to wrap my head around it. This year is passing by at warp speed, which to a preggo is awesome! Michael and I will welcome our baby in October with loving, open arms. As we draw closer to God through the pregnancy, our excitement builds. I have the giddiest feeling knowing He has chosen us to be parents to another one of his angels on earth! YAY!

Today's love dare is the one I was dreading the most because I knew it would come up eventually—forgiveness! We all struggle with forgiveness. When it comes to my marriage, I hope I don't hold anything against my hubby indefinitely. When it comes to other relationships, I struggle with forgiveness more than any other issue.

I've held onto some hurts and wrongs done to me. In entries from the past year, I have shared about my anger and resentment. Anything shared was the tip of the issue. Some of it is deep-rooted and disturbing. I long to say honestly that I have forgiven everyone.

I'm working with God on this. I've had small breakthroughs, but they are mini ones. I need to make more progress. An analogy in today's reading hit home. It was about seeing the people in your life in a prison-like setting.

The prison represents a room in your heart where we are caged with others in our life. Our bitterness, hurts, unforgiveness, and anger, when left to fester, imprison us. I want freedom. I don't want to be trapped, imprisoned. He meant for each of us to be free.

Reading the rest of this chapter alone is worth the price of the book. It reveals what unforgiveness is doing to each of us. The hurt I see every day in myself and others usually stems from unforgiveness. I guess it's time I step up and start forgiving. Though not easy, the end result is beautiful and freeing—worth forgiving others and releasing my grudges to God. What about you? Are you being held captive by being unforgiving?

On another note, I was able to blow bubbles for a precious angel baby, Emalee Graycen Whaley, tonight. She was born a year ago. Please join me in lifting up her family and friends. Today was bittersweet for them, celebrating without her physically here on earth. Michael and I celebrated our precious Lilian Grace with over a hundred people just a couple of months ago.

Grief is hard, and it doesn't necessarily get easier over time, but the love, grace, and mercy my heavenly Father gives me will provide me with rest and make it bearable. God made Lilian's birthday wonderful with the Warrior Princess Trail Run event. We're excited that many of you have already volunteered to be a part of it next year. It's humbling and exciting! Praise God for turning something so tragic into something so fabulous and incredibly beautiful!

Our little firecracker

JULY 5, 2011

177 › Eleven-Month Angelversary

Firecrackers sound like bombs going off in our ears, but their beautiful colors light up the night sky with sparkles. Lilian Grace was our little firecracker. She rumbled into our lives and blessed us with the beautiful colors of her life. What colors are you displaying to those around you?

Michael and I slipped away to Kansas City on Saturday to hang out together, then finished the trip visiting good friends of the family (the Martins) and their newest arrival. The shopping was fun, and we found "The Who" the exact stuffed toy rabbit Lilian had but in chocolate brown this time. YAY! Now we won't be tempted to give up Lily's rabbit to the newest member—they have their own!

The food was incredible as always at The Plaza. I'm normally not adventurous in my food choices, but Kansas City somehow gets me to venture out—and I am never disappointed. DELICIOUSNESS—enough said!

Now to update you about my experience with *The Love Dare*.

The Love Dare: Day 26

Saturday, July 2, 2011: Today talks about our personal responsibility. I know I get in my own way all the time. I've learned through the years to look at myself first, then at everything else before trying to decide where things went wrong. This is a valuable lesson I continue to learn, because as a human, I often forget. We tend to blame someone else the first chance we get.

I love how the book talks about pride, humility, and honesty. Pride is our number one enemy. It can cause so much damage. I'm praying God will help us all to be more humble than prideful!

The Love Dare: Day 27

📜 Sunday, July 3, 2011: Today is about encouraging. We can show love to our spouse and others by giving them space to be themselves. Something that caught my attention was not projecting my all-or-nothing personality onto Michael. He is his own person. I'm sharing two important Scriptures that speak to encouraging anyone in our lives:

"Strengthen the feeble hands, steady the knees that give way" (Isaiah 35:3).

"Therefore encourage one another and build each other up, just as in fact you are doing . . . encourage the disheartened, help the weak, be patient with everyone" (1 Thessalonians 5:11, 14).

The Love Dare: Day 28

📜 Monday, July 4, 2011: Today's dare is about sacrifice. The main question to ask others every day is "How can I help you?" This is a great question not only for our spouses but for our children, families, close friends, and coworkers. The book reminds us to notice others' needs and try to meet them. *"'For I was hungry and you gave me something to eat, I was thirsty and you gave me something to drink, I was a stranger and you invited me in, I needed clothes and you clothed me, I was sick and you looked after me, I was in prison and you came to visit me'" (Matthew 25:35–36).*

If we are honest, we think too often about what others can do for us, instead of vice versa. Love means sacrificing. We aren't always going to be in the best mood to help or be there for someone. I'm learning to help with a sacrificing heart within reason because it's important!

For Independence Day, Michael and I saw my big Cooper and Poteet clans—what a blessing! It's been two years since we attended the July 4 family festivities. I even got to see one of my great-grandfather's nephews again. I love listening to him. It sends me straight back to when I was nine years old, hearing my great-grandpa talking and laughing—good memories!

The Love Dare: Day 29

Tuesday, July 5, 2011: Love's motivation is today's theme in *The Love Dare*. It talks about obeying your parents and the motivation behind it before love and respect carry on to your spouse. I love how the reading emphasized the importance of looking to God for our motivation in love and life. One verse stood out to me: *"Whatever you do, work at it with all your heart, as working for the Lord, not for human masters" (Colossians 3:23).*

When I think about ultimately working for the Lord, it puts everyday life in a different perspective and motivates me to do my best. The book mentions how to honor the Lord. Think about how much you are honoring God in how you love. Does this thought kindle happiness or sadness? Slow down and ponder how love is hard. The last sentence in today's reading reminds us of the heights we can go to when we love others like God loves them.

Now on to what today is—an eleven-month angelversary celebration! My baby girl, our lil missionary, celebrates eleven months in heaven. I admit this post is being typed before July 5. I can't seem to stop typing these days. Eleven months on July 5, 2011. I don't know if this feeling will ever completely go away. Perhaps I don't want it to go away—the feeling that she was here recently is comforting. But our journey with her is over in a physical sense, and another chapter without her has begun.

We all lose people at some point in our lives but, for me, losing a child ranks the highest as the worst thing to live through. God created a beautiful bond between a mother and child starting inside the womb. My child felt like an extension of my heart outside my body. When a child dies, so does some of the mother's heart, because they are forever and eternally linked as God made it to be.

Do I remember everything from the past year? No, I've crammed in a lot and been in survival mode, hoping I don't crack or lose any more of my heart, soul, or self. God has given me new eyes and the desire to make Lilian's life a legacy to be proud of—a mission that can be continued by any of us as we live out the journeys God graciously chose for each of us.

I have a month before the reality of a year gone by hits. I have much to look back on and smile about through the tears that come and go daily. God has blessed me abundantly with adventures for healing, changing, and moving in the direction He's leading me. I can't lie and say I wouldn't trade it for the world. I would trade it in a heartbeat to feel Lilian against me or see her gorgeous smile in front of me.

I'm posting a photo from Lilian's first doctor appointment. It looks like Lilian is thanking God for all the things. The fact is, when comparing my two children through ultrasounds, Lilian never should have been able to live. By God's miraculous ways, she got to be here. When I see this photo, I like to think she is praising God for getting to live out her mission so all of us could be changed for the better. It's like God let her see a snapshot of us and she was thanking Him—knowing that enduring her pain and suffering was worth it.

Joy and praises to God for making us a family!

I pray that all of us are half as strong as Lilian Grace was for us. If we were all so determined to glorify God with our lives, I think it would make our heavenly Father proud. Don't let life get you down and flustered to the point you miss His love and the blessings He's bestowed upon you. I'm not able to see Lilian Grace again on this earth nor the children that could have been ours before her, but I will see them one day in heaven. How amazing that will be!

Dear Lilian Grace, my most precious gift from God,

A year ago, you were all dressed up and taking pics with fireworks brought by a dear friend (Sandra Burton). You were precious in every way as you wore your red, white, and blue proudly. Again, I find myself thanking you for all the precious moments you fought for so your daddy and I could enjoy them.

Another month and we will celebrate a year since you jumped into the arms of Jesus. That day is forever tattooed on my heart, soul, and mind. I'm glad God's been gracious in giving me all those other memories we share. Your brother or sister will be here in no time. I pray I will be what he or she needs—like I prayed I could be for you.

I'm thankful for all the lessons God taught me through you. I hope each month you are in heaven gets sweeter and sweeter and sweeter. I dream about joining you one day and know it will be an even bigger celebration for us both. I am forever linked to you through God. He gave me a feeling I will never forget. You made me a better person, better than I'd ever be without you!

I'm still in awe of you and your abilities. Your daddy and I are still mesmerized by all of you. I know of more angels who have joined you lately. Show them the ropes up there and remind them to come down and visit their families every now and then.

I love you to the moon and back and for all eternity. The broken pieces of my heart are mending, but I will never forget you.

Love,
Your Grateful Mother,
Chrissy

> PS: "Precious Child" by Stowegood caught my ear from her album On Angel's Wings. My dreams had to alter when you left. I've been letting go of the dreams of seeing you dance in a tutu or swim around the pool like a water baby. My dreams now consist of you being alive and well yet never here. A bright light always surrounds you when I dream of you.

I highly recommend this song for a grieving parent. It covers many facets of grief. I long to hold my baby girl another day. My feelings are still fresh, and I'm not sure how I will navigate them once I have another child. God will reveal it all in time. Do yourself a favor and listen to this song. It will bring comfort and tears wrapped in love.

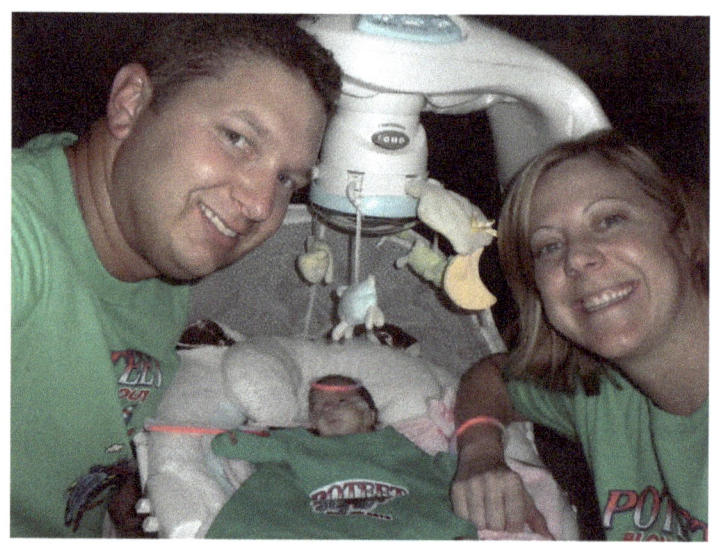

Forever celebrating our Warrior Princess

JULY 6, 2011

178 › Treasurable

Yesterday and today have been vastly different for me. Yesterday, I was on my last leg, tired and grumpy, trying to stay above water. After ten hours of sleep, I am happier and awake today—swimming strong in the water. I'm getting chores and to-dos accomplished. PRAISE GOD! I'm reminded how sleep is essential for life. If we don't sleep, others know and wish we did!

I watched *The Bad Mother's Handbook* during my downtime this afternoon. I cried and cried and cried as I reflected on my attitude toward everything. Sometimes you don't know how God is working, but He is.

I know it's not a Christian movie, but it did challenge me. In my life, God has moved me to a happier place. Though there are times I can't see the happy ending, I know He's working it out while I get out of His way. I need to work on my definitions of success and failure to strengthen and change my outlook!

Now back to *The Love Dare*.

The Love Dare: Day 30

Today is about unity. God demonstrates unity, togetherness, and oneness through the Trinity, in His Word, and across creation. When Michael and I are on the same page, everything works better and smoother, and we are happier. I want to ensure we have a oneness that can't be broken. Sadly, so many suffer loss through divorce—it can happen to anyone.

Being unified with others means being part of a community. There are boundless benefits to working with others in my family, church, and work. Without unity, things get messy. Do you feel unified with your spouse and those around you?

Okay, I have ten days to go in *The Love Dare,* and I confess I'm wearing down. It's been a heavy load of mental work but worth the results. My relationship with my husband is moving in a positive direction, and we are benefiting immensely. I'm involving him in my decisions more than before.

A word of caution: you can't skimp on time. You must give each other time to think through and do each exercise. I asked Michael the twenty questions in the back of the book while driving to Kansas City. He was a good sport and answered all of them—as did I. That experience was gold. I know where Michael is now, and that is priceless! He's an introvert at heart, so you can imagine how much he's winning the jackpot by marrying an extreme extrovert like me.

We get so wrapped up in the daily grind that time flies, and we wake up one day realizing that X number of years have gone by. Where did the time go? When did he or she change? Am I really where I want to be or should be? These and more questions come up all the time. I'm glad that after almost ten years together—and eight of those married—that we find ourselves living in the present.

Don't get me wrong—I sometimes catch myself holding him to who he was ten years ago. Although we've faced many of the same trials together, I'm finally learning we processed them differently. Those experiences have made us different people than we were on our first date. I'm praying we can keep up with each other because the past is gone and today is all we have. Treasure one another and avoid taking one another for granted. Distractions, time, and trials can rip couples apart. Discover and rediscover each other when needed to keep love alive—and avoid complacency.

Penguin Quest 2011

JULY 8, 2011

179 › Top Priorities & Front Seats

The Love Dare: Day 31

Thursday, July 7, 2011: Today's dare hit close to home. I remember as a child dreaming about my wedding day along with the kids God would bless us with. In those daydreams, reality wasn't welcome. A daydreaming child doesn't think about the hardships of life and the sacrifices they'll have to make when they get married. We had no clue as children—innocence reigned in the magic kingdom of Disney movies.

I want to make sure I'm where I need to be so I can experience the fullness of God and what He has for me in my daily walk. I hope I can keep my priorities straight in the fact that Michael and our children are first, then extended family, and lastly, everything else.

Praise God my husband hangs in there with me year after year. He frequently takes a back seat while others ride shotgun with me day to day. Not only have I put my family ahead of Michael, but my career, education, dreams, wants, needs, and priorities also frequently ride in my front passenger seat. God is patient, grace-filled, and merciful. I'm a proud family person, but I need to adjust the hierarchy since I'm married and soon we'll be parents to another child.

How are you doing in leaving and cleaving? If you are single or divorced, take advantage of the time you have to work on your goals and dreams. God may have someone right around the corner. You deserve to have all your ducks in a row—whether single or married. We often take our partners for granted. It's a blessing to have a companion for life. Each person deserves to be whole, happy, and graciously living out God's plan for them. Instead of fighting, griping, arguing, or being discontent, try to focus on getting yourself to a good place. It will improve your happiness and marriage!

Since I started making Michael my priority, we are both much happier. I have less guilt, and hopefully it will be nonexistent one day. I'm healthier and happier because I'm not torn trying to make everyone happy. God gives me permission to focus on my husband. I'm glad He gave me an affirmation today. I love and appreciate when He does that because I need them! It's how I know I'm getting something right—FINALLY!

I got approved to go on another road trip, so my little sis and I will be burning rubber this week to see a very close friend of mine, currently living in Florida. My brother and I were blessed to do a big road trip to Camp Orkila for my internship in Eastsound, Washington back in 2002, and I loved the adventure and memories we made. Now I pray my sis and I make as many memories on this trip. It'll be an adventure as always. I can't wait!

I can't forget to write about the wacky penguin statue adventure my girlfriend Joy (Arneecher) and I had today. I got it in my head that I wanted to find all the large penguin statues in Tulsa. There was a project fundraiser for the Tulsa Zoo back in 2002 for which local businesses purchased six-foot penguins to design and display. I felt like a kid again when we found them! And the designs were beautiful and creative. We got a list of locations from the Metro Chamber.

If you ever need something random to do and have no money, go on the penguin adventure. We got pictures with only five of the penguins but unraveled lots of history regarding the mysterious disappearances of many. There were sixty-five initially. I felt like a detective trying to unlock the secrets of where in the world did that penguin go. When I get back from my trip, Joy and I will resume our quest to take pictures with all sixty-five or at least learn the stories behind their locations!

Always be creative and adventurous in life. If you are bored, stop being bored. There's unlimited free entertainment in the world—you just have to think outside the box!

The Love Dare: Day 32

Friday, July 8, 2011: Today's challenge in *The Love Dare* is intimate—it's about sex. God designed sex to be a wonderful experience of oneness with our spouse. I'll leave it at that!

On another note, I want to thank all who commented on my guestbook, email, or Facebook. You all are always good at providing encouragement just when I need it most. As I share my random thoughts, my heart is healing. I know reading my entries isn't easy, but I feel led to share what God is teaching me. He's always trying to get our attention. I appreciate all of you who read and walk alongside me.

God is Bigger than we allow Him to be. May He continue to hold you while you walk with Him. I love you all!

Finding more penguins

JULY 17, 2011

180 › Bumps & Blessings

The movement in my belly feels different tonight. The lil bumps in my womb are energetic as "The Who" moves around inside. My sister has rain sounds playing on her phone, and the baby is loving it.

Growing another miracle inside of me a year later, after I thought it might not be possible, is mind-blowing. I'm realizing how deep God's love is and how amazing His miraculous ways can be. I've set so many limits on Him throughout the years when it came to my life. I'm glad those limits have never contained Him.

I've been extremely blessed to watch baby after baby be born this summer to families who were at their limit on waiting and trying. A negative result was their norm until now, when they are finally holding their own miracle in their hands—beautiful, handsome, and adorable in every way. For many, having babies comes naturally and easily and is trouble free. For the rest of us, trying to have a baby is disappointing and leaves us empty-handed time after time, but God has been tremendously generous giving each family their own miracle.

Praise God to the highest limit and beyond! Each baby photo makes me more ecstatic about meeting "The Who," no matter if they are a boy or a girl. I can't wait to meet another one of God's children whom He so graciously is letting me borrow. As I rest here in my thoughts and excitement, I get these overwhelming tears of joy, peace, and love. May God bless you in whatever you need right now! May He grant you the desires of your heart! Trust Him to bless you beyond anything you could ever want, hope, or need.

Sometimes—always—it's hard to wait for God's timing. That's coming from a girl who has wanted more than anything to be a mommy. I finally got to be one for Lilian Grace. Even though she had to return to her heavenly Father so soon, I still got a taste of motherhood and continue to be her mommy.

Now her little brother or sister will be here in less than sixteen weeks, and I hope this little miracle gets to stay longer. I have no clue what God has in store, but my desire is to watch them grow up and experience all God has for them!

This life—for me—hasn't always been an easy street, but I know God has my back. When you are at the end of your rope, let go and fall into His arms. Let Him carry you until you're able to walk next to Him. If it seems like nothing is working out right now, God's probably working to make the next part of your journey perfect and exactly what you need!

The past eleven months since Lilian Grace passed away have been a mix of hard days and healing moments. God has blessed me with opportunities to travel and work with others. This trip with my sister is yet another eye opener for me, revealing more of God's healing power.

I have three more days of this trip and four more days until I turn double-three. There are twenty-four more days till Lilian's one-year angelversary and 110 days, give or take, until "The Who" arrives. I find myself breathless and overcome by multiple emotions. It's all coming at a fast pace; I hope I find peace and joy in it all. My plans are never better than what God has in store for me. I wish I had more patience. Here's to hoping you and I remain in Him while trusting that He's working it all out for the good.

Now the crickets are sounding with the rain on my sister's phone. I picture myself with "The Who" on a porch swing, listening to a rainstorm as Lilian Grace watches from heaven's window. She's singing a lullaby to us—praying for goodness, strength, love, and courage. I feel blessed and surrounded by my angels—at peace and madly in love with my babies! God has given me the desires of my heart!

What a wonderful daydream! It's more of a reality than I could ever hope for. Did God really give me the desires of my heart? Yes—a husband who loves, protects, and provides for me and my children who give me the chance to be a mommy! He keeps providing in His time!

May you let the desires of your heart be daydreams that one day become reality, because your heavenly Father loves you and desires to provide them. Rest in Him and enjoy His love and protection every single day!

I will continue *The Love Dare* challenges when I return from my trip. Hope you all are trusting God in your walk! Love you!

328 Chrissy L. Whitten

Happy birthday to me

JULY 18, 2011

181 › Stripped Away

Saturday was my thirty-third birthday! I wasn't prepared for my emotions to run wild. I cried off and on the whole day. I kept it together when around others but afterward broke down in tears. You'd think one birthday with my daughter a year ago wouldn't have embedded itself so deeply into my heart and soul. I had thirty-one other birthdays when she wasn't here, yet one with her was all it took to make this next one unbearable.

It feels like my thirty-second birthday (from last year) just happened. I spent much of the day at the hospital with Lilian Grace. It felt like we were one step away from losing her forever. I remember going out with my girlfriends to eat and watch a movie—pumping when I could and trying to have fun away from my baby girl. Now and forevermore, I will have to be without her. Having her here was the greatest birthday wish come true! It only took one birthday with her to never want another birthday without her. Blowing candles and making wishes will continue but with a reminiscent mindset.

I know I can't bring her back—I just wish it didn't hurt so bad. The heart really is a funny compass. It can steer you in all sorts of directions. That's why it's important to lead it. Only having a few weeks left until we celebrate Lilian's first angelversary could be another reason I'm emotional. Oh, and there are the pregnancy hormones on top of all that.

Not only did "not having her" get to me, so did dealing with negative people. I've heard things from random people this past week, and I just have to say—maybe I shouldn't—I feel they could possibly be soldiers in the devil's army. You know who you are. If you haven't said a negative comment or been distasteful with your feedback about my grieving journey, this does not apply to you. I thank you for your awesomeness and compassion. I wish everyone were like you.

To those "devil warriors" here, I have a statement to share. If you have nothing but bad things to say about my journal entries or my life, then please stop reading it. No one is making you. I don't put a gun against your head to read this. I enjoy opening up so others can learn and walk with me. I'm not trying to say I know everything, nor have I gotten it all figured out. I'm trying to walk my journey and grow spiritually. So—again—if reading my stuff, seeing my pictures, or anything else related to me bothers you, please don't read it, look at my photos, or be around me.

I'm blessed by all the amazing people I get to spend time with. I communicate with them on the phone and in person. I don't need people who are life suckers in my life. I need honest people who genuinely love me and want me to be a better version of myself. I don't need unhappy people who want to drag me down with them. I want to keep living and learning through all circumstances.

As for the soap box, "Strip Me" by Natasha Bedingfield is the perfect song for those who judge and ridicule me. I'm constantly second-guessing myself and thinking I'm not enough. My brain rarely shuts off. Since Lilian died, I've been fighting the old and new versions of Chrissy.

If you strip me down to the bones, I'm broken and searching, too, for what really matters. When Lilian stripped my blinders, I started seeing life for what it is. I no longer care about things that just don't matter.

The negative people I mentioned prefer the old me. Which isn't surprising since I was easy to walk all over and take for granted. I bent over backward until my back broke.

I'm still Chrissy but more direct. I do what I say and say what I do. Who you see is who I am. No one can take away what God has done in my life and through my daughter. I'm not going back. This is who I am now!

Free to be me

Preggo on vacay

JULY 26, 2011

182 › Roots & Leads

I'm back from traveling and thought I'd finish up the mini summaries of *The Love Dare* for those who are patiently waiting. I love traveling, but I am officially retiring from travel until way after "The Who" arrives. It's been a jam-packed summer! Praising God and praying for things to be a little less hectic!

The Love Dare: Day 33

📜 Saturday, July 9, 2011: Today's entry takes us back to making sure your spouse is part of your decision making. I have failed many times with Michael on this one. If I didn't like his input or decision, I'd just do what I wanted and go on with it. Usually not a good idea. I'm trying to step aside and give Michael the reins. It sucks, but I know I should do it more.

During my time grieving, I've been able to hand over the reins more. I am not the same person I was before losing Lilian Grace. I think people forget how weak I really am. I know I've become stronger, but not as strong as you'd think. I'm more emotional (believe it or not) and short-fused. Making decisions is harder for me, and dealing with people is not my cup of tea. I'm hoping Michael leads and knows he gets more input than ever before.

The Love Dare: Day 34

📜 Sunday, July 10, 2011: Today is about celebrating godliness in your spouse. Michael has become a stronger Christian man over the past few years—PRAISE GOD! I rejoice that he has a relationship with God, which is the most important thing to me.

I celebrate him with the happiest heart because I know Michael is trying and it matters. When we are trying to walk the Christian walk, we sometimes forget we are sinners—mere humans. We're going to mess up and sin. I pray God guides our steps, helps us sin less, and makes us more like Him!

The Love Dare: Day 35

📜 The entry starts out describing the strength of sequoia trees, their endurance, and incredible growth. How amazing would it be if someone described me or my marriage as a sequoia tree? They stand firm and tall while growing stronger through each storm. The trunk of the tree is important, yet the roots underneath are what enable them to endure a long life.

I know I've talked about God as our foundation, but this is a great reminder. If God is your foundation, you can't be moved unless God decides to move you Himself. Be strongly rooted in the Word, and God can help you move any mountain that comes your way. God remains the reason why Michael and I have survived the last ten years together, especially through our journey with Lilian Grace and up to now. I pray we always keep Him as our center and foundation!

The dare talks about finding a marriage mentor during your walk through marriage. Sadly, it seems like good marriage mentors are few and far between. Here's to praying God will build up all the relationships in our lives so they can be shining examples for us. May our own marriage be an example for others.

The Love Dare: Day 36

📜 I love the verse in today's reading: *"Your word is a lamp for my feet, a light on my path" (Psalm 119:105).* I treasure this verse because it reminds me to be in the word daily, go to church, and walk my talk.

I don't read the Bible daily, yet I'm reading it more than I ever have. There's room for improvement. It's important to use your time wisely, so why not pick up the Bible or a Bible study guide and start feeding your soul? It will change your life! Haven't found a church yet? Don't give up. Your tribe is out there—keep searching. Always walk your talk to the best of your abilities, have integrity, and persevere.

I only have four more summaries to post for you tomorrow about *The Love Dare*. I hope you've enjoyed it. I've learned a lot from it myself. Always remember to keep learning, especially about yourself and others. Work on your relationships. We have room to grow until God calls us home. If you're not learning, you're not living.

The Love Dare in action

JULY 27, 2011

183 › Listen, Pray, Dream

Drum roll please—here's the final posting of *The Love Dare*! Yippee and praise God! Hope you enjoy the final four summaries.

Over the next couple of months, I'll post more entries about grieving. I've asked this before, but if you have any stories to share about how God changed your life through our journey with Lilian Grace, please post it in the guestbook if you have not. I want to include them. I love you all. Enjoy!

The Love Dare: Day 37

📜 Wednesday, July 13, 2011: Today's dare is about praying together on a daily basis. Michael and I don't pray together daily, but we do pray together often. One thing I love about prayer time with Michael, whether at church, home, or anywhere together, is that we hold hands. It reminds me that we are one with each other and God. Even after years of marriage, we still do this every time, and I hope we always do. I can't wait to add "The Who" to our tradition. I just love it!

I know praying together is very important. This is something I will be asking Michael to do more. We used to pray before most meals but got away from it. This is one practice that we need to bring back—even praying at night before going to bed. When was the last time you prayed with someone?

The Love Dare: Day 38

Thursday, July 14, 2011: Today's theme is that love fulfills dreams. It's about knowing what your mate would love to obtain, then helping them get there. This could work for my single friends too. It's hard to find extra time to turn a dream into reality. How can we encourage and help others achieve their goals? I enjoy a worthy project. I've always been a doer, yet my ADHD gets in the way sometimes. I've made a lot of to-do lists for my hopes, dreams, and projects over the last ten years. I'm bulldozing, cleaning, and accomplishing more now. I've decluttered my brain and created room for new hopes, dreams, and projects—just in time for "The Who" to arrive!

Love makes the world a better place. Are you helping your spouse seek bigger and better things—a better version of them? I'm tired of saying, "I'm going to do this or that," "I wish I could do that for him," or "I wish we could . . ." I'm ready to start living outside the box. I don't want to wake up one day and wonder where I went wrong or wish I had pursued my dreams.

The Love Dare: Day 39

Friday, July 15, 2011: *"Love never fails" (1 Corinthians 13:8).* This is a strong Scripture. Love never fails—we fail when love is not in us. Love is not something that comes and goes—it's a choice. We choose to love or not. Today is about writing a letter to your spouse to let them know you will love them until death. Loving someone no matter what they do or who they are is easier said than done. I pray that no matter what, I can love Michael until one or both of us leaves the earth.

Some of you didn't have a choice with your spouse. They

chose for you when they left. I pray your next marriage is a forever commitment filled with abundant love!

Remember that love is a choice. Enough said!

The Love Dare: Day 40

Saturday, July 16, 2011: The last day—praise God. This has been extremely challenging for me. There have been days I've soared and others I've failed. This is a resource I will use more than once in my lifetime. We are continuously changing as individuals, so we need to check in frequently with ourselves and our spouse to see where we are. If you don't know who you are, how do you expect others to know?

Today's challenge is to write out a renewal of our vows. For my single or divorced friends, write out a renewal about your commitment to God to work on yourself, your relationship with Him, and your relationships with those around you. When you allow God to heal you, His love will exist in you. We are all on a journey that requires dealing with drama, adjusting to change, committing to our faith and family, and walking toward the promised eternity God has for us.

I have not written the renewal yet. Michael and I plan to renew our vows at ten years, which will be December 2013. Until then, I'm choosing to love him no matter what and giving him the reins to lead our household. May God be with you at whatever point you are at in your journey, whether married, divorced, widowed, or single. God has hopes and dreams for you. He wants to give you the desires of your heart, so work on yourself and your relationship with Him—everything else will come in time!

340 Chrissy L. Whitten

Till death do us part

AUGUST 3, 2011

184 › Chipped Shoulder

I have decided to follow Jesus—no turning back, no turning back. I remember singing this song many years ago. I was young when I decided to follow my heavenly Father no matter where He leads. It's a desire that wells up and bursts out of my soul. Sadly, the devil battles me daily to wear me out. He wins more than I like to admit.

So I must be doing something right—if the devil feels so threatened by me he has to attack me that often. Hmm, interesting to say the least! It's a different perspective—knowing Jesus has led me so far, I am now a threat to the evil one. I'd like to say it's something I've accomplished, but it's not.

Truly, I pray that God's light shines through all the holes in my heart. The less there is of me, the more room there is for His glorious light to shine. If I could make this life less about me and more about Him, then I would feel like less of a failure. I'm successful when I step aside and let Him lead—it takes my breath away!

I'm working on accepting myself and others for who we are. As we get closer to "The Who" arriving, I'm realizing I have unfinished business with myself, projects, people, and more. I'm a doer, yet I tend to do only those things I want to do.

This summer has me doing projects I have put off for years. Do you have any? As I've been decluttering my mind, heart, and home, I've discovered hurts and pains that I've carried since I was a kid.

Though I had a fun-filled childhood, I've still accumulated disappointments, hurts, and pains throughout my thirty-three years. I guess we call that the infamous chip on the shoulder. I imagine that's normal, right? It would be interesting to see the size of everyone's chip!

That chip on the shoulder causes each of us to overreact to anything that reminds us of those disappointments, hurts, or pains. I know I tend to snap when someone gets close to my chip. I've noticed others do too.

I'm praying God removes the chip on my shoulder, which means the following to me:

1. Facing the past—good, bad, or indifferent.
2. Resolving those things discovered.
3. Releasing the hold they've had on me.
4. Forgiving myself and others.
5. Walking my journey without that chip on my shoulder. Being whole and happy without the grievances weighing on me.

It requires time and thought, but I don't want a year or twenty to pass and I still have this chip on my shoulder that makes me and everyone else miserable and bitter. Are you tired of it? I am!

A huge factor is that some of my issues are with people who are not ready to face the truth or hear it. Our realities are different. I've been looking through all my old pictures and memorabilia this week. I'm starting to see some stuff in a different light—some good and not so good. I can usually admit when I'm wrong. That's the first step. Remember when I wrote about theoretically putting your problem on a chair in the middle of a room, then walking around it to observe from all angles (book one, entry 34)? Well, I'm starting to write a list of what's in my head and heart. I'm going to look at each issue in the chair and walk around it to plan the best course of action.

Just saying "get over it" or "move on" is not going to work for me. Yep, I said it. Apparently, when you don't deal with life, it bites you big time in the rear! People explode, and everyone around them gets hit with the impact. People ignore you or are just done. Any of these and more don't resolve anything! You've got to find a way to make it right or bury the hatchet.

Going to a pastor or therapist can be helpful in more ways than one. I think many people look at that as being weak, but to me, if someone does this, they are stronger than any of us. After I get my projects done, which won't be long, I'll be heading back to the grief counselor to do some more work.

Until that time, I've got unfinished projects and books to read. I hope you realize it's never too late to start the healing process and transform your life from unhappy and unfulfilled to happy and fulfilled. God is waiting to heal each of us—starting with the tiniest hurts to the ginormous holes. I'm praying each of us makes a little progress every day.

How amazing would it be if we all were free of that chip on our shoulder and had whole hearts and happy souls? It would be grand! We sure could accomplish more for the Father's kingdom!

Now for this week—a week of realizing I have been on the grieving journey for a year exactly this Friday, August 5, 2010. A year? It just doesn't seem like it's been a year since Lilian Grace took her last breath here on earth. This past year has been filled with changing, adjusting, and healing—processing, processing, and more processing. Today, I can smile when I look in the mirror because I'm starting to see the me who God sees. It feels good to smile!

Yesterday, Michael and I had a radiology ultrasound at

the hospital. Lo and behold, the tech who scanned Lilian Grace greeted us. This was no coincidence. I believe it was a divine appointment along our grieving journey. She remembered us just as we did her. I tried to keep the tears back because this pregnancy is making me face my fear of reliving the trials we went through with Lilian Grace. I'm just thankful God keeps giving me the people I need to help me process it all. She was exactly who we needed to see. It was like God was reassuring us about our newest miracle while acknowledging our last one. I never get tired of remembering and talking about Lilian Grace!

I was blessed to have Dave, Michelle, Caeden, and Dash Anderson at our house last night and today. Their angel baby, Rhyder, is in heaven with Lily. I needed to see them more than I thought. The conversations we had were healing reminders and good prep for today! Thank you, Andersons, for coming and blessing us through this journey. It's important to share and learn!

Another dear friend, Sandra (Wright), spent the afternoon with me. We had some deep conversation that reminded me of what I've learned and what I still need to work on. She was with me the day we had to rush Lilian Grace to the hospital for her last visit. It was a crazy day; I was very thankful she was with us.

I didn't expect the week to be like this, yet only by God's hand did it play out so well. I knew I needed time with people, but I didn't know how, when, or who. I'm glad God made it happen. Tomorrow, Rachel (Foley) and I will go through Lilian Grace's belongings and treasures. I want to organize her things and give them another resting place in our home. I've put it off for a year. After doing some projects and feeling good afterward, I'm ready. Ready for what? I'm not sure. I'll always miss her, but I need to prepare our home to welcome another child too.

As a grieving mother, I cry tears of sadness because I miss Lilian and tears of joy for the child who will be joining our family. Grief is a path I wish on no one. It's a journey you can't relate to unless you've experienced it firsthand. I will say, though, that you don't have to relate to me to be there for me—that's the best advice I can give anyone. I want to feel like I'm not going crazy. I'm tired of correcting people. "The Who" will be my second baby—God willing. Lilian Grace will always be our first child. Nothing will change that.

Regarding Lilian's one-year angelversary on Friday, August 5, 2011, people have asked if we are doing anything special. Michael and I will be going on a special date with our children—one in heaven and one in the womb. We will eat like kings and queens while celebrating God's grace, love, peace, comfort, perseverance, guidance, and more during that special time together. This will be an annual tradition for our little family. I think it's fitting because when Michael and I sat holding Lilian as she left us, it was the three of us and God. Yes, we had staff watching us, but we were oblivious to them all. We were in our own little world as we said our goodbyes.

We appreciate you asking and walking with us to this point in our journey. I've thought of a few things you can do remotely with us on Lilian's special day if you'd like. We would love it!

1. Go out with your family and eat like kings and queens.
2. Wear the Lily T-shirt or any of her birthday colors: red, blue, green, black, and pink.
3. Say a prayer for all the trisomy families who have children here or in heaven.
4. Make a donation to The Warrior Princess Foundation.

Thank you for being with me as always through this journey. It's been a ride I wanted off of since it started, yet I'm so thankful for the experience. It's made me a better person and mother. The humbleness, the fire burning away the junk, and the realization I am not even close to being perfect were valuable lessons learned.

Life is precious, and tomorrow is not guaranteed. We can be called to heaven at any point. When it's our time, it's game over. I pray God comforts us through the journey and supplies our every need. More posts to come!

Just the three of us

AUGUST 4, 2011

185 › Before the Morning

"Before the Morning" by Josh Wilson is an essential song for this week. The grieving journey is up and down. I believe God is molding my hurts into something beautiful. Tomorrow, I get to share the fabulous poem that Lilian Grace's eye specialist wrote for us. It's perfect in every way. We just got it a few weeks ago.

I've decided to go ahead and post the letter I wrote to Lilian Grace on my birthday that was meant for tomorrow. That way I can write a fresh one on her actual angelversary! My birthday was tough for me. I was hurting and barely breathing, but I tried to keep moving.

I'm realizing there are good days, then there are bad ones. Rachel (Foley) and I started going through Lilian Grace's things in her keepsake chest and green Rubbermaid containers. We got the chest cleaned out and took snapshots of the items for her Shutterfly books that I will be doing soon. As we did this, I could remember everything about each clothing item she wore, toys she played with, and jewelry I slipped on her lil body. The smells, the people, and her reactions all flooded back.

When Rachel left, I had a panic attack. I took a nap to get myself back in order for the rest of my day. I have to remember I'm not Superwoman. I have limits and overwhelming emotions. I still have major processing to do. I can't tell anyone else how to do things, but I can suggest being brave enough to try to process life every day regardless of your situation.

As each item was folded up and placed into its resting place, I could feel the uneasiness tied to each item release. Talk about a strange feeling where my memory is a blessing by God's grace yet is scorched by the fires. God helps me remember the important takeaways as needed so I remember the significance of the battles—praise Him on high!

I'm not even close to being done yet, but I have time this month. My goal is to complete this project by the end of next weekend. People have asked me why I feel I have to do this. It's what works for me. I am fortunate to have Lilian Grace's cremains in our bedroom resting in a tiny, beautiful urn. It may seem crazy to someone else, but it helps me. Just like taking photos of all her stuff—I want to preserve all the memories I can.

I'm not sure which way this journey will take me tomorrow, but I know God has given me wonderful techniques and the ability to process and grow. All the hurt I've felt this past year since she left was meant to make a better way, life, and future. I accept what I cannot change and pray for the things I struggle to accept.

The letter I wrote to Lilian on Saturday, July 16, 2011, is below. Remember that I just needed to get it out. I'm only doing well at this point because God's got me in His arms. I felt it might be beneficial for you to see a darker side of my grief. Here's to releasing and getting it all out! Love you all!

Lilian:

I'm writing this to you on my thirty-third birthday. This morning I find myself processing a common statement that mommies say when they miss their earthly child(ren). They usually say something like, "I'm already missing my baby, and it's only been a few minutes or an hour. I don't know if I can make it for a blank amount of hours until I see him or her later today or tomorrow." I could go on and on, but the point is that they miss their babies. It's such a normal thing for a mommy, yet I see person after person who judges me or my other angel mommies when we can't figure out how to make the missing go away.

See, mothers with earthly children are cured in seconds once they pick up their child and love, kiss, and hug them from wherever they have been. For me (and other angel mommies), I'm never cured when it comes to you. Mommy doesn't ever get to see, hold, love, hug, or kiss you in person. I don't get to be with you. I wish there was something someone could invent to make this feeling go away.

It's been a year since I had to let go of you on earth physically, and not a day goes by that I don't have to face trying to shake the feeling of missing you so deeply. Naturally, other mothers with living children miss their child who is at the babysitter's, grandparents' house, camp, school, or wherever. I wish those negative people would consider how they would feel if missing their child was permanent—forever and without a choice. What if my child never gets to come back to me here on earth? Hopefully, it makes people think a little more when judging an angel mommy.

I know, Lilian, that I can't change the journey. I'm still trying to adjust, but today I find it harder after thinking about all these mommies who get to be mommies to earthly children. They miss them even when they will still get to see them. Well, I gave myself a break and realized that I'm doing better than I thought. It's natural to miss and want you because you are my baby forever.

It's a natural thing for a mother to miss her children when they are not present with them. Therefore, I accept that I will always miss you and wish I could see you and watch you grow. I just hope that missing you doesn't cause me to disappear into the nothing that tries to grab at me every so often.

God has been bigger than my imagination and understanding. He comforts me when things are good, bad, and indifferent. When the missing hurts more than I can bear, He picks me up into His arms and provides comfort and love as He holds me tight. I could not do this without Him. I would be nothing—nothing at all—without Him.

Sweetheart, I remember at three in the morning when the song "No Air" blasted from my phone as you were leaving us. I sat there almost numb because I didn't want to hold you back selfishly. God held me and reassured me it was your time to go as He comforted me, so I knew it was going to be okay—not at first, but eventually, it would all be okay. I would rise from the ashes and be okay.

As the alarms all went off and person after person rushed into your room to try to save you, I smiled and thought, I'm so proud of my baby girl. You fought so hard and surpassed your first breath—103 days' worth of breathing. You fought so we could all learn and live. I *could finally know and feel what it's like to be a mommy, so I smiled more.*

Tears came, of course, through the cracked smile, because I really wanted to keep you here with us. I wanted so desperately to never let you go, but I wanted what you needed and saw you had to finish what you came here to do. A mother discovering that truth and actually stepping aside is not as natural, but trusting God made it possible. It is what a mother should do!

I know the doctors, nurses, and other staff kept your body breathing with a machine, but I knew you were already gone—my mother's instinct. That's why, when your daddy and I were told later in the day that we were doing stuff to you instead of for you, the decision to take you off the machines wasn't a struggle. I knew you were already healed and living life large!

You were finally getting to breathe on your own and be a baby without all the machines and medicine! All the older angels are getting to play with you and help you grow! Knowing all this helps me carry on! You are healed! Praise God!

Now when Daddy and I held you for the last time, it was hard, because I knew I wouldn't be getting you back. I knew I'd never physically be with you after the funeral home took you in the van. Sorry, Mommy keeps bawling through this letter. God just needed me to deal with this finally. The hardest thing I had to do was put you—a lifeless body, my baby—in that van and watch it drive away with you, all alone, in the back without me. Deep down, I knew that you were stronger than I could ever be. You did what you were supposed to do, and you didn't let anyone stop you.

There came a time in your days here that I knew you were smarter, braver, kinder, and much more. You did what God needed you to do, and I am forever grateful! I hope I can do this and keep going, even with the judgmental and negative people that can suck the life out of anyone.

I wish I didn't know so many like this. I wish I and others didn't have to go through the ridicule on a daily basis sometimes. It makes my heart sad, baby girl, that people can be so wrapped up in themselves and selfish beyond measure. I praise God that there are at least decent human beings who are selfless and positive. They get it and don't judge! I'm glad there are more like this than the others.

I pray for both—for all—that one day God can finally break through their cold hearts so He can live there like I see Him do so graciously in others' hearts—even in my own!

Sweet Lily, you know I'd do anything to hold you one more time. I know, though, if I did, I'd always want more! One more would never be enough. I will happily miss you until we meet again in heaven. I love you to the moon and back and for all eternity.

Your Mommy—period!

AUGUST 5, 2011

186 › One-Year Angelversary

Yesterday, I was in the worst mood. It was just like the day before Lilian's one-year birthday anniversary. I dreaded it with every ounce of my being. I'm glad yesterday was the worst day because the devil was not going to ruin Lilian Grace's one-year angelversary no matter what!

I can type to you and say with a huge smile on my face that Michael and I got some time together with Lilian Grace and "The Who"—our little family lived it up today. We started with dessert at Peachwave before gearing up to do some shopping. It was delicious, by the way!

Next, we got quite a bit of shopping in. My hubby bought me the sweetest bracelet from James Avery that he had specially picked out. It reads, "And Lo, I am with you always." How perfect is that? Pretty perfect if you ask me. We both got great items to add to our wardrobe. We ended up with a second dessert—GODIVA this round. Oh yes—chocolate is our best friend!

We proceeded to our favorite little taste of heaven, Mahogany Steakhouse, and feasted like kings and queens. Michael and I talked about our children—reminiscing and dreaming of the future. It was the most perfect moment! I felt excited, and my belly was pleased—even "The Who" was jumping with joy at the delicious meal. We're afraid they'll demand steak, au gratin potatoes, and asparagus with hollandaise sauce when brought into the world!

To follow this up, Michael agreed to do a mini photo shoot of me at Lilian's last place before leaving this earth.

There is a beautiful animated kids' garden on the back side of the Children's Hospital. We parked right where we had said our last goodbye to our sweet baby girl and took all the cute pictures. It made my heart even happier.

Needless to say, God blessed our time together just as he has blessed our journey the entire time. Lilian Grace is in a much better place where she is being raised by the greatest Father there will ever be. My heart shines brightly knowing we'll get to see her one day and dance with her again.

Michael and I have discovered that any of us can easily stay in the gutter. We can get so scared about what's outside that gutter that we just stay in it—wallowing around and hoping change will come to us. By the grace of God, we've chosen to get out of it, no matter how scared we are to continue the walk He has for us. I'm glad we grabbed on to each other's hands and His so we could get out of our gutter. This journey, no matter how hard, is breathtaking and more adventurous than we could ever hope for. God truly keeps blessing us daily. I can't wait to keep walking with Him along with our little family.

Thank you all for being with us today in your thoughts and prayers. We could feel them throughout the day. No parent wants to have to face something like this, but God has provided us with the essentials to get us through it. We love you deeply. Now here's a letter to my angel I'd love to share.

Lilian Grace—my sweet Lil Squeaker and baby angel,

You are my sunshine and twinkling star. I love you to the moon and back and for all eternity. I hope you got to feast like your father, sibling-to-be, and I did tonight. We had our own piece of heaven on earth as we sat as a little family. Your younger sibling was rolling around and making sure we knew they were a part of our celebration for you.

I feel that as your mommy, I'm starting to figure out what to say to people when they ask about you. I get very happy when I get to talk about you. Just a week ago today, Jennifer, Gage, and Logan Watkins came to visit me. The boys asked all sorts of questions about you and let me show off all your gorgeous pictures as I told little stories about each one. My soul jumped and leaped with joy and enthusiasm. I'm so glad God brought them here so I could do that.

Other people also love to hear about you, and we talk openly. I hope you can look down and hear all the wonderful stories I tell about you. Today, I saw people I've never met dress up in honor of your special day. Tears of joy and happiness came over me as I was tagged in each picture on social media so I could see. Sweetie pie, God was able to reach across the world with your story. I know He is proud of you just like we are.

As I took pictures at the special children's garden behind the Children's Hospital, I could sense you there. I wish we could have taken pictures there with you. You would have loved all the bright colors and larger than life animals and flowers. I know that heaven has to be way sweeter than that little area. I imagine you with glistening angel wings fluttering around and enjoying every minute of your heavenly life.

Mommy was very sad and in a bad mood yesterday, but I got my act together. We actually had a fabulous day honoring and remembering you. It's always easy to get happy when thinking of you. I shall never forget your warm little body in my arms and feeling your heart beat up against mine when we got to kangaroo! Oh, this mother shall never forget the feelings you brought me every single minute. I can still remember how you smelled—sweet as honey and flowers.

Today marks your first whole year in heaven. I still cannot fathom how quickly it has come and gone. I remember your great-great-grandma Cooper telling me that life flies fast and to make sure not to miss out. She always reminded me to be in this life and let God lead the way. I'm glad I listened. I feel when it comes to you that I finally got my act together and lived life loud. I'm trying to continue to do so today because of our many adventures together.

Baby girl, you may have been here only 103 days, but you engraved God's light into our hearts forever. I praise His name on High for giving you to us, even if He had to take you back so soon. I still believe that I would do our journey over and over a million times if He wanted us to, because you were worth it all!

May you get to see all of God's wonders and ways in His glorious light and love. May God continue to touch lives with your story forever. I can't wait for us to meet your younger brother or sister. Please make sure to tell them to trust in God and do His will just like you did.

> *I guess I need to close this letter. Know this—you are the greatest angel I've ever met to date. You are the key that opened all the doors I had closed, locked, or lost the key to. You are God's miracle who changed thousands of lives just by being who God created you to be. You are my baby girl for all eternity. You, my Lily Bug, will forever be loved and missed.*
>
> *Love,*
> *Your Mommy for Eternity,*
> *Chrissy*

I continue to love how God brings people into our lives to help comfort us and give us what we need at the right time. Two more songs were shared with us: "What It Means to Be Loved" by Mark Schultz and "The Dance" by Garth Brooks. I've listened to them several times. I love that God brings me beautiful music to soothe my brokenness and grief. I wanted to give Lilian the world, but God gave her eternity in heaven—that's a pretty big upgrade. As long as I keep my focus on God, I will continue to dance among the pain and sorrow. There's a certain sweetness when you rise above hardships and come to a better understanding of why life contains struggles, battles, and chaos.

All we wanted for Lilian Grace was for her to be completely loved and for us to step out of the way so she could do God's will. Though our journey with Lilian Grace was painful for many hours, days, and weeks, the dance with her was worth every heartache and broken piece of our heart and soul. I would never want to take any of it back. Though I'd love to have her here with us still, I wouldn't want to interfere with God's glorious plans.

Please enjoy the poem that Lilian's eye specialist, Dr. Groves wrote and presented to us:

Love in Christ

Lovely little one
Into His hands now home
Loving Him as we cry here on earth
Into the night, she has total freedom now
A new creation as promised and a new day dawns soon for us
No more sorrow, no more pain, no more tears with a healed heart has come

Gracefully dancing for her King, gentle rains of grace for you and me
Running, running, joyfully as we roll in His love
Angels around, yes the angels abound
Come into the healing rain and see sweet Lilian now
Exquisitely, unbelievably, eternally free enjoying His touch

While we still here hurt
He the Father holds her near
Into His love she melts
Tenderly sweetly she is now whole
Together with her King
Eternally at peace
Now safely home

(Dr. Steve Groves)

A NOTE FROM THE AUTHOR

Thank you for reading this segment of my story. I published these journal entries for readers of my first book, *The Fight,* and to offer people a close look at how wild and rich the grief journey was for me while I pursued comfort from the Creator. I stumbled and fell while trying to process my loss, but I learned lessons daily and grew personally and spiritually. This prepared me to climb what comes next in book three. I encourage you to own the strength training your trials render and to remember you are never alone.

If you found *The Fall to the Climb* helpful or healing, please recommend it by leaving a review on Amazon, Goodreads, or wherever you browse for books online. Who do you know who is grieving? Lend or gift a copy to them in lieu of flowers. You can also donate a copy to your local library or church. I pray this book reaches those who need it most.

Publishing my journals has been challenging because it's evident the enemy is after me when I work on it. Yet I am blessed to know that readers are benefitting from the lessons God taught me through hard seasons. May God's wisdom train you to recover and soar beyond each loss in life.

Your story's not over yet. Continue climbing! Glimpse a view of what God has in store for you in Scripture. It's extravagant and praiseworthy! God is working for your good. Don't give up. The mountaintop is just ahead.

Blessings,
Chrissy

Whitten Silver Dollar City trip in 2022

BOOK COVER LEGEND

Circle Window

God knows our future. He created us in His image with a beginning and an ending to our story that brings us full circle. It's not a smooth, round circle; the curves represent the bumps, turns, and twists on our journey.

› **Angel Wing:** Book two walks you through my first year of grief. The angel wing represents our one-year celebration of Lilian's life, memories of her, and her milestones. When we grieve, we are under the protection of our Father's wings. The white and blue colors symbolize our faith and a calming, peaceful energy.
› **Dragonfly:** The dragonfly has landed, signifying a change of course toward a new destination. We can rest upon God's strength and goodness as He carries us along our grief journey. He will work all our pain and suffering out for the good of His kingdom. The devil will not prevail. *"You intended to harm me, but God intended it for good to accomplish what is now being done, the saving of many lives"* *(Genesis 50:20).*
› **Bears:** Part of Native American culture, the bear is a sacred animal that represents power and courage in the spiritual and physical realms. Twelve years after Lilian's departure, our family of five is depicted as a sleuth of bears. We look forward to reuniting with Lilian and loved ones in heaven.

🐻 **Chrissy:** As a mama bear, I am protective of my cubs. Every day, I wake up and choose to be brave by getting out of bed. It's tempting to hibernate, but in Ezra 10:4, we are instructed to rise up with courage and do hard things, because we are not alone. I remind my family to keep getting up no matter how hard it is.

🐻 **Lilian:** As the oldest cub, she is now a spirit that watches over us. She showed great fighting ability and honorably earned her wings. In the painting, mama bear and family keep Lily's memory alive while holding onto sweet memories and her spirit.

- **Silver Metal:** Silver stands for intuition, self-reflection, inner wisdom, healing, protection, love, clarity, awareness, focus, persistence, and subtle strength.
- **Ladybugs:** The black-and-red insect has been linked to good luck and happiness. The ladybug pays homage to one of Lilian Grace's nicknames, Lily Bug. Her life ultimately brought me an unspeakable happiness only God can provide. The two ladybugs represent the book artist and her husband. She absolutely loves ladybugs. They have both encouraged me along my book journey; I would not have made it without them.
- **Lily Flower:** Her name, along with the swirling mix of blue, green, and purple, bind the following key words and phrases: innocence, purity, grace, growth, dignity, passion, tranquility, harmony, sweetness, humility, loyalty, wisdom, love's good fortune, rebirth, and Christ's second coming.
- **Lily's Butterfly:** The pink, yellow, and purple butterfly fits the firstborn of our family. She is tender, loving, compassionate, comforting, kind, and joyful. She proved to be a light from above while inspiring us to look to God in all things. She was His little missionary. Lilian's butterfly has been transformed into an angelic-like representation of her transition from life to death. The frayed wings are

evidence of her fight against earthly pain and sorrow, yet she flew into her heavenly Father's presence when it was finished. She is positioned perfectly under the angel wing, as the promise in Psalm 91:4 states, *"He will cover you with his feathers, and under his wings you will find refuge; his faithfulness will be your shield and rampart."*

- **Green Emerald Stones:** The emerald is known as the stone of the heart. It promotes balance between each part of us—the physical, emotional, mental, and spiritual. Lily's journey strengthened our faith as God met and guided us through adversities. The teardrop shape matches Lilian's upside-down teardrop pupils. The six stones divided by the lily flower represent the six years and three and a half months it took to get Lilian here from our wedding date to her birth!
- **Mountain:** We all face mountains that feel like Mt. Everest. When I changed my perspective, the mountain/trial before me became an exquisite training opportunity for the future. Mountains exude constancy, firmness, and stillness. Climbing one gives us a higher perspective from a loftier point of view. It's easy to get stuck on the mountainside. There were plenty of mountain highs and valley lows before, during, and following Lilian Grace's death. Sometimes we must fall back and choose a different path before we can start climbing again. We must get out of our own way and God's way to reach the top.
- **Pine Trees:** After Lilian's death, life didn't stop, even though our hearts shattered. Life went on, and although it was challenging, each day delivered a dose of renewal and purpose for our spirits. The pine trees represent eternal life and regeneration.
- **Tree of Life:** Michael and I keep our feet rooted in Christ like a tree rooted deep in the ground. He is our source of

essentials for survival, and we grow stronger as our relationship with Him matures. Our family trees are filled with strong people and even include Native American lineage from the Cherokee and Chickasaw tribes. This tree is a reminder of our roots and our intent to keep growing with God's strength. We are His warriors, battling whatever confronts us physically or spiritually. Our church and family members are the hands and feet of Jesus reaching out like branches from a tree. They rejuvenate us and encourage us to press on each day toward triumph. The tree is in full bloom because spring has arrived. The previous tree's branches were pruned and stripped of their leaves. We felt that way through the winter season of Lilian's fight, but God nourished us and grew us into something more beautiful. Though we are heartbroken, God helped us flourish after a difficult season. Trust His process and lean into Him always.

> **Turtle:** We must stay grounded through the chaos and emotions of grief if we want to survive. The turtle exemplifies being grounded as we slow down and pace ourselves through all the processing. It's essential to offer grace to ourselves and others through grief.
> **Swirls of Wind:** While grieving, we feel whirlwinds of change blowing around us. It can affect our physical, mental, emotional, and spiritual health. It can be scary, so hold on tight to God and trust He is taking you to a better place.
> **Waterfall:** Waterfalls revive and purify. They flow freely and purposely, shaping and molding the earth beneath. They are a source of water. Is Jesus your source of living water? We need to fill ourselves up with Him so we can pour into others. His water is healing, and His grace and unconditional love will support you through any journey.

God opens and closes doors for us, helping us live a purposeful life.

Door Background

› **Blue, Purple, and Brown Weathered Wood:** These colors represent grief and serve as a reminder to keep swimming. Don't let dark water overtake you. Keep your eyes on Jesus.

Pinecone Doorknob

A doorknob allows everyone to open and close doors to opportunities. The pinecone is a symbol of eternal life. We each have free will and decide whether to accept Christ or not. I pray God will show you that He is here and wants a relationship with you. If you already have a relationship with Him, He wants more time with you. He yearns to have a daily relationship with each of us. Eternity is not far off.

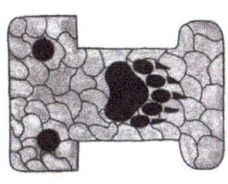
Door Hinge

The bear paw claws symbolize healing. A hinge demonstrates how to be flexible during the healing process. Cracks appear in the metal to signify our brokenness. Healing takes time; there's not a definite finish line. But we can make progress by moving through doors when they open.

Door Knocker

God loves us unconditionally and wants to give us good gifts. In Mathew 7:7, Jesus reminds us to ask, seek, and knock on the door we want to go through. He will open it when the time is right.

› **Acorn with Oak Leaves:** We seek the positive potential of life on the other side of a door while building strength where we stand like an oak tree.

› **Cracks in the Door Handle:** The heartbreaks of life create a compelling story full of emotional growth that we can share with those around us. The cracks are scars that signify a stronger awareness of what's important and wisdom that's learned through courageous living.

Keyhole Plate

In each stage of life, we pass through a door to the unknown. Trusting in God's eternal perspective keeps me moving. When I am afraid, God opens the door and walks me across the threshold. His grace and mercy will help you adjust and adapt through each transition.

› **Red Oak Tree Leaves:** God provides peace and comfort by communicating through His wondrous creation. The red oak tree leaves denote grounding, stability, healing, security, power, and survival.

› **Acorns:** Perseverance is so important. During tough times, we have to persevere using the strength God gives us. The acorn is associated with life, strength, and perseverance. When I think about what an acorn goes through to become a glorious, towering tree, I am reminded of Job. Don't ever

THE FALL TO THE CLIMB

give up. There will be a day when you appreciate the training and your transformation.

› **Squirrel:** These little critters are associated with focused energy, balance between action and rest, resourcefulness, the importance of having a plan, and preparing for the future. They demonstrate being mindful of the seeds we plant and how those seeds benefit people.

› **Glowing Light within the Keyhole:** God will be with us wherever we go, and His light within us illuminates His goodness and grace in the darkness around us. Are you allowing God to shine brightly in your circumstances? It's easy to overlook the positive in a hard situation, but people take notice when you allow His light to shine through your brokenness.

› **Wind:** The wind is symbolic of the Holy Spirit. When we ask Jesus into our hearts, the Holy Spirit dwells within us, and we are never alone. Though we cannot see Him, we know by His mighty ways that He is here. *"The wind blows wherever it pleases. You hear its sound, but you cannot tell where it comes from or where it is going. So it is with everyone born of the Spirit"* (John 3:8).

Skeleton Key

God provides the keys or tools necessary to open the doors that lead to the purpose He has in store for us.

› **Flaming Sun (bow):** The flowing flames demonstrate the fires of adversity we battle every day in our grief. The sun's shape reminds us to look to the Son for all things. When we step aside, His light shines brightly.

> **Compass (center of bow):** A crucial instrument when climbing an unfamiliar mountain. God has divinely designed you and placed you in the world for such a time as this to further His kingdom. His Word is the compass that will lead us home to heaven. Our journeys vary in length, yet God will bring us to Himself in His perfect time.
> **Acorn with Oak Leaves (middle of stem):** We will be victorious when we ask God to partner with us. In the same way an acorn miraculously grows into a mighty oak tree, so we will grow spiritually. God grants power and authority to those who are one with Him.
> **Silver Metal:** Silver was valuable in biblical times. There's value in trusting God and standing on His Word. Believe He will work all things out for good in His timing. That's the key to getting through grief.
> **Emerald Stone (bottom of bow):** Lilian's two-month birthday color was green. It represents life, growth, moving forward, and my time with the 4-H program (since I had to depart from it when Lily arrived). For her two-month birthday, we encouraged people to eat something extra healthy because each of us is worth filling up with good stuff. A car can't go without good gas, so we need to take care of ourselves! We all take our health for granted sometimes. The single stone represents God as our source of life.
> **Five (in the key ward):** Lilian's angelversary, August 5, 2010, is etched in the key ward. On the fifth of each month, I pray for others as they fall and climb through challenges toward their purpose.

The little cardinal on the spine is Lily visiting after she earned her wings. Legend has it that these beautiful birds are visitors from heaven. It seems as if they always show up at the appropriate time.

Red Cardinal

Back Cover

› **Bears:** Part of Native American culture, the bear is a sacred animal that represents power and courage in the spiritual and physical realms. Twelve years after Lilian's departure, our family of five is depicted as a sleuth of bears. We look forward to reuniting with Lilian and loved ones in heaven.

🐻 **Michael:** As papa bear, he protects and leads our family. He has not backed down from his role in making sure our family is safe, secure, and thriving. He works hard and provides adventure and care.

🐻 **Piper:** As the middle cub, she is flourishing and adventurous. She loves animals to an extreme level. She is helpful, sweet, loving, and brave.

🐻 **Daphne:** As the youngest cub, she keeps us on our toes. Her empathy for people is through the roof. She is determined, sweet, invested, and courageous.

› **Flying Dragonfly:** As a family, we are constantly reminded of Lilian Grace. Every time we see a dragonfly, we say hello to her. From adventurous trips to school activities, we can always count on a dragonfly to appear in flight. We feel like she's still a part of it all, and we are thankful for God's goodness. When we travel, we trust God to protect and direct us through the good, bad, and everyday activities.

Dragonfly

Dragonflies symbolize change. Without change, we can't evolve into the person God created us to be. To change is to level up in the game of life and grow wiser because of our experiences. Change is inevitable. We can't grow or make things better without it.

› **Bear Claws (praising):** The bear claws are lifted toward God, signifying our praises for His protection and our connection to Him whether in the valley deep or on the mountaintop.

› **Colors (green, brown, blue, and yellow):** The overall color scheme communicates growth, harmony, fruitfulness, joy, peace, truth, creativity, simplicity, and tranquility. Lean on God and enjoy the experience of flying with Him!

› **Flying Position:** When a dragonfly's wings are open in flight, it creates a cross. We think about Jesus paying the price for our sin as He hung on the cross. He carries us through our journey just as He carried his cross. He sacrificed everything for you and me.

› **Silver Heart:** Though Lilian earned her wings, God helps us heal with reminders of her beautiful heart. A light radiated from within her. Lilian's legacy is laced with God's glory!

› **Burgundy Lilies:** Just like our Lilian, burgundy lilies are known for vitality. God renews our strength and energy daily, especially when we are grieving. Continuing Lilian's legacy renews my vitality.

› **Green Circle:** The green circle represents nature. The elements of water, wind, and fire are in the design of the dragonfly. Together they attribute healing, cleansing, strength, communication, transformation, purification, and breath of life.

› **Wind (tail):** The wind is symbolic of the Holy Spirit. When we ask Jesus into our hearts, the Holy Spirit dwells within us, and we are never alone. Though we cannot see Him, we know by His mighty ways that He is here. *"The wind blows wherever it pleases. You hear its sound, but you cannot tell where it comes from or where it is going. So it is with everyone born of the Spirit" (John 3:8).*

› **Upside-down Teardrop:** Lilian's pupils were the shape of upside-down teardrops. Our world felt upside-down during that time. Our tears are now a mix of joy and sorrow. Lilian's fight is over and made good, but we will always miss her.

MEMORY VERSES

🗡 "His divine power has given us everything we need for a godly life through our knowledge of him who called us by his own glory and goodness. Through these he has given us his very great and precious promises, so that through them you may participate in the divine nature, having escaped the corruption in the world caused by evil desires. For this very reason, make every effort to add to your faith goodness; and to goodness, knowledge; and to knowledge, self-control; and to self-control, perseverance; and to perseverance, godliness; and to godliness, mutual affection; and to mutual affection, love. For if you possess these qualities in increasing measure, they will keep you from being ineffective and unproductive in your knowledge of our Lord Jesus Christ" (2 Peter 1:3–8).

🗡 "Take delight in the LORD, and he will give you the desires of your heart. Commit your way to the LORD; trust in him and he will do this: He will make your righteous reward shine like the dawn, your vindication like the noonday sun. Be still before the LORD and wait patiently for him" (Psalm 37:4–7).

🗡 "So that Christ may dwell in your hearts through faith. And I pray that you, being rooted and established in love, may have power, together with all the Lord's holy people, to grasp how wide and long and high and deep is the love of Christ, and to know this love that surpasses knowledge—that you may be filled to the measure of all the fullness of God" (Ephesians 3:17–19).

🗡 "For this reason I kneel before the Father, from whom every *family in heaven and on earth derives its name. I pray that out of his glorious riches he may strengthen you with power through his Spirit in your inner being" (Ephesians 3:14–16).*

⚔ *"A cheerful heart is good medicine, but a crushed spirit dries up the bones" (Proverbs 17:22).*

⚔ *"He said to me: 'It is done. I am the Alpha and the Omega, the Beginning and the End. To the thirsty I will give water without cost from the spring of the water of life. Those who are victorious will inherit all this, and I will be their God and they will be my children'" (Revelation 21:6–7).*

⚔ *"After that, we who are still alive and are left will be caught up together with them in the clouds to meet the Lord in the air. And so we will be with the Lord forever" (1 Thessalonians 4:17).*

⚔ *"I eagerly expect and hope that I will in no way be ashamed, but will have sufficient courage so that now as always Christ will be exalted in my body, whether by life or by death. For to me, to live is Christ and to die is gain. If I am to go on living in the body, this will mean fruitful labor for me. Yet what shall I choose? I do not know! I am torn between the two: I desire to depart and be with Christ, which is better by far" (Philippians 1:20–23).*

⚔ *"He will wipe every tear from their eyes. There will be no more death or mourning or crying or pain, for the old order of things has passed away" (Revelation 21:4).*

⚔ *"Keep your lives free from the love of money and be content* with what you have, because God has said, '**Never will I leave you; never will I forsake you.**' So we say with confidence, 'The Lord is my helper; I will not be afraid. What can mere mortals do to me?' Remember your leaders, who spoke the word of God to you. Consider the outcome of their way of life and imitate their faith. Jesus Christ is the same yesterday and today and forever" (Hebrews 13:5–8, boldface added by author).

⚔ "Be strong and courageous. Do not be afraid or terrified because of them, for the LORD your God goes with you; **he will never leave you nor forsake you**" (Deuteronomy 31:6, boldface added by author).

⚔ "God is our refuge and strength, an ever-present help in trouble. Therefore we will not fear, though the earth give way and the mountains fall into the heart of the sea, though its waters roar and foam and the mountains quake with their surging.... The LORD Almighty is with us" (Psalm 46:1–3, 7).

⚔ "May the God of hope fill you with all joy and peace as you trust in him, so that you may overflow with hope by the power of the Holy Spirit" (Romans 15:13).

⚔ "And let us consider how we may spur one another on toward love and good deeds, not giving up meeting together, as some are in the habit of doing, but encouraging one another— and all the more as you see the Day approaching" (Hebrews 10:24–25).

⚔ "I am the vine; you are the branches. If you remain in me and I in you, you will bear much fruit; apart from me you can *do nothing" (John 15:5).*

⚔ *"This is the confidence we have in approaching God: that if we ask anything according to his will, he hears us. And if we know that he hears us—whatever we ask—we know that we have what we asked of him" (1 John 5:14–15).*

PLAYLIST

♪ "Beauty Will Rise" by Steven Curtis Chapman
♪ "Answer" by Sarah McLachlan
♪ "Goodnight My Angel" by Billy Joel
♪ "Held" by Natalie Grant
♪ "You Hold Me Now" by Hillsong
♪ "You Haven't Seen the Last of Me" by Cher
♪ "On the Radio" by Regina Spector
♪ "Peace on Earth" by Chris Rice
♪ "O Holy Night" by Whitney Houston
♪ "Come Thou Fount of Every Blessing" by Chris Rice
♪ "Borrowed Angels" by Kristin Chenoweth
♪ "I'm Alive" by Celine Dion
♪ "One Last Christmas" by Matthew West
♪ "Set the World on Fire" by Britt Nicole
♪ "The Climb" by Miley Cyrus
♪ "From the Inside Out" by Hillsong United
♪ "The Wonder Pets!" by Wonder Pets
♪ "Losing My Way" by Justin Timberlake
♪ "Firework" by Katy Perry
♪ "I Will Carry You" by Selah
♪ "In My Life" by Better Midler
♪ "I Will Glory in the Cross" by Dottie Rambo
♪ "Stronger" by Mandisa
♪ "It Is Well" by Mary Mary
♪ "Never Wave My Flag" by Mary Mary
♪ "Destined" by Avalon

♪ "Said and Done" by Michael Boggs
♪ "He Is with You" by Mandisa
♪ "While I'm Waiting" by John Waller
♪ "Blessings" by Laura Story
♪ "Precious Child" by Stowegood
♪ "Strip Me" by Natasha Bedingfield
♪ "I Have Decided to Follow Jesus" by Jaden Lavik
♪ "Before the Morning" by Josh Wilson
♪ "What It Means to Be Loved" by Mark Schultz
♪ "The Dance" by Garth Brooks

https://open.spotify.com/playlist/1pRbBcQ5iAI1AEfp5Se6dT?si=82877844d9124fd1

ACKNOWLEDGEMENTS

To my family: Life has dealt us an abundance of adversity, but we haven't given up. Thank you for supporting me, even when it doesn't make sense. Money is not the motivation behind this project, people are. If one person benefits from reading this book, my job is done. I'm thankful you see and understand this is a God-given mission I must accomplish.

To my friends: Thank you for your nonstop support! You've attended my book signings and speaking events, prayed for me through sickness, and listened to me process life. I love my tribe that spreads across the United States.

To my team (the warrior tribe): Despite the enemy's attacks and in between everyday life, you keep plugging away to help me publish my journals. I can't thank you enough for your commitment to each project we work on together. God has woven our talents into two beautiful tapestries now. Your gifts, passion, and follow through impress me to no end. Thank you for not giving up!

To everyone in my life: Our paths have crossed for a reason. If you've attended a book signing or speaking event, read my story, or supported me at any point in my journey, I thank you from the bottom of my heart. My life is amazing because God purposefully placed all of you in it. I wouldn't have made it through the hardest times of my life without your help and love.

May God guide, direct, and protect each of you. He is our Healer and Lord of Heaven's Armies. Look to Him in battle. He'll not only bring you through it, He'll harvest goodness from the very things that brought you pain. Don't give up. I'm proof that you can survive and thrive. I love you all and hope the best is yet to come for you and your family!

ABOUT THE AUTHOR

Chrissy L. Whitten holds a bachelor of science in leisure service management and a master of interdisciplinary studies in educational psychology, REMS, and leisure service management from Oklahoma State University (OSU). She has over thirty years' experience working in youth programming and teaching fitness. She grew up in the Cushing and Stillwater, Oklahoma, communities before marrying her husband, Michael, in December 2003.

She lived in Sand Springs, Oklahoma, for fourteen years, where she was the Tulsa County 4-H extension educator for five years and Juntos 4-H educator for over a year and a half. She founded the Warrior Princess Foundation after Lilian passed away and ran it for five years to raise money for trisomy 13 and 18 children. She organized seven races with Ken TZ Childress and numerous donors and volunteers who helped with fundraising efforts. It was a healing experience.

Michael's work moved them to Tuttle, Oklahoma, with their two children (on earth), Piper and Daphne. She enjoys going on adventures around the world with her family, discovering and exploring together. She loves getting involved with her church and volunteering for her girls' schools and extracurricular activities where needed.

She has been healing and recovering from a recent health scare but loves challenging herself. She's run many ultras—50Ks, fifty milers, seventy milers, hundred milers, and anything between. She has a wonderful buckle collection for completing hundreds of miles. She even participated in a virtual treadmill run where she completed 402.7 miles and 318,146 feet at a 15 percent incline from December 1–25, 2020, in forty-one runs. Her last race was the 9th Annual Snowdrop ULTRA 55 Hour Race & Relay in Texas in December 2021. She walked one hundred miles.

She facilitates Calm Waters grief student support groups in schools in the communities of Blanchard, Bridge Creek, Mustang, Moore, Newcastle, Tuttle, and Yukon and virtually throughout the state of Oklahoma. She teaches local fitness classes—barre, Pilates, PiYo, kickboxing, yoga, and fitness mix at Steppin' Out Dance Studio.

She has been working on the *Journals from a Warrior's Mother* project for over twelve years. Chrissy wrote her first journal entry shortly after her firstborn entered the world on April 25, 2010. She's ecstatic to share book two of four with the world after battling countless distractions, difficulties, and detours. She continues to learn, adjust, and grow.

MORE FROM CHRISSY L. WHITTEN

Are you worn from fighting your own battle? Where is God in it all, and what is the purpose of your pain? If you need empathy and hope or simply want to gain perspective from a little warrior's mother, *The Fight* is for you. *The Fight* (book one) is available as an eBook or in paperback. Illustrations by artist Tammy Edwards and photos of the Whitten family are printed in color in the Collector's Edition.

Coming Soon in 2023

The Fight Study Guide
and
The Fall to the Climb Study Guide

To learn more about Chrissy, visit
https://chrissylwhitten.com.

REVIEW PLEA

Thank you for reading *The Fall to the Climb*! I hope you enjoyed it. I would love to know if this book resonated with you and how you found it helpful. Your feedback will make the study guides and my future books better. Please take two minutes now to leave a helpful review on Amazon and Goodreads. Thank you, and happy trails!

Chrissy L. Whitten

www.ingramcontent.com/pod-product-compliance
Lightning Source LLC
Chambersburg PA
CBHW041303110526
44590CB00028B/4235